JOURNAL FOR THE STUDY OF THE OLD TESTAMENT
SUPPLEMENT SERIES
396

The Human and the Divine in History

Herodotus and the Book of Daniel

Paul Niskanen

T & T CLARK INTERNATIONAL
A Continuum imprint
LONDON • NEW YORK

Published by T&T Clark International
The Tower Building, 11 York Road, London SE1 7NX
15 East 26th Street, Suite 1703, New York, NY 10010

www.tandtclark.com

British Library Cataloguing-in-Publication Data
A catalogue record for this book is available from the British Library

Typeset and edited for Continuum by Forthcoming Publications Ltd
www.forthcomingpublications.com

Printed on acid-free paper in Great Britain by The Bath Press, Bath

ISBN 0-5670-8213-X

CONTENTS

Abbreviations   vii

Chapter 1
HERODOTUS AND BIBLICAL STUDIES   1
   1. Introduction   1
   2. Herodotus   4
   3. Herodotus and Daniel   6
   4. Judaism and Hellenism   9
   5. Studies of Herodotus and Hebrew Historiography   13
      a. Mandell and Freedman   13
      b. Flemming Nielsen   17
   6. Studies of Herodotus and Jewish Historical Novellas   20
      a. Esther   21
      b. Judith   23

Chapter 2
DANIEL AND CLASSICAL STUDIES   26
   1. Daniel 2 and 7: The Theory of a Succession of World Empires   27
      a. The *Bhaman Yasht* and the *Denkard*   31
      b. The Babylonian Dynastic Prophecy   34
      c. The Herodotean Tradition   35
   2. Daniel 11: Greek History Told as Prophecy   43
   3. Herodotus in the Hellenistic Period   47

Chapter 3
THE HUMAN IN HISTORY   52
   1. The King in Daniel   54
      a. The Kings in the Court Tales   55
      b. The King in the Dream Visions   59
   2. The King in Herodotus   65
      a. Croesus   65
      b. Cyrus   67
      c. Cambyses   68
      d. Darius   72
      e. Xerxes   73
   3. The Sage   75
      a. Daniel the Sage in the Court Tales   75
      b. Daniel the Seer in the Dream Visions   78
      c. The Wise Advisor in Herodotus   78

Chapter 4
THE DIVINE IN HISTORY   83
   1. The Divine in Daniel   85
      a. Dreams and Signs   86
      b. Heavenly Combatants   91
   2. The Divine in Herodotus   93
      a. Oracles   94
      b. Dreams   95
   3. Heavenly Figures and Local Gods   98

Chapter 5
DANIEL'S THEOLOGY OF HISTORY   104
   1. Daniel as Greek *Historia*   104
   2. Daniel as Apocalypse   106
   3. Daniel's Theology of History   109
      a. Continuity with Biblical Traditions   109
      b. The Influence of Greek Historiography   113
      c. The Scope of History in Daniel   117
      d. The Typological Use of History   119
      e. The Human and the Divine   121

Appendix
THE TEXT OF DANIEL 11.2B   126

Bibliography   128
Index of References   135
Index of Authors   142

ABBREVIATIONS

AB	Anchor Bible
ABD	David Noel Freedman (ed.), *The Anchor Bible Dictionary* (New York: Doubleday, 1992)
AJP	*American Journal of Philology*
ANET	James B. Pritchard (ed.), *Ancient Near Eastern Texts Relating to the Old Testament* (Princeton: Princeton University Press, 1950)
BDB	Francis Brown, S.R. Driver and Charles A. Briggs, *A Hebrew and English Lexicon of the Old Testament* (Oxford: Clarendon Press, 1907)
BHS	*Biblia hebraica stuttgartensia*
BSO(A)S	*Bulletin of the School of Oriental (and African) Studies*
CBQMS	*Catholic Biblical Quarterly*, Monograph Series
CP	*Classical Philology*
CQ	*Classical Quarterly*
FGrH	*Die Fragmente der griechischen Historiker* (ed. F. Jacoby; Leiden: E.J. Brill, 1954–64)
FOTL	The Forms of the Old Testament Literature
HDR	Harvard Dissertations in Religion
HSS	Harvard Semitic Studies
ICC	International Critical Commentary
JAL	Jewish Apocryphal Literature Series
JBL	*Journal of Biblical Literature*
JSOT	*Journal for the Study of the Old Testament*
JSOTSup	*Journal for the Study of the Old Testament*, Supplement Series
JTS	*Journal of Theological Studies*
LCL	Loeb Classical Library
LSJ	H.G. Liddell, Robert Scott and H. Stuart Jones, *Greek–English Lexicon* (Oxford: Clarendon Press, 9th edn, 1968)
LXX	Septuagint
MT	Masoretic Text
NJBC	R.E. Brown, J.A. Fitzmyer, and R.E. Murphy (eds.), *The New Jerome Biblical Commentary* (Englewood Cliffs, NJ: Prentice–Hall, 1990)
NRSV	New Revised Standard Version
NTS	*New Testament Studies*
OTP	James Charlesworth (ed.), *Old Testament Pseudepigrapha*
OTS	*Oudtestamentische Studiën*
SBL	Society of Biblical Literature
SBLDS	SBL Dissertation Series
SHANE	Studies in the History of the Ancient Near East
TB	Theologische Bücherei
TDNT	Gerhard Kittel and Gerhard Friedrich (eds.), *Theological Dictionary of the New Testament* (trans. Geoffrey W. Bromiley; 10 vols.; Grand Rapids: Eerdmans, 1964–)
VT	*Vetus Testamentum*

Chapter 1

HERODOTUS AND BIBLICAL STUDIES

1. *Introduction*

Any study which proposes to investigate the relationship between texts as seemingly disparate as the book of Daniel and the *Histories* of Herodotus cannot proceed without a substantial word of both introduction and explanation. Given that innumerable volumes have been written on either one of these works, yet virtually nothing has been said of them together,[1] the question must be asked whether this current state of affairs exists with good reason or whether something has been lacking or overlooked in the scholarship. A careful reading of the book of Daniel and of the relevant scholarship reveals two types of oversight that have frequently been made in the study of Daniel. The first is that the historical elements in Daniel have been either largely ignored, or discounted, or subordinated to the eschatological component of the book.[2] This tendency can be seen, for example, in the work of Martin Noth who, while admitting the presence of historiographical material in the book of Daniel, denies that it has any value as such. With reference to Daniel, he writes:

> The apocalyptic writings absorbed all sorts of material current at that time concerning the idea of world epochs and world empires, and perhaps too all sorts of material concerning symbols for historical manifestations and powers. But they considerably depleted this material and robbed it of its original content and real

1.   The one notable exception of which I am aware is found in the writings of Arnaldo Momigliano, 'Biblical Studies and Classical Studies', in S. Berti (ed.), *Essays on Ancient and Modern Judaism* (trans. M. Masella-Gayley; Chicago: University of Chicago Press, 1994), pp. 3-9 (7). One of the most recent and thorough scholarly commentaries on Daniel (J.J. Collins, *Daniel: A Commentary on the Book of Daniel, with an essay 'The Influence of Daniel on the New Testament', by Adela Yarbro Collins* [ed. F.M. Cross; Hermeneia; Minneapolis: Fortress Press, 1993]) cites no less than 59 passages from Herodotus, but these citations are mostly to corroborate details found in Daniel with independent historical accounts of similar phenomena in antiquity (e.g. the colossus in ch. 3 of Daniel is compared with the descriptions of large statues in Herodotus, Diodorus, and Pliny, pp. 180-81).

2.   This was so even in antiquity. Josephus emphasized that Daniel prophesied future events and even established when they would happen (*Ant.* 10.11.7), but the most significant contribution to the eschatologically weighted interpretation of Daniel is Mt. 24.15-16: 'So when you see the desolating sacrilege standing in the holy place, as was spoken of by the prophet Daniel (let the reader understand), then those in Judea must flee to the mountains' (NRSV—all biblical citations are from the NRSV unless otherwise indicated). The fulfillment of the prophecy of Daniel is taken by Matthew as a sign that 'the end will come' (Mt. 24.14).

value by merely applying it to make the motley colouring and changeable nature of world history more vivid... The apocalyptic writings...do not recognize definite laws in the development of history...

We must accept the judgment that 'the concept of history...scarcely plays any marked role' for the apocalyptic writings.[3]

This negative judgment was echoed by Gerhard von Rad who questioned 'whether apocalyptic literature had any existential relationship with history at all'.[4]

The second oversight is that the influence of Greek sources in Daniel has been minimized in favor of Mesopotamian[5] or Iranian[6] sources; this in spite of the fact that Daniel was certainly written in the middle of the second century BCE, a time when over a century of Hellenistic rule and the diffusion of Greek culture were making a definite impact on the Jews of Palestine. Without denying the influence of the previously mentioned eastern cultures on aspects of the language and thought of Daniel,[7] I see undeniable evidence of Greek influence as well, which has seldom been addressed in depth.[8] In the first place, there is the notable presence of Greek loan-words in the book of Daniel.[9] The Greek origin of several of the musical

3.   M. Noth, 'The Understanding of History in Old Testament Apocalyptic', in his *The Laws in the Pentateuch and Other Studies* (trans. D.R. Ap-Thomas; Edinburgh: Oliver & Boyd, 1966), pp. 194-214 (214) (citing L. Köhler, Hebrew Man [trans. P.R. Ackroyd: New York: Abingdon Press, 1956], p. 136).

4.   G. von Rad, *Old Testament Theology* (trans. D.M.G. Stalker; 2 vols.; New York: Harper & Row, 1965), I, p. 304.

5.   The possibility that the vision in Dan. 2 was originally a Babylonian composition has been suggested in various ways by E. Bickerman, *Four Strange Books of the Bible* (New York: Schocken Books, 1967), pp. 63-64; and J.J. Collins, 'The Court-Tales in Daniel and the Development of Apocalyptic', *JBL* 94 (1975), pp. 218-34 (222). There has also been speculation as to a possible link between the book of Daniel and the very fragmentary Babylonian 'Dynastic Prophecy', published by A.K. Grayson in *Babylonian Historical-Literary Texts* (Toronto: University of Toronto Press, 1975), pp. 24-37. See, e.g., W.G. Lambert, *The Background of Jewish Apocalyptic* (London: Athlone, 1978).

6.   The primary Iranian text cited as a source for the material in chs. 2 and 7 of Daniel is the *Bahman Yasht*. The first to suggest that this text (which in its present form dates to no earlier than the ninth century CE) comes from an earlier Hellenistic text that was used by the author of Daniel was E. Meyer, *Ursprung und Anfänge des Christentums* (Berlin: Cotta, 1921), II, p. 190. Meyer's hypothesis has gained widespread acceptance, having been taken up in the latter half of the twentieth century by S.K. Eddy, *The King is Dead: Studies in the Near Eastern Resistance to Hellenism 334–31 B.C.* (Lincoln: University of Nebraska Press, 1961), p. 17; D. Flusser, 'The Four Empires in the Fourth Sybil and in the Book of Daniel', *Israel Oriental Studies* 2 (1972) pp. 148-75; and Collins, *Daniel*, pp. 55, 163-65.

7.   Mesopotamian and Persian background is evident especially when considering the Aramaic portions of the book of Daniel. That the court tales of chs. 1–6 originated in the eastern Diaspora is a widely held, though not uncontested hypothesis. See Collins, *Daniel*, p. 48.

8.   Here a notable exception is T.F. Glasson, *Greek Influence in Jewish Eschatology* (London: SPCK, 1961). Even this work, however, has surprisingly few references to Daniel, covering as it does a broad range of Old and New Testament texts as well as Pseudepigrapha (especially 1 Enoch). Furthermore, his study is limited to influences involving eschatology.

9.   P.W. Coxon, 'Greek Loan-Words and Alleged Greek Loan Translations in the Book of Daniel', *Transactions of the Glasgow University Oriental Society* 25 (1973–74), pp. 24-40.

instruments mentioned in ch. 3 is unquestionable. קיתרוס is equivalent to the Greek κίθαρις, while פסנתרין and סומפניה correspond to ψαλτήριον and συμφωνία respectively.[10] Furthermore, the significance which the advent of Greek hegemony had for the author of Daniel is expressed quite clearly in the vivid description of the fourth beast in the vision of ch. 7, emphasizing its uniqueness—its difference from the three that preceded it (Dan. 7.7). Daniel dwells at length upon this fourth beast, wishing to gain certainty as to its meaning (7.19). It is not merely one among several images, representing just another kingdom among many; rather, it is a primary concern of his. This fourth beast—representing the 'Greek' kingdom from its origins in the time of Alexander to the persecution of Antiochus IV—obviously left a deep and disturbing impression on the author of Daniel. It would be a grave mistake, then, to overlook or to underestimate the impact and influence of this fourth kingdom on the book of Daniel. The second half of the book of Daniel is in fact inextricably tied to the kingdom of the Greeks. To view the book of Daniel simply as anti-Greek, and therefore as neither affected nor influenced by the surrounding forces of Hellenism which it opposed, is to neglect the fact that 'exclusivism never prevented the unconscious or surreptitious assimilation of foreign ideas'.[11]

In this study, then, I will address these two issues: (1) the historical elements or, more precisely, the theology of history that is found in Daniel, and (2) the Greek influence (particularly in the realm of historiography) on the book of Daniel. Since the second of these will help to illustrate the first, I will begin by demonstrating that the author of the book of Daniel was familiar with Greek historiography in general and the *Histories* of Herodotus in particular. Through a comparative reading of these two texts, I will then illuminate how the book of Daniel contains a theology of history that is neither as deterministic nor as exclusively eschatological as scholars have portrayed it. By comparing the human and divine characters in these two works and the roles they play in the unfolding of history, I hope to demonstrate that Daniel, like Herodotus, has a keen interest in both the human and the supernatural causes of historical events. It is my contention that the apocalyptic visions of Daniel do not merely point to an end of history, passively awaiting its consummation. Rather, they reveal a profound interest in contemporary history and the dynamic relationship between the human and divine realms within this ongoing history.

The recognition of historical concerns as well as Greek influences within the book of Daniel does not necessarily lead to a direct relationship with Greek historiography in general nor with Herodotus in particular. The explicit link between Daniel and Herodotus was first suggested to me by the work of Arnaldo Momigliano who pointed to the fact that the well-known theory of a succession of world empires found in many Greek and Roman historians appears for the first time in the *Histories* of Herodotus, while outside of Greek historiography this theory first shows up in the book of Daniel.[12] This observation became for me the starting point

---

10. P. Grelot, 'L'Orchestre de Daniel III, 5, 7, 10, 15', *VT* 29 (1979), pp. 23-38 (28-29, 33-38).

11. A. Momigliano, 'Jews and Greeks', in Berti (ed.), *Essays on Ancient and Modern Judaism*, pp. 10-28 (12).

12. Momigliano, 'Biblical Studies', p. 7.

from which to further explore the book of Daniel in relation to Herodotus and the Greek historiographical tradition stemming from him. As I began this exploration, I was struck by the degree to which the historiographical material in Daniel mirrored the Herodotean tradition, both in its broad temporal and spatial scope as well as in its efforts to explain the causes of events on both the human and divine levels. It is my conviction that reading the texts of Herodotus and Daniel together can prove illuminating for the historical material in Daniel by providing a context for its origin and a key for its interpretation.

2. Herodotus

Herodotus of Halicarnassus lived from about 484 to 425 BCE.[13] Little is known with certainty about his life. The tradition associates him with a period of exile spent on the island of Samos, a sojourn in Athens (where he is said to have been friends with Sophocles), and the foundation of the colony of Thurii in southern Italy. What can be stated with a high degree of probability is that he traveled extensively through-out the Mediterranean, and that he did most of his research and writing in the third quarter of the fifth century. So, even as the Peloponnesian War was breaking out (431 BCE), Herodotus was looking back and inquiring about an earlier conflict, not only to glorify 'great and marvelous deeds', but also 'to show why the two peoples fought with each other' (1.1).[14] At the very outset of his work, Herodotus clearly states his intention of uncovering causes, of explaining the 'why' behind the events he narrates. In doing so, Herodotus takes history in a new direction, moving beyond the earlier chroniclers of the Greek city-states. These earlier local historians, or horographers, had but 'one single and unvarying object, that of bringing to the common knowledge of all whatever records or traditions were to be found'.[15] Herodotus, by contrast, not only collected and reported information on a wide vari-ety of topics—including genealogy, ethnography, geography, and politics—he also gave unity to the wealth of far-ranging events he recounted by highlighting their causal relations. He does not merely relate what happened, but also why it hap-pened. And as Charles Fornara has pointed out, the novelty of Herodotus consists as well in his description of how things happened.[16] His exhaustive and intricately detailed narrative of the Persian War is entirely without precedent. It is this new and original venture that justifies his bearing the title, known to us from Cicero, as the 'father of history'.[17]

---

13. For a discussion of his dates and biographical information, see the introduction by J. Marincola in *Herodotus: The Histories* (trans. A. de Sélincourt; revised with introductory matter and notes by J. Marincola; New York: Penguin Books, 1996), p. x.

14. All translations of Herodotus unless otherwise noted are from the edition of Aubrey de Sélincourt revised by John Marincola (New York: Penguin Books, 1996).

15. C. Fornara, *The Nature of History in Ancient Greece and Rome* (Berkeley: University of California Press, 1983), p. 22.

16. Fornara, *The Nature of History*, pp. 29-30.

17. Cicero, *Laws* 1.1.5.

The history that Herodotus wrote had a profound impact on subsequent historiography. Not only was he the first historian to give an analytical description of a war, he was also probably the first to use ethnographic and constitutional studies to explain the war in itself and in its consequences.[18] His choice of the main subject matter for his investigations—the Persian War and its concomitant circumstances—defined the very substance of historiography for those who followed him.[19] The reciprocal relevance of customs, institutions, and war discovered by Herodotus remained profoundly connected to historical research. As Momigliano has stated, it was Herodotus who introduced the rule that historians must explain the events of which they write.[20] It is in this explaining of events that both Herodotus and his followers as well as the writers of biblical history differ most dramatically from their neighbors and predecessors in antiquity. It has long been noted that the great sweep of historical narrative found in the books of the Hebrew Scriptures is without peer or precedent among the writings of the ancient Near East. More recent studies have suggested, however, that a suitable comparison can be made between the Hebrew texts and Herodotus.

In selecting Herodotus, then, as the reference point from which I hope to gain greater insight into the historiographical material in Daniel, I am following the lead of such scholars as Elias Bickerman[21] and John Van Seters[22] who began to give attention to the work of Herodotus in the study of historiography in ancient Israel. Until very recently, this crossover into the world of Greek historiography on the part of biblical scholars of Israel's history was almost unheard of. Among the reasons Van Seters cites for the almost total neglect of Greek influences on Israelite historiography by Old Testament scholars is the long-standing supposed contrast between Greek and Hebrew thought.[23] This distinction, which was perhaps most explicitly formulated in the work of Thorlief Boman,[24] can be seen in the work of

18. A. Momigliano, *Storiografia Greca* (Turin: Einaudi, 1982), p. 6.

19. This fact is seen most clearly in his immediate successor in the field of historiography, Thucydides. Although Thucydides claimed that serious history could only be written about contemporary events which can reliably be attested, thus breaking with Herodotus's method of inquiring into past events and distant lands; nevertheless, his choice of the Peloponnesian War as his subject imitates Herodotus's own focus upon the Persian War.

20. Momigliano, *Storiografia Greca*, p. 7.

21. E. Bickerman, 'The Historical Foundations of Postbiblical Judaism', in L. Finkelstein (ed.), *The Jews: Their History* (New York: Schocken Books, 4th edn, 1974), pp. 72-118 (80-84).

22. J. Van Seters, *In Search of History: Historiography in the Ancient World and in the Origins of Biblical History* (New Haven: Yale University Press, 1983), Chapter 2 *passim*.

23. Van Seters, *In Search of History*, p. 8. The other reason he gives is the dating of Herodotus (which is firmly established in the fifth century) compared with the customary dating of the rise of Israelite historiography in the tenth century. He disputes the latter dating to make his case for a comparison. With regard to the book of Daniel, the relative dates do not pose a problem. Since Daniel can be dated securely to the middle of the second century, there is no chronological difficulty in positing influence from Herodotus.

24. T. Boman, *Hebrew Thought Compared with Greek* (trans. J.L. Moreau; London: SCM Press, 1960).

such eminent biblical theologians as Rudolph Bultmann[25] and Gerhard von Rad.[26] Their assertions that Greeks and Hebrews had completely different ideas about such fundamental notions as knowledge and time inevitably led to their concluding that the Greek and Hebrew concepts of history were entirely different from one another. While it would be foolish to claim that there are in fact no fundamental differences in thought or perspective between distinct cultures, the radical differentiation that was often proposed has now been shown to be untenable in many respects.[27] The doors have thus been opened to new inquiries into the mutual influences between Jews and Greeks in antiquity, especially in regard to what can now be seen as a very similar development of historiography in these two cultures. With particular reference to Herodotus, the work of Sara Mandell and David Noel Freedman[28] as well as that of Flemming Nielsen[29] have followed Van Seters in studying the historiography of ancient Israel alongside the *Histories* of Herodotus. I will examine these works and their conclusions in some detail below.

3. *Herodotus and Daniel*

While the wall separating biblical and classical historiography has thus begun to come down, permitting such comparative studies as those of Van Seters, Mandell and Freedman, and Nielsen, there is yet another wall which has impeded the study of Daniel and Herodotus together. This is the wall within biblical studies which has separated apocalyptic literature from the earlier historical and prophetic texts of the Hebrew Scriptures.[30] Apocalyptic literature has often been bracketed aside as a phenomenon that is late, foreign, degenerate, or of little theological value when compared with earlier traditions in Israel. These divisive and deprecating judgments were to a large extent overcome by the work of Paul Hanson, who stressed the continuity between prophecy and apocalyptic.[31] Nevertheless, his analysis perpetuated yet another inequitable division: the emphasis on the eschatological aspect of

---

25. See, for example, his article on the word γιγνώσκω in *TDNT*, I, pp. 689-719, where he distinguishes between the notion of knowledge held by the Jews and that found among the Greeks. Elsewhere he explicitly states that the Old Testament conception of history differs dramatically from the Greek conception. See his 'History and Eschatology in the New Testament', *NTS* 1 (1954–55), pp. 5-16 (5).

26. Von Rad (*Old Testament Theology*, II, p. 108) also overstates the differences between Hebrew and Greek thought which leads to his exaggerated contrast between Greek and Jewish concepts of time and history.

27. See A. Momigliano, 'Time in Ancient Historiography', in his *Essays in Ancient and Modern Historiography* (Oxford: Basil Blackwell, 1977), pp. 179-204. See also J. Barr, *Biblical Words for Time* (London: SCM Press, 1962).

28. S. Mandell and D.N. Freedman, *The Relationship between Herodotus' History and Primary History* (Atlanta: Scholars Press, 1993).

29. F.A.J. Nielsen, *The Tragedy in History: Herodotus and the Deuteronomistic History* (JSOTSup, 251; Sheffield: Sheffield Academic Press, 1997).

30. See, e.g., von Rad, *Old Testament Theology*, II, pp. 303-305.

31. P. Hanson, *The Dawn of Apocalyptic* (Philadelphia: Fortress Press, 1975).

apocalyptic literature to the neglect of its historical components.[32] While acknowledging that history is recounted in apocalyptic literature, Hanson downplays the historiographical material as merely setting the stage for eschatological prophecies by establishing the seer's credibility through *ex eventu* prophecies. In fact, the historiographical material present in the symbolic visions of Daniel (chs. 2, 7, 8, and 11) is seldom given much attention by scholars. When it is addressed, it is generally turned on its head to support the negative judgments of Noth and von Rad that apocalyptic writers had no interest in history. Such is the case with Stanley Brice Frost in his paper entitled 'Apocalyptic and History' where he describes apocalyptic as 'a rejection of history as the medium in which religious truth is to be sought and expressed'.[33] I am aware of only one brief article by G.I. Davies that gives a positive assessment of the historiographical component of apocalyptic literature.[34] His fundamental assertion—'that the preoccupation of the apocalyptic writers with historiography is a major element of their activity'[35]—holds true most especially, I will argue, for the book of Daniel. When one looks closely at such marvelously detailed and accurate (albeit symbolic) historical narrations as ch. 11 of Daniel, it becomes difficult to maintain that 'mundane history has become insignificant in the eyes of the apocalyptists',[36] as it likewise does to speak of 'the notorious historical inaccuracies of the apocalyptic writers'.[37] One would in fact be hard pressed to find a more verifiably accurate historical account in the pages of the Hebrew Scriptures than one does in this remarkable chapter of Daniel.

So, there have been these two barriers in place which have impeded the study of Daniel and Herodotus together: the wall between the Greek and Hebrew worlds, as well as the wall between apocalyptic and historiography. Both of these, upon closer inspection, prove to be illusory. There is no reason why the texts of Daniel and Herodotus cannot be studied together. Indeed, once we get beyond the assumptions that Athens has nothing to do with Jerusalem and that apocalyptic has nothing to do with history, the texts themselves invite a comparison. As previously mentioned, the great classical historian, Arnaldo Momigliano, pointed out this invitation. Being quite familiar with ancient Jewish as well as ancient Greek texts, he noticed that the theory of a succession of world empires (which appears in several Greek and Roman historians) shows up for the first time in Herodotus, who speaks of the Medes succeeding the Assyrians in mastery over Asia (1.95), and subsequently of the Persians succeeding the Medes (1.130). In the fifth century, the same series of

---

32. Hanson, *Dawn of Apocalyptic*, p. 28.

33. S.B. Frost, 'Apocalyptic and History', in J.P. Hyatt (ed.), *The Bible in Modern Scholarship: Papers Read at the 100th Meeting of the Society of Biblical Literature, December 28-30, 1964* (Nashville: Abingdon Press, 1965), pp. 98-113 (98-99).

34. G.I. Davies, 'Apocalyptic and Historiography', *JSOT* 5 (1978), pp. 15-28. A positive, albeit qualified, judgment of the historiographic interests of apocalyptic literature was also given in the dissertation of B.W. Jones, 'Ideas of History in the Book of Daniel' (unpublished doctoral dissertation, Graduate Theological Union, 1972), pp. 271-77.

35. G.I. Davies, 'Apocalyptic and Historiography', p. 15.

36. Frost, 'Apocalyptic and History', p. 110.

37. Frost, 'Apocalyptic and History', p. 111.

successive empires reappeared in the *Persika* of Ctesias, who obviously imitated the pattern established by Herodotus even as he attempted to correct him. Soon after the conquest of Alexander, the Macedonians were added to the sequence. At the end of the fourth century, Demetrius of Phalerum spoke of the Macedonians as successors to the Persians in their rule over the world.[38] From the second century BCE onward, the theory of imperial succession is widely attested in Greek and Roman historians including Polybius, Aemilius Sura, Diodorus Siculus, Dionysius of Halicarnassus, and Trogus Pompeius. Outside of Greece and Rome, this theory is first witnessed in ch. 2 of the book of Daniel.[39] If this theory is rooted in the Greek conception of history, with its 'specific interest for political and military phe-nomena',[40] then the book of Daniel not only owes something of its own distinctive view of history to the Greek tradition going back to Herodotus, but it is also quite possibly the first non-Greek work to appropriate and transform this Greek theory.

If the final author/editor of the book of Daniel wrote shortly before the restora-tion of the temple and the death of Antiochus IV,[41] it is certainly not inconceivable to suppose that he knew directly or indirectly of Herodotus's *Histories*. According to the second book of Maccabees, a significant number of Jews in Jerusalem had embraced a Greek way of life, including a Greek education, in the years just previ-ous to these events (2 Macc. 4.10-15). Even among those Jews who did not fall into the so-called Hellenizing party there was no lack of individuals who spoke, read, and wrote Greek. Such was certainly the case with Judas Maccabeus's envoy to Rome, Eupolemus (1 Macc. 8.17; 2 Macc. 4.11). In addition to bearing a Greek name, he must have been familiar with the *lingua franca* of the day to be able to function as an international ambassador. If, as seems likely, this Eupolemus is also to be identified with the second-century BCE Jewish historian of the same name, then there is even a precedent for a Palestinian Jew of the second century, conver-sant in both Greek and Hebrew, who was also familiar with a certain amount of Greek historiography.[42] Yet scholars have been slow to appreciate the depth of Greek influence in Palestine. If we no longer see Hellenization only or primarily as

38.	Preserved in Polybius 29.21.4.

39.	A. Momigliano, 'Daniel and the Greek Theory of Imperial Succession', in Berti (ed.), *Essays on Ancient and Modern Judaism*, pp. 29-35.

40.	Momigliano, 'Daniel and the Greek Theory', p. 30.

41.	Such a dating has received an overwhelming consensus based upon the 'incorrect' prophecies in Daniel concerning the time of the restoration of the Temple (8.14; 12.11-12) and the circumstances of Antiochus IV's death (11.45).

42.	See F. Fallon, 'Eupolemus: A New Translation and Introduction', in *OTP*, II, pp. 861-72. On the relationship between Eupolemus and both Herodotus and Ctesias, see B.Z. Wacholder, *Eupolemus: A Study of Judaeo-Greek Literature* (Cincinnati: Hebrew Union College, 1974), pp. 230-34. He argues that Eupolemus used an intermediary source which combined accounts of Herodotus and Ctesias. His main argument for a dependence upon Greek sources is the appearance of a Median ally to Nebuchadnezzar in his campaign against Jerusalem—Astibares by name (the passage is preserved in Eusebius, *Praeparatio Evangelica* 9.39.4). There is no biblical account mentioning a Median ally; and the otherwise unknown Astibares (Cyaxares was the Median king at this time) appears to be the invention of Ctesias who created an artificial list of Median kings which included this name (see Diodorus Siculus 2.32.5–34.6).

a phenomenon of the Diaspora, there is still a certain unwillingness to see it as something more than an apostate political movement in Palestine.[43] Therefore, it will be helpful to take a closer look at the interaction between Jewish and Greek culture that preceded the composition of the book of Daniel. Only if we can broaden our understanding of Hellenization in Palestine to include its influence upon pious Jews—Jews who fiercely opposed Antiochus IV—will a comparison between Daniel and Herodotus make sense.

4. *Judaism and Hellenism*

'What has Athens to do with Jerusalem?' The rhetorical question, posed by Tertullian[44] early in the third century CE, was raised as well—if not in those exact same words—in Palestine four centuries earlier. By the symbolism of these two cities, Tertullian referred to the Academy and the Church, denying the validity and usefulness of 'pagan' Greek philosophy for the believing community. In a similar manner, certain devout Jews of the second century BCE viewed the proliferation of Greek education and customs as harmful and incompatible with their religious way of life. Yet, in spite of the negative appraisal of all things Greek by both Tertullian and those Jews of the Maccabean era who decried the 'extreme of Hellenization' (2 Macc. 4.13), both the Church of the third century CE and Judaism of the second century BCE were (and would become to an even greater extent) influenced by Greek ideas.

The understanding of the impact and influence of the Greek world upon Judaism (and/or vice versa) has been one of the more fascinating questions left to us by antiquity. As Erich Gruen has so poetically stated, 'The interaction of Jew and Greek in antiquity still weaves a spell'.[45] While there is still much that is obscure about this interaction, particularly with regard to the situation in Palestine and the beginnings of the Hellenization attested to in 2 Maccabees, two points should be made clear. First of all, 'Judaism' and 'Hellenism' were neither competing systems nor incompatible concepts.[46] Tertullian notwithstanding, Athens and Jerusalem were not mutually exclusive. A Jew could possess a Greek education and even have an affinity for Greek culture and still be a Torah-observant Jew grounded in the traditions of Israel. The presence of a thoroughly 'Hellenized' Jew such as Eupolemus on the side of Judas Maccabeus who fought for the ancestral religion dramatically illustrates this point. Secondly, the contrast between Palestinian Judaism as the pure form of the faith and Hellenistic Judaism as the tainted or watered-down

---

43. See, e.g., L.H. Feldman, 'How Much Hellenism in Jewish Palestine?', *Hebrew Union College Annual* 57 (1986), pp. 83-111. He argues that the lack of evidence for any large-scale apostasy in Palestine means that Hellenization had no deep impact upon the populace, as if Hellenization and apostasy were equivalent.

44. Tertullian, *De Praescriptione Haereticorum* 7.

45. E.S. Gruen, *Heritage and Hellenism: The Reinvention of Jewish Tradition* (Berkeley: University of California Press, 1998), p. xiii.

46. Gruen, *Heritage and Hellenism*, p. iv.

version cannot be maintained.[47] It has been such simplistic dichotomies as these which have led to the almost automatic attribution of many Hellenistic–Jewish writings to the Diaspora with little or no basis for such a designation.[48] It is often simply assumed that good Greek writing and clearly Greek ideas are not likely to be found in Palestinian Judaism. In a similar manner, these long-held assumptions continue to impede the study of the influence of Greek culture on Palestinian–Jewish texts such as Daniel. There is, however, no compelling reason to maintain that a Palestinian Jew of the second century BCE who wrote in Hebrew was *ipso facto* ignorant of or opposed to Greek ideas. One might say that for centuries Tertullian had the last word and the prevailing view held that Athens in fact had little or nothing to do with Jerusalem. A very brief look at the history of scholarship concerning the relationship between Judaism and Hellenism can help to explain the persistence of this separatist view.

The term 'Hellenism' in connection with Jewish culture has been around at least since the time in which the second book of Maccabees was written (c. 100 BCE). The term used in 2 Macc. 4.13—Ἑλληνισμός—clearly refers to the adoption of Greek customs by the Jews in Jerusalem. This is made explicit in the surrounding context of 4.9-15 through numerous examples. Among the Greek innovations are the establishment of a γυμνάσιον and ἐφηβεῖον for the intellectual and physical education of the young Jewish men. The city of Jerusalem was also refounded as a πόλις with the name of Antioch (Ἀντιόχεια), while a number of its populace were enrolled as citizens of this new Greek city (4.9). Greek athletic contests figure prominently in the picture of decadence painted by the author of 2 Maccabees (4.14) and mention is even made of the distinctive Greek fashions taken up by the newly Hellenized (4.12). This description in 2 Maccabees, involving as it does the educational, political, and recreational dimensions of life, presents us with something of the breadth and depth of impact which Greek culture had upon Jewish Jerusalem. However, the vast literature produced by modern scholarship around the word 'Hellenism' took its initial cue not from this passage in 2 Maccabees, but from the contrast expressed in the Acts of the Apostles 6.1 between Hellenists (Ἑλληνισταί) and Hebrews (Ἑβραῖοι). Here the terms refer explicitly to speakers of Greek and Hebrew (or Aramaic).[49] The distinction is primarily one of language.

47. Gruen, *Heritage and Hellenism*, p. xv.
48. See, e.g., H. Attridge, 'Philo the Epic Poet', in *OTP*, II, p. 781. He states that it is more likely that the poem originated in Alexandria than in Palestine. This assertion (made in spite of the fact that the focus of the poem is Jerusalem) rests solely on the high Greek literary character of the poem which is assumed to be incompatible with a Palestinian provenance. Tessa Rajak, writing specifically about Judeo-Greek historiography, correctly states that it would be a mistake to assign this literature particularly to the Diaspora, and that 'not all of those normally regarded as Alexandrian Jewish writers can, from their fragments, be assigned even as a probability to that milieu' (T. Rajak, 'The Sense of History in Jewish Intertestamental Writing', in *Crises and Perspectives: Studies in Ancient Near Eastern Polytheism, Biblical Theology, Palestinian Archaeology and Intertestamental Literature: Papers Read at the Joint British–Dutch Old Testament Conference held at Cambridge, UK 1985* [OTS, 24; Leiden: E.J. Brill, 1986], pp. 124-45 [132]).
49. J.A. Fitzmyer, *The Acts of the Apostles: A New Translation with Introduction and Commentary* (AB, 31; New York: Doubleday, 1998), p. 347.

The assumption was often made (rightly or wrongly) that the Greek speakers were Jews from the Diaspora, while the Hebrew speakers were native Palestinians.[50] In the scholarship of the seventeenth century it was this linguistic aspect which shaped the understanding of Hellenism.[51] It was debated whether or not these Ἑλληνισταί spoke a special Greek dialect, while the idea of a Hellenistic language came to indicate the Greek of the New Testament as well as that of the Greek versions of the Hebrew Scriptures. The eighteenth century saw the notion of Hellenism expand to include not only the language, but also the thought of Greek-speaking Jews.

It was Johann Gustav Droysen who expanded the notion of Hellenism beyond the realm of Greek-speaking (or Greek-thinking) Jews. In fact, he came to disregard the Jewish part of the equation almost entirely. For him, Hellenism was the language and thought found among all of the peoples conquered by Alexander.[52] Influenced by Hegelian notions of history, Droysen presented Hellenism as the synthesis of Greek and Oriental ideas that would eventually lead to Christianity. This depiction of Hellenism as a world culture emphasized the depth of interaction between Jew and Greek while at the same time noting that this particular interaction was not unique, but rather part of a more widespread phenomenon. The drawback to this portrayal of Hellenism is that it contributed to the illusion of a programmatic blending of cultures which has proven difficult to maintain.[53] Furthermore, Droysen's initial focus on non-Jewish Oriental cultures (including Egyptian, Babylonian and Syrian) in the making of a Hellenistic culture reinforced the ancient assumption that Athens and Jerusalem simply do not mix. The Hellenistic synthesis of Greece and the 'pagan' Orient came to be viewed as something extraneous to Palestinian Judaism. Jewish involvement in this 'Hellenistic world' was reserved for those Jews living in the Diaspora. This sharp differentiation between the thoroughgoing

50.   The text itself does not mention this. There is the comment a few verses later that one of the seven deacons (Nicolaus) appointed to assist the Greek speakers was himself a native of Antioch (Acts 6.5). But this special mention regarding the origin of Nicolaus who was a convert seems to suggest that the others were long-time residents of Jerusalem and Judea. Furthermore, the very structure of Acts of the Apostles in which the Christian mission does not spread beyond Judea until ch. 8 suggests that the Greek-speaking Jews were themselves residents of Judea.

51.   A brief summary of the scholarship is provided by A. Momigliano, 'J.G. Droysen between Greeks and Jews', in *idem, Essays in Ancient and Modern Historiography*, pp. 307-23 (309-10). A more lengthy discussion of the history of the term 'Hellenism' is found in R. Laqueur, *Hellenismus* (Giessen: Alfred Töpelmann, 1925).

52.   Momigliano, 'J.G. Droysen', pp. 309-10.

53.   As Martin Hengel has noted ('The Interpenetration of Judaism and Hellenism in the Pre-Maccabean Period', in W.D. Davies and L. Finkelstein [eds.], *The Cambridge History of Judaism*, [Cambridge: Cambridge University Press, 1989], II, pp. 167-228 [168]) this interpretation has its origins in antiquity, especially in Plutarch's idealized characterization of Alexander as one who brings civilization, law and peace (*De fortuna aut virtute Alexandri Magni* 4.328b). In modern times, this idea was championed especially by W.W. Tarn, *Alexander the Great* (2 vols.; Cambridge: Cambridge University Press, 1948), I, especially pp. 121-48; and *idem, Hellenistic Civilisation* (London: Edward Arnold & Co., 3rd edn, 1952), especially pp. 210-38, regarding Hellenism and the Jews. In reality, the concerns of Alexander, the Diadochi and their successors had more to do with securing and extending power than with spreading civilization and culture.

Hellenism of Judaism in the Diaspora and the traditional, normative, or mainline Judaism in Palestine remains stubbornly influential, especially on a popular level. Nevertheless, it can also be found explicitly and implicitly in some modern scholarly works.[54] This distinction has been shown, however, to be overstated and untenable in its extreme form. The work of scholars such as Elias Bickerman and Martin Hengel has pointed out the extent to which Palestinian Judaism also was influenced by Greek culture.

Bickerman's influence has been enormous in recognizing and appreciating the influence of Greek culture upon Judaism in the Hellenistic period. From his authoritative work on the Maccabean revolt, *Der Gott der Makkabäer*,[55] to his final posthumous publication, *The Jews in the Greek Age*,[56] he has presented clear and compelling arguments for a significant impact of Greek language, thought and customs on Judaism (including Palestinian Judaism) in the final three centuries BCE. Following in Bickerman's footsteps, Hengel's *magnum opus*, *Judaism and Hellenism*, has pushed the argument to the point where Hellenistic influence can be seen 'not only in the realm of the pro-Hellenistic upper class and in late wisdom, but at the very point where the bitterest defensive action was being fought against the destructive forces of Hellenism'.[57] It is in fact around this point that we must situate the book of Daniel.

So, the studies of Bickerman and Hengel have greatly increased our understanding and awareness of Hellenization in Palestine. They have brought scholarship back full circle to the point where we can ask serious questions about Greek influences in Palestinian–Jewish writings. With regard to Herodotus in particular, Bickerman preceded the work of more recent comparative studies by several decades in pointing to various ways in which the Chronicler is similar to Herodotus and Greek historiography as opposed to Oriental historiography.[58] Morton Smith summarized Bickerman's analysis around six points: (1) both Herodotus and the Chronicler do not simply transcribe, but correct their sources according to their own standards; (2) they do not merely provide a chronicle, but seek to explain history; (3) their explanation is related to the divine, particularly as expressed through retribution; (4) they make their point through speeches of wise counselors and foreboders of doom; (5) their accounts become more detailed as they approach their own time, although neither reaches the author's present day; (6) they give a large place to the reproduction of official records.[59] Although Bickerman was content to enumerate these similarities without arguing for some deeper relationship to explain them, he suggests a world in which Jew and Greek (including their histories and

54. E.g. Feldman, 'How Much Hellenism in Jewish Palestine?'.

55. E. Bickerman, *Der Gott der Makkabäer* (Berlin: Schocken Verlag, 1937).

56. E. Bickerman, *The Jews in the Greek Age* (Cambridge, MA: Harvard University Press, 1988).

57. M. Hengel, *Judaism and Hellenism: Studies in their Encounter in Palestine during the Early Hellenistic Period* (2 vols.; Philadelphia: Fortress Press, 1974), I, p. 311.

58. Bickerman, 'Historical Foundations', pp. 80-84.

59. M. Smith, *Palestinian Parties and Politics that Shaped the Old Testament* (London: SCM Press, 2nd corrected edn, 1987), p. 129.

historiographers) are not wholly other. Even though he elsewhere insists on the mutual ignorance between Athens and Jerusalem before the coming of Alexander, it is an ignorance mitigated by Phoenician traders who introduced goods from Rhodes, Cyprus and Athens into Palestine beginning in the seventh century.[60] The discoveries in Palestine of Greek pottery dating as far back as the eighth century and of Judean coins modeled after the Athenian drachma prior to the time of Alexander effectively dispel the myth of total segregation between Jerusalem and Athens.[61]

5. *Studies of Herodotus and Hebrew Historiography*

If Bickerman hesitated to develop a theory to explain the similarities between the *Histories* of Herodotus and the books of Chronicles, he did so with good reason. If (as seems likely) the Chronicler wrote before the eastward march of Alexander which made possible the more direct contacts between Jews and Greeks, any direct link between Chronicles and Herodotus would be difficult to maintain. The archaeological evidence of a certain shared material culture was not a substantial foundation upon which to build a theory of a common literary tradition. More recent scholars, however, taking a more literary approach, have sought to define explicitly the relationship they perceive between Herodotus and various blocks of Hebrew historiography. It is to these recent studies of Herodotus and Hebrew historiography that I now turn.

a. *Mandell and Freedman*
The first of two recent major studies to appear was the work of Sara Mandell and David Noel Freedman, titled *The Relationship between Herodotus' History and Primary History*. Believing that the parallels between the two works 'were too numerous to be accidental or merely characteristic of a shared genre',[62] they attempt a literary-critical study of the two texts. This they do from the perspective of analytic (i.e. 'new') criticism, the basic tenet of which is that 'a literary text does and, indeed, must stand alone as a self-contained artifactual or iconic entity'.[63] While purporting to work within this theoretical structure, they often draw into their argument assumptions that are foreign to the method they propose. These assumptions include speculation about the literary history of the Hebrew Bible that is somewhat dubious. Such is the case with their presuming that Ezra was the man responsible for the present shape of the Pentateuch and Former Prophets.[64] They

---

60. Bickerman, *The Jews in the Greek Age*, p. 20.
61. Momigliano, 'Jews and Greeks', p. 10. The impact of oriental cultures on Greece has also been documented in various studies. See, e.g., M.C. Astour, *Hellenosemitica: An Ethnic and Cultural Study in West Semitic Impact on Mycenaean Greece* (Leiden: E.J. Brill, 1965); S.P. Morris, *Daidalos and the Origins of Greek Art* (Princeton, NJ: Princeton University Press, 1992), especially the chapter 'From Ugarit to the Aegean'.
62. Mandell and Freedman, *The Relationship*, p. ix.
63. Mandell and Freedman, *The Relationship*, p. 10.
64. Mandell and Freedman, *The Relationship*, pp. ix and 89. This central role ascribed to Ezra in the formation of the Hebrew Scriptures does have a long history behind it. It is witnessed as early

persist in this identification throughout their work in spite of their own claim to hold to 'the basic axiom of Analytic Criticism, whereby a narrative cannot be used as a source of exact knowledge about its real author'.[65] One need not take the minimalist view, which doubts even the historicity of Ezra,[66] in order to see the difficulties of ascribing such a central role to him in the 'final redaction' of the biblical text.

Regarding Herodotus as well, Mandell and Freedman arrive at some conclusions in violation of their 'basic axiom'. For instance, they infer that Herodotus must certainly have known Aramaic in order to travel so extensively throughout the Persian Empire.[67] This itself implies that he actually accomplished the travels of his implied narrator. Again, without necessarily disagreeing with either of these propositions, it can be seen that they are extraneous to the method set forth by Mandell and Freedman. This often speculative approach of Mandell and Freedman allows them to make much more elaborate claims as to the relationship between Herodotus and what they refer to as 'Primary History'. For example, they can conclude either that Herodotus was familiar with Primary History through an Aramaic translation or that the many similarities may be explained as the work of Alexandrian grammarians who redacted both texts sometime between the third century BCE and the first century CE.[68]

In addition to the highly speculative nature of their conclusions, the very nature of their evidence is at times quite weak. The similarities and parallels which they are able to enumerate between the *Histories* of Herodotus and Primary History are not in and of themselves any more sufficient for establishing a literary dependence than were those noted by Bickerman. Among the examples they cite are: (1) both works are national epics; (2) both have been divided at some point in their history into nine books; (3) both are about the same length; (4) both begin with a prehistory that includes myths, folk-tales and legends treated as factual occurrences; (5) both show a shift in their basic format at the point where the 'homeland' becomes the scene of action; (6) in both historic causation is tied to divine will.[69] Some of these are in fact highly questionable. If one bases a comparison on such criteria as the approximate length of a work or its division into a certain number of books (no matter when this division occurred!), there is no telling how many literary connections one might deduce amid all the world's literature that has ever been written.

as the pseudepigraphal *4 Ezra* (c. 100 CE), which tells of Ezra's commission by God to write twenty-four books to be made public (corresponding to the Hebrew canon) as well as seventy books to be reserved for the wise (*4 Ezra* 14.37-48).

    65. Mandell and Freedman, *The Relationship*, p. 11.

    66. See Nielsen, *The Tragedy in History*, p. 16, who also cites the studies of Lester Grabbe ('Reconstructing History from the Book of Ezra', in P.R. Davies [ed.], *Second Temple Studies*. I. *Persian Period* [JSOTSup, 117; Sheffield: JSOT Press, 1991], pp. 98-106) and G. Garbini (*History and Ideology in Ancient Israel* [New York: Crossroad, 1988]) concerning historical problems regarding Ezra.

    67. Mandell and Freedman, *The Relationship*, p. 175.

    68. Mandell and Freedman, *The Relationship*, pp. 176-77.

    69. Mandell and Freedman, *The Relationship*, p. x.

The fact remains that if Herodotus knew either directly or indirectly this 'work of Ezra' and even went so far as to model to some extent his own work upon it as they suggest, it becomes inexplicable that he recounts no stories of the Israelites. More likely is the conclusion of Nielsen that Herodotus simply had never heard about the Israelites.[70] This verdict is supported by the ethnographic information reported by Herodotus himself. He refers to Syria-Palestine (1.105; 2.106; 3.91; 4.39) but its inhabitants are always referred to as Syrians (1.104; 7.89). Furthermore, the only Palestinian city between Phoenicia and Egypt that he mentions is Ashkelon (1.105) along the main coastal trade route from which the small district of Judea was isolated. One *may* doubt whether Herodotus visited every place he claims to have seen, but one *should* doubt whether he visited or knew of a country and people of which he makes no mention.

In spite of its limitations, the study of Mandell and Freedman has its merits. Primary among these is its recognition of the fact that both Herodotus and the so-called Primary History tie historical causation closely to the divine will.[71] Both portray the divine, whether as a singular God or a multiplicity of gods, as taking an active role in historical events. The gods in Herodotus aid the Greeks in their battle against the Persians (8.13, 37-38, 65) in much the same way as the God of Israel helps the Israelites in battle. Strengthening the comparison is the fact that the many gods which Herodotus acknowledges are in fact treated as a single divine historical force acting upon the world. As Ivan Linforth has noted: 'though the multiplicity of gods is never called in question, there is a disposition to speak of the divine element in the world as if it were characterized by the indivisibility of the god of the pure monotheist'.[72] Thus the two works share the idea of a singular divine agent who acts in history. Furthermore, the divine will is often expressed in both works through dreams, oracles, or prophecies which either encourage a course of action or tell what will in fact happen by God's design.

Closely related to this divine role in history, Mandell and Freedman have noted that both works narrate their history in what may be described as a tragic mode of presentation.[73] The close relationship of Herodotus' *Histories* to Attic tragedy has in fact long been noted.[74] It is a relationship born of their common roots in Greek epic. Most recently, Nielsen took this tragic mode of presentation as the focal point for comparing Herodotus to the Deuteronomistic History.[75] Mandell and Freedman themselves enumerate several literary connections between Herodotus and the

---

70. Nielsen, *The Tragedy in History*, p. 17 n. 17.

71. Mandell and Freedman, *The Relationship*, pp. 69, 143-45.

72. I. Linforth, 'Named and Unnamed Gods in Herodotus', in L. Tarán (ed.), *Studies in Herodotus and Plato* (New York: Garland Publishing, 1987), pp. 75-119 (94).

73. Mandell and Freedman, *The Relationship*, p. 175.

74. See J.L. Myres, *Herodotus: Father of History* (Oxford: Clarendon Press, 1953), p. 27.

75. Nielsen (*The Tragedy in History*, p. 46) refers to H. Fohl, *Tragische Kunst bei Herodot: Inaugural-Dissertation zur Erlangung der Doktorwürde der hohen philosophischen Fakultät der Universität Rostock* (Borna-Leipzig: Buchdruckerei Robert Noske, 1913) as the standard work on this subject.

tragic genre:[76] (1) the clarity or vividness of the narrative which both employ; (2) the lack of description of the natural world behind the narrative or of description 'for its own sake'; (3) the absence of psychological and physiological analysis; (4) the theological dimension which comes into play; and (5) the inclusion of direct speech within the narrative. It is perhaps more novel to view the historical books of the Hebrew Scriptures as a tragic drama. While Mandell and Freedman do point out that Primary History shares many of these features common to Herodotus and Attic tragedy, they do not fully develop this point. Their conclusion contains only a brief description of what they consider to be the main tragic theme in both works: Mandell and Freedman see as a main theme in both works the idea that disunity (of the Israelites during the conquest and of the Greeks during the Persian War) leads to a future tragic downfall.[77] It seems doubtful, however, that this failure of the Israelites to unify constitutes the main tragic theme of the Hebrew Scriptures. Rather, it is the failure of the people to keep the covenant that leads to their tragic dispossession of the land. As far as Herodotus is concerned, it is questionable to call any signs of Greek disunity tragic since the fall of the Greek city-states (to which Mandell and Freedman allude as the tragic consequence foreboded by this disunity[78]) lies entirely outside of the narrative. The 'disunity' in Herodotus, if it serves a literary function, would seem rather to be employed to highlight the exploits of individual groups within the Greek coalition, giving pride of place to the Athenians for their role in turning back the Persians.

A final word that must be said in regard to the study of Mandell and Freedman is that in spite of their arguments suggesting a direct relationship between Herodotus's *Histories* and the Primary History, the chronological and cultural difficulties which they sidestep remain. The problem of dating the biblical text has to be more critically addressed before any direct relationship can be maintained. Simply proposing that Ezra arranged the text into its present form some time in the middle of the fifth century will not do. Furthermore, the assumption that Herodotus knew Aramaic and therefore may have become acquainted with an Aramaic translation or Targum of Primary History[79] is pure speculation. There is in fact no evidence that Herodotus even knew Aramaic[80] (Herodotus himself on one occasion mentions his dependence upon an interpreter[81]) and certainly no hint that he was familiar with

---

76. Mandell and Freedman, *The Relationship*, pp. 70-71.

77. Mandell and Freedman, *The Relationship*, p. 186. The examples of disunity they cite for Israel are the complaints of Aaron and Miriam (Num. 12), the false reports of the scouts (13.25-33), the threat of revolt (14.1-10), and the rebellions of Korah (16.1-11) and of Dathan and Abiram (16.12-24). From Herodotus they emphasize the Spartans arriving too late at the battle of Marathon.

78. Mandell and Freedman, *The Relationship*, p. 187.

79. Mandell and Freedman, *The Relationship*, p. 175.

80. For a generally negative evaluation of Herodotus's knowledge of foreign languages see W. Schmid, *Geschichte der griechischen Literatur: Die griechische Literatur in der Zeit der attischen Hegemonie vor dem Eingreifen der Sophistik* (Munich: Beck, 1934), pp. 557-58.

81. At 2.125 he relates how an Egyptian inscription on the pyramid of Cheops was read to him by an interpreter. It has been noted that Herodotus most likely used paid guides and interpreters as a matter of course. See D. Asheri, *Erodoto: Libro I: La Lidia e la Persia* (Milan: Fondazione Lorenzo Valla, 1988), p. xxix.

any of the traditions in the Hebrew Bible since he recounts none of them, nor even mentions the Jewish people. These would be curious omissions indeed, considering the breadth of material recounted by Herodotus both from what he claims to have seen with his own eyes and from what he reports to have heard from the various peoples he encountered in his journeys.

If the direct or indirect dependence of Herodotus upon the biblical text which Mandell and Freedman suggest cannot be supported, the alternatives, then, would be either to ascribe some kind of literary priority to Herodotus or to posit no connection at all, attributing the similarities between the texts (if not wholly to coincidence) to the shared literary genre and similar historical circumstances in which each work was produced. With regard to this latter possibility, Arnaldo Momigliano has pointed out that at least from the fifth century BCE both Jews and Greeks 'had constantly to refer to the reality of the Persian Empire'.[82] More specifically, he gives two examples of the parallel development of strongly nationalistic civilizations in Greece and Israel 'in reaction to the cosmopolitan and tolerant despotism of the Persians'.[83] He notes first of all the activity of Themistocles and Nehemiah in the construction of walls to isolate and protect their cities of Athens and Jerusalem. Secondly, he indicates how Ezra's denunciation of mixed marriages in Judea is paralleled by Pericles' laws on Athenian citizenship. Whether the development of Jewish and Greek historiography fits into this picture of nascent nationalism against a Persian background is an interesting question. It must be stated, however, that while Chronicles and Ezra–Nehemiah (the material to which Momigliano is referring in his article) originate in the Persian period, it has not been established that the great bulk of Israelite historiography (the Primary History of Mandell and Freedman) arose at this relatively late date. Although there are some scholars who date this material to the Persian[84] or even the Hellenistic[85] period, the majority of scholars maintain that the major compositional and redactional stages in Israelite historiography belong to the late monarchic and exilic periods.

b. *Flemming Nielsen*
Following the work of Mandell and Freedman by a few years was Flemming Nielsen's book, *The Tragedy in History: Herodotus and the Deuteronomistic History*. As its title suggests, it takes a more focused look at these two great works, examining them around one key feature already mentioned by Mandell and Freedman —the tragic mode of presentation. Flemming operates from a position which is the chronological opposite of Mandell and Freedman, postulating a later date for Hebrew historiography and thereby raising the question 'how and to what extent

---

82. Momigliano, 'Biblical Studies', p. 7.
83. A. Momigliano, 'Eastern Elements in Post-Exilic Jewish, and Greek, Historiography', in his *Essays in Ancient and Modern Historiography*, pp. 25-35 (25).
84. See, e.g., P.R. Davies, *In Search of 'Ancient Israel'* (JSOTSup, 148; Sheffield: JSOT Press, 1992); and T.L. Thompson, *Early History of the Israelite People: From the Written and Archaeological Sources* (SHANE, 4; Leiden: E.J. Brill, 1992).
85. See N.P. Lemche, 'The Old Testament—A Hellenistic Book', *JSOT* 7 (1993), pp. 163-93.

Herodotus may have been among the sources of inspiration for the Old Testament historiography'.[86] Other than this chronological priority which he presupposes, his assumptions are more modest. Citing the work of Claus Westermann, he even admits that the Deuteronomistic History, which is half of his comparison, may never have existed.[87] Nevertheless, he accepts this literary unit consisting of the books of Deuteronomy through Kings as a working hypothesis.

Without trying to establish an explicitly direct relationship between Herodotus and the Deuteronomistic History, Nielsen attempts to demonstrate that the latter, no less than the former, has a decidedly tragic element. This he identifies as the 'tragic view of the relationship between God and humanity'.[88] He highlights this element of tragedy by a comparison with Herodotus around five main themes:[89] (1) 'the idea of an immense distance between god and man'; (2) that 'man should keep to his proper place seen in relation to the deity'; (3) 'the idea of the deceptive deity who leads humans to bring about their own misfortune'; (4) 'equilibrium, often in the form of a *hubris–nemesis* motif'; and (5) that 'people are blessed or cursed by the deity on account of their lineage'. The most significant of these themes in Herodotus is clearly the fourth, to which the first and second can be seen as closely related. The well-known Greek idea that excessive pride inevitably meets with destruction is found throughout the *Histories*. It must be stated, however, that what Nielsen refers to as a *hubris–nemesis* motif in the Deuteronomistic History should be more properly defined (especially in the main examples he cites from Deut. 29.25-27; 2 Kgs 17.7-8, 19-20; 22.16-17) as the covenant dynamic whereby the people receive either blessing or curse based on their fidelity to their covenant obligations. It is not exactly the same as the well-known Greek idea encountered so often in Herodotus in which *hubris* is met with divine wrath or retribution. The primary sin that is punished with destruction in the Deuteronomistic History is not pride at all, but infidelity to the covenant, which is more precisely defined as apostasy—the worship of other gods:

> They will conclude, 'It is because they abandoned the covenant of the LORD, the God of their ancestors, which he made with them when he brought them out of the land of Egypt. They turned and served other gods, worshiping them, gods whom they had not known and whom he had not allotted to them; so the anger of the LORD was kindled against that land, bringing on it every curse written in this book'. (Deut. 29.25-27)

Even among the 'lesser stories' from the Deuteronomistic History which Nielsen cites as examples of this *hubris–nemesis* motif, there are marked differences from the parallels he finds in Herodotus. For example, he mentions the extreme imbalance of power between two opposing forces as an overstepping of bounds—a

---

86. Nielsen, *The Tragedy in History*, p. 15.
87. Nielsen, *The Tragedy in History*, p. 18. See also C. Westermann, *Die Geschichtsbücher des Alten Testaments: Gab es ein deuteronomistisches Geschichtswerk?* (Theologische Bücherei, 87; Gütersloh: Chr. Kaiser/Gütersloher Verlagshaus, 1994).
88. Nielsen, *The Tragedy in History*, p. 18.
89. Nielsen, *The Tragedy in History*, pp. 114-17.

situation to which the deity seeks to return balance. One can think of the classic example from Herodotus in which the shipwreck of the Persian fleet is explained as being caused by God who wished to reduce it to the size of the Greek fleet (8.13). The corresponding example, which Nielsen cites from Judges 7, of Gideon's victory over the Midianites works in an entirely different way. There the Lord wishes to reduce the number of Israel's forces, which are already outnumbered by the Midianites. The imbalance is increased rather than decreased. The passage emphasizes the value of quality over quantity, but most importantly it points to the Lord as the hero of Israel whose action alone brings victory:

> The LORD said to Gideon, 'The troops with you are too many for me to give the Midianites into their hand. Israel would only take the credit away from me, saying, "My own hand has delivered me."' (Judg. 7.2)

There is no mention of *hubris* at all with regard to the vast numbers of the Midianites (Judg. 7.12). The entire focus of the narrative is on Israel's relationship with God. It is they who must avoid attributing to themselves what belongs to God. In contrast to Herodotus's tragic portrayal of foreign personalities (of which Xerxes is the prime example), the Deuteronomistic History is focused squarely on Israel. The Midianite princes, Oreb and Zeeb, whom Gideon defeats are ultimately insignificant to the story. Even the most significant foreign power in the entire Deuteronomistic History—Nebuchadnezzar, who brings the history to a close—does not say a word or have a personality. These foreign rulers are merely instruments of divine retribution in the tragic story of Israel's relationship to God.

Ultimately, in terms of defining the relationship between Herodotus and the Deuteronomistic History, Nielsen's aim is somewhat more modest than that of Mandell and Freedman. Accepting as he does the chronological priority of Herodotus, he vaguely states that this earlier work 'should be viewed as being part of a greater, literary context to which the later work belongs'.[90] If his approach is more sober and realistic than that of Mandell and Freedman, it is also to a certain extent disappointing. If the Deuteronomistic History was written in the Hellenistic period as Nielsen maintains, and if it has striking affinities with the *Histories* of Herodotus (more than with any other work from the surviving Greek tradition), why is there the willingness to assert that 'the Hellenic tradition…influenced the Deuteronomistic history'[91] but the unwillingness to maintain a more direct influence by Herodotus? Nielsen does not explain or elaborate how this influence may have been mediated through the vague category of the 'Hellenic tradition'. If by this he refers to historiographers subsequent to Herodotus, there would be little sense in the focus of his study as he has set it up. The same can be said if he is alluding to the possibility of a link, if not with Herodotus himself, with Attic tragedy or perhaps with the Greek epic tradition, thus making the *Histories* and the Deuteronomistic History half-siblings or cousins who share at least one common ancestor.

---

90. Nielsen, *The Tragedy in History*, p. 17.
91. Nielsen, *The Tragedy in History*, p. 164.

One senses that the more generic connection proposed by Nielsen stems from the unanswered questions that remain regarding the origins of Hebrew historiography. This is the same difficulty which Mandell and Freedman attempted to deal with. Of the two texts being compared we have a lot more 'facts' about one of them than the other. We can state with a good deal of certainty who wrote the *Histories*; we know with a fair amount of precision when they were written. Although questions of sources and method do continue to puzzle and intrigue scholars, we know that Herodotus read and imitated Homer to a great extent.[92] Herodotus himself also explicitly states that he knew the work of the historian Hecataeus of Miletus (2.143; 6.137). And while we have only fragments of the latter's writings, that is more than remains of such works as the book of Jashar cited in Josh. 10.13 and 2 Sam. 1.18.

The major drawback to Nielsen's work is a kind of circular argument that posits a Hellenistic date for the Deuteronomistic History based on the presumed presence of Greek traditions within it. The Greek influence 'proves' the late dating, while the late dating 'proves' that the direction in which the traditions moved was from Greece to Israel. I find Nielsen's dating of the Deuteronomistic History to the Hellenistic period no less problematic than Mandell and Freedman's ascribing the compilation of Primary History to Ezra in the middle of the fifth century. Both hypotheses seem motivated by a desire to compare the Hebrew texts in question with Herodotus' *Histories* based upon their many similarities. Both appear to force the evidence to fit the theory. In spite of their ingenuity, neither the arguments of Mandell and Freedman nor those of Nielsen come to grips with the prevailing view that the writing of Israel's first history, whether Primary or Deuteronomistic, was for all intents and purposes completed during the period of exile in the sixth-century BCE.[93]

6. *Studies of Herodotus and Jewish Historical Novellas*

The difficulties involved with relative dating and the cultural conditions which would make possible a true literary influence of Herodotus in Israel or Judea (or vice versa as Mandell and Freedman suggest) make the establishment of any direct dependence between Herodotus and the history writers of ancient Israel problematic. These problems do not continue, however, once we enter the Hellenistic age. After Alexander, there is no longer a question of Herodotus's precedence with respect to the literature of this era. Furthermore, there is no difficulty in positing the dissemination of the *Histories* to a non-Greek audience at a time when the Greek

---

92. See L. Huber, 'Herodots Homerverständnis', in H. Flashar and K. Gaiser (eds.), *Synusia: Festgabe für Wolfgang Schadewalt zum 15 März 1965* (Pfullingen: Neske, 1965), pp. 29-52.

93. Although Martin Noth's original hypothesis concerning the Deuteronomistic History ('Das deuteronomistische Werk [Dtr]', in *idem, Überlieferungsgeschichtliche Studien: Die sammelnden und bearbeitenden Geschichtswerk im Alten Testament* [Schriften der Königsberger gelehrten Gesellschaft: Geisteswissenschaftliche Klasse, 18; Halle: Max Niemeyer, 1943], pp. 45-152) has mutated into numerous forms often involving several layers of redaction, the dating of the final stages of compositional or redactional activity to the period of the exile is fairly consistent.

language was becoming more extensively spoken and a Greek education was actively sought by many people within the lands conquered by Alexander. While we do not have from this time period a great Jewish history that would correspond to the work of Herodotus, we do have shorter works of narrative—historical novellas—which correspond in many ways to the λόγοι which make up Herodotus's more extensive work. The stories of Esther, Judith, and Daniel all show elements of both form and content which may be traced back to the *Histories* of Herodotus. It is in these shorter and later works of historical fiction that we can perhaps see more clearly the influence of Herodotus. While there have been no major studies on the relationship of any of these books with Herodotus, there are a number of shorter works in which similarities have been highlighted.

a. *Esther*

The book of Esther, like so many of the λόγοι in Herodotus, takes place in the setting of the Persian court. The mere fact says nothing of itself. There are Jewish stories that take place in Babylonian and Egyptian courts as well. The setting merely reflects the reality of post-exilic Judaism which was in fact subject to a historical succession and a geographical variety of kingdoms with which it had to reckon. More significant are the similar motifs which have been noted between the two works. A number of these parallels were listed in a brief essay in 1958 by E. Pfeiffer.[94] More recently Inge Hofmann and Anton Vorbichler have outlined nine motifs which they find in common between the book of Esther and Herodotus:[95] (1) the great expanse of the Persian Empire (Est. 1.1; 8.9; 9.30; Herodotus 3.89-97); (2) the 'prostitution' of the queen (Est. 1.11; Herodotus 1.8); (3) the wearing of the king's clothes by another (Est. 6.7-11; Herodotus 7.15-17); (4) the rise and fall of the king's favorite (Est. 3.1; 7.6-10; Herodotus 1.108, 119); (5) the pledge to grant a request (Est. 5.3; 6.2; Herodotus 9.109); (6) the fulfillment of the request (Est. 9.12-15; Herodotus 9.110-13); (7) the desecration of the dead (Est. 9.14; Herodotus 3.79; 8.238; 9.79); (8) the exhortation to rescue the nation (Est. 4.13-14; Herodotus 3.68-69); and (9) the extermination of the enemy and the victory celebration (Est. 9.18-19; Herodotus 3.79). The degree of correspondence between these alleged parallels varies quite a bit. The desire of King Ahasuerus to show off the beauty of his queen, Vashti, to his subjects (Est. 1.11) corresponds quite closely with the wish of King Candaules that his friend Gyges see his wife's beauty (Herodotus 1.8). Other parallels are much more general. Elements such as the expanse of the Persian Empire or the desecration of the dead are certainly not peculiar to the texts in question, but might be regarded as historical givens: the former an undeniable political fact and the latter a well-known practice towards one's enemies.

---

94. E. Pfeiffer, 'Herodots Geschichten und das Buch Esther', *Deutsches Pfarrerblatt* 62 (1958), pp. 544-45.

95. I. Hofmann and A. Vorbichler, 'Herodot und der Schreiber des Esther-Buches', *Zeitschrift für Missionswissenschaft und Religionswissenschaft* 66 (1982), pp. 294-302.

One might also note that the common motifs which Herodotus shares with Esther according to Hofmann and Vorbichler are scattered throughout the *Histories*. Nevertheless, there is a core λόγος in which one finds the majority of these parallels. This is the story of the revenge upon the Magi, or the Magophonia, found in Herodotus 3.61-79. Lawrence M. Wills has done a closer analysis of this text in relation to the book of Esther in his book *The Jew in the Court of the Foreign King*.[96] First of all, he focuses on the similarities between the dialogues between Otanes and Phaidyme on the one hand and Mordechai and Esther on the other. In both cases 'an older, male family member takes advantage of his relation with a young female family member in the harem to carry out an urgent mission'.[97] The young female family member hesitates, invoking the difficulty and danger involved in the mission. But the older male relative reminds her of her heritage and duty, urging her to proceed, which she finally does.[98]

The other similarities detected by Wills are less convincing. For example, it is hard to see how the lists of seven eunuchs and seven sages in Esther 1 correspond to the seven conspirators against the Magi in Herodotus as Wills suggests.[99] Their offices and roles in the narratives are entirely different; the only similarity is in their number. Even if one disregards Wills's lesser arguments, however, a strong case remains for some connection between the tales preserved in Herodotus and Esther. The major problem in further defining this relationship is the 'difficulty in differentiating Herodotus's sources and his own editorial work'.[100] Herodotus himself often refers to his oral sources—what was reported to him by the peoples he encountered. Are the similarities between Esther and Herodotus the result of common legendary material—widely circulating folk-tales—which both employed? Or might there be a more direct literary connection? Wills at least hints at the latter possibility by noting that the parallels between Herodotus's Magophonia and the book of Esther are limited to what he discerns to be the redactional sections of Esther.[101] Furthermore, Ctesias's account of the Magophonia (*Persika* 10–14) does not share the close similarities to Esther that Herodotus's account does.[102] While these similarities might be explained by common use of well-known folk tales, the possibility of a closer relationship remains and warrants further investigation.

96. L.M. Wills, *The Jew in the Court of the Foreign King: Ancient Jewish Court Legends* (Harvard Dissertations in Religion, 26; Minneapolis: Fortress Press, 1990), pp. 182-85.

97. Wills, *The Jew in the Court*, p. 183.

98. Wills, *The Jew in the Court*, p. 184.

99. Wills, *The Jew in the Court*, p. 184.

100. Wills, *The Jew in the Court*, p. 56.

101. Wills, *The Jew in the Court*, p. 185. Similarly, he notes that the only portion of Esther that resembles the Egyptian *Instruction of Onkhsheshonq* is what he calls the Mordechai/Haman source. Wills uses literary-critical and linguistic evidence in his source analysis. He distinguishes between what he calls 'the source of Esther' and the redactional sections largely on syntactical observations. He lists a number of these on pp. 157-58. His most important criterion is the infrequent use of converted verbs in the redactional sections compared to the overwhelming preference for these forms in the source story.

102. Wills, *The Jew in the Court*, p. 182 n. 43.

b. *Judith*

The book of Judith presents us with yet another Jewish historical novella, although its historical setting is manifestly fictitious. While a precise dating of the book is difficult, it contains several unmistakable Greek elements which suggest some time after Alexander. Among the typically Hellenistic customs related in Judith are the wearing of garlands (3.7), the worship of a king as god (3.8), reclining while eating (12.15), and the use of olive wreaths (15.13). The book of Judith does not fit into the genre of 'court narrative' as do Esther and the first part of the book of Daniel. Although it shares some similar elements to these works (such as the wise counsel of Achior the Ammonite to the Assyrian commander, Holofernes, in ch. 5), the Jews themselves do not participate in the court of the foreign power. Rather, they are locked in a bloody struggle against them. This military element, when combined with the element of the wise counselor mentioned above, provides us once again with a striking parallel to Herodotus's *Histories*.

The dual scenes of battlefield and council chamber form the backdrop for a most intriguing analysis of Herodotus and the book of Judith put forward by Arnaldo Momigliano.[103] His study of the two texts produced the following observations. Militarily, the second part of book 7 in Herodotus centers around the defense of Thermopylae, a narrow mountain pass. Corresponding to this, the first part of the book of Judith recounts the defense of Bethulia, which is also described as being situated at a narrow pass through the mountains. In addition to this similar military scene, the ideological scene in this section of Herodotus is dominated by the counsel of Demaratus to Xerxes. Demaratus explains that the Spartans are the best of fighters and never retreat in battle because, being free, they obey their only master which is the Law. Similarly, the ideological focus in Judith is on Achior's counsel to Holophernes that the Jews cannot be defeated in battle unless they sin against their God. In addition to this double parallel, Judith (deceitfully) offers to reveal the secret mountain path to the Assyrians, just as in the *Histories* Ephialtes does in fact for the Persians. Momigliano concludes that the similarity of structure between the two passages forces us to ask whether the author of Judith knew Herodotus directly or indirectly. While not fully committing himself to a positive response to this question, he allows it a high degree of probability.

Adding weight to Momigliano's conjecture are the insights of Moses Hadas who noted that the opening chapters of Judith describing 'the king's enormous wealth and power, his wrath at being crossed, his council, his long preparations which put the whole world in turmoil, and then the massive and seemingly irresistible movement of the huge armament'[104] correspond to Herodotus's description of Xerxes and his campaign. The similarities are even found at the level of phraseology such as the request for 'earth and water' (Jdt. 2.7) as a sign of submission.[105] Picking up on this latter element, Mark Stephen Caponigro carries the argument yet a step

---

103. Momigliano, 'Biblical Studies', p. 8.

104. M. Hadas, *Hellenistic Culture* (Morningside Heights, NY: Columbia University Press, 1959), p. 167.

105. Hadas, *Hellenistic Culture*, p. 168.

further. Caponigro bases his argument on several key passages in the LXX text of Judith that are difficult to understand by themselves. These passages become more explicable, however, when they are seen as 'less than perfectly coherent adaptations of Herodotean material to a new and different story'.[106]

The first such passage identified by Caponigro is the aforementioned Jdt. 2.7 in which Nebuchadnezzar says to Holofernes: 'Tell them to prepare earth and water, for I am coming against them in my anger, and will cover the whole face of the earth with the feet of my troops, to whom I will hand them over to be plundered'. As Caponigro points out, nowhere does the book of Judith explain the meaning of preparing earth and water.[107] Apparently the demand was meant to be understood, yet there are no biblical precedents and our own understanding of this practice depends upon Herodotus. Furthermore, this symbolic gesture of surrender is curiously out of place since Nebuchadnezzar's intention is not to accept such a surrender but to destroy totally the countries that offended him. Caponigro argues that the inclusion of this puzzling element in the narrative is an allusion to the wrath of Darius and Xerxes as part of the author's characterization of Nebuchadnezzar. It is, as he puts it, the 'Xerxizing' of the portrait of Nebuchadnezzar.[108]

A second passage highlighted by Caponigro is the palace conference in Jdt. 2.1-3. As he notes, this brief text 'does not recall any obvious biblical precedent' and 'is not consistent with the characterization of the utterly autocratic and resolute Nebuchadnezzar established in chap. 1'.[109] The apparent inconsistency makes sense if we again infer that the author is trying to paint Nebuchadnezzar to look like Xerxes who also summoned a conference of nobles to debate the invasion of Greece (7.8-11).

Finally, Caponigro raises the question of Bethulia in Jdt. 3.9-10.[110] There is again no precedent in the Bible of an invader having to pass through the northern hill country to reach Judea. The Jordan and coastal valleys provided much easier access. But as it is the author's intention to have the confrontation between Judith and Holofernes take place in this remote village, there must be some reason for the army of Holofernes to be detained there long enough for the story to unfold. This is accomplished by modeling Bethulia on Thermopylae—each is described as a narrow pass which cannot be skirted on the way to the respective Jewish and Greek heartlands. Caponigro further notes how the parallel to Thermopylae made in Jdt. 4.7 is quickly dropped once it has served its purpose. The scene of the guarded mountain pass quickly becomes a besieged city so that it is Judith alone—not mountain fighters—who brings about the defeat of the enemy.

The combined analyses of Momigliano, Hadas and Caponigro provide a powerful argument that the author of Judith had some familiarity with Herodotus. This

---

106. M.S. Caponigro, 'Judith, Holding the Tale of Herodotus', in J.C. VanderKam (ed.), *'No One Spoke Ill of Her': Essays on Judith* (SBL: Early Judaism and Its Literature, 2; Atlanta: Scholars Press, 1992), pp. 47-59 (47).

107. Caponigro, 'Judith', p. 49.

108. Caponigro, 'Judith', p. 51.

109. Caponigro, 'Judith', p. 51.

110. Caponigro, 'Judith', pp. 53-56.

highly probable connection between Judith and Herodotus will be important to keep in mind as we proceed in Chapter 2 to look at the book of Daniel. For, like Daniel, Judith was in all likelihood written around the time of the Maccabean revolt.[111] More significantly, Judith was almost certainly originally written in a Semitic language[112] (probably Hebrew) just as Daniel was composed in Hebrew and Aramaic. If it appears likely that the author of Judith knew Herodotus—something which I shall also argue for Daniel—then there is a more solid case for the hypothesis that a Jewish writer in the middle of the second century BCE could in fact read Greek and yet choose to write in Hebrew. The book of Judith becomes added evidence for overcoming the scholarly bias 'of attributing a Greek literary education only to those Jewish writers who wrote Greek of a good quality, not to those who wrote it colloquially or barbarically, and *a fortiori* not to those who wrote in a Semitic language'.[113]

111.   As was previously mentioned, a definite dating of Judith is difficult, but there are indications of a time near that of Judas Maccabeus. Among these are Nebuchadnezzar's desire to be worshipped as a god (3.8) as a reflection of Antiochus IV, the political and military authority of the high priest (4.6), and the inclusion of many place names in Judith at which Judas is known to have fought (e.g. Jamnia and Azotus in Jdt. 2.28 and Beth-horon in Jdt. 4.4). It may also be the case that the very name Judith is meant to be the female equivalent of Judas Maccabeus, although it may simply be meant to connote the Jewish nation.

112.   For a presentation of the linguistic evidence see C.A. Moore, *Judith* (AB, 40; Garden City, NY: Doubleday, 1985), pp. 66-67. An opposing opinion, however, is held by Toni Craven who maintains that 'the Greek text could have been written from the outset in elegant hebraicised Greek' (*Artistry and Faith in the Book of Judith* [SBLDS, 70; Chico: Scholars Press, 1983], p. 5). While there can be no absolute certainty in this matter barring the discovery of an ancient Jewish manuscript of Judith, I find the philological and linguistic evidence presented by Moore to be more convincing.

113.   Caponigro, 'Judith', p. 58.

Chapter 2

DANIEL AND CLASSICAL STUDIES

As we have seen in the previous chapter, there have been a number of recent studies which have begun to look at the *Histories* of Herodotus in relationship to different books or sections of the Hebrew Scriptures. These works have been undertaken, not surprisingly, by scholars trained in the field of biblical studies. They have looked at Herodotus in relation to Jewish histories such as the Deuteronomistic History and Primary History, and they have also noted the impact of Herodotus on Jewish novellas like Esther and Judith. The book of Daniel, regrettably, does not figure among these studies. Only one scholar, a historian working within the field of classical studies, has raised the question of a connection between Daniel and Herodotus. Biblical scholars have so far been reluctant to investigate the possibility of Greek influences in Daniel. As mentioned in the previous chapter, there have been two main reasons for this lack of investigation: (1) the perceived wall between the Greek and Hebrew worlds, and (2) the wall erected between apocalyptic and earlier 'historical' biblical traditions. As the first barrier has given way to the studies discussed in Chapter 1, it is the second barrier that has proven more persistent. Yet, as we have seen, it too is illusory. The label of 'apocalypse' which the book of Daniel bears[1] should not impede the investigation and appreciation of its historical and narrative elements in which it bears many similarities to the work of Herodotus. Indeed, as I hope to demonstrate in this study, the apocalyptic visions of Daniel show a profound interest in history that is in continuity with

---

1.   It is interesting to note that some recent scholarly works have rightly observed that the book of Daniel does not fit neatly into widely held conceptions of apocalyptic literature. It is somewhat confusing, however, to state that Daniel should not be called 'apocalyptic' (the conclusion of both G.W. Buchanan, *The Book of Daniel: Intertextual Commentary on the Book of Daniel* [Lewiston, NY: Edwin Mellen Press, 1999], and G. Boccaccini, 'E' Daniele un testo apocalittico? Una (ri)definizione del pensiero del Libro di Daniele in rapporto al Libro dei Sogni e all'Apocalittica', *Henoch* 9 [1987], pp. 267-302). Since Daniel is so clearly imitated by later apocalypses such as *4 Ezra* and the New Testament book of Revelation (not to mention the fact that it is itself one of the earliest exemplars of the apocalyptic genre), it makes more sense to reconsider some of the assumptions that have gone into the modern constructs of the 'apocalyptic' social setting and worldview. In any event, the work of Boccaccini in particular has been significant for dispelling some of the 'apocalyptic' stereotypes in regard to the book of Daniel by pointing out that Daniel 'offers a comprehensive vision of history and of individual destiny' (G. Boccaccini, 'Daniel and the Dream Visions', in *idem*, *Middle Judaism: Jewish Thought, 300 BCE to 200 CE* [Minneapolis: Fortress Press, 1991], pp. 126-60 (160).

earlier biblical writings. If this historical concern in the book of Daniel has not been readily recognized, it is perhaps due to the fact that Daniel adds a new, decidedly Greek emphasis to the biblical historical traditions.

Therefore I now proceed with the task of establishing a basis for the claim that the *Histories* of Herodotus were known and used by the author of Daniel. This will be done by first demonstrating a correspondence between historical elements in these two works—a correspondence that goes deeper than the parallels often drawn between Daniel and Near Eastern literature. I will then support the case for a direct relationship by arguing that the *Histories* of Herodotus continued to be widely read and influential in the Hellenistic age throughout the Greek-speaking world, a world to which the book of Daniel definitely belonged.

1. *Daniel 2 and 7: The Theory of a Succession of World Empires*

As previously stated, the one scholar who has insightfully pointed to a connection between the book of Daniel and the world of Greek historiography was Arnaldo Momigliano. He raised the question of Daniel's dependence upon Greek historiography in an address at the Society of Biblical Literature's centennial conference in 1980.[2] The focus of his address was on the historical research which is common to both classical and biblical scholars. In this context, he proposed a fruitful collaboration between scholars in these two fields. Such a collaboration, at least with regard to the questions he raised concerning the book of Daniel, has unfortunately not been realized. It was Momigliano himself who followed up on his address by writing a brief article—'Daniel and the Greek Theory of Imperial Succession'[3]—in which he developed his arguments for Greek influence in the book of Daniel based upon the theory of four successive empires found in chs. 2 and 7 of Daniel.

Momigliano focuses on the first of these dream visions which, being older, served as a model for the material in ch. 7. His argument for Greek influence is very specific, being concentrated on the single element of the theory of a succession of world empires which is communicated by the vision. By zeroing in on this one element in the passage, Momigliano helps to cut through some of the more general arguments of scholars who have sought to locate the origins of this dream vision in the context of Iranian or Mesopotamian mytho-historical works. He points out quite clearly that while these latter works may indeed share some common elements with the visions in Daniel, the one thing that they certainly do not share is the idea of a succession of four world empires. He is willing to grant that the book of Daniel drew upon these eastern traditions for other elements which show up in ch. 2 and elsewhere in Daniel, but the theory of imperial succession can only have come from Greece.

The evidence marshaled by Momigliano is impressive. First, he demonstrates that there did in fact exist the concept of imperial succession as a recurring theme in

---

2. Momigliano, 'Biblical Studies', p. 7.
3. Momigliano, 'Daniel and the Greek Theory'.

Greek historiography.[4] Beginning with Herodotus and Ctesias, who each epito-mized Asian history in the three successive empires of Assyria, Media, and Persia (Herodotus 1.95; 1.130; Ctesias = *FGrH* 688), Momigliano shows how 'the theory of imperial succession was a constant in Greek political and historical thought'.[5] From its origins in the fifth century, this theory naturally grew to include the Macedonian kingdom as the fourth in the series after the conquests of Alexander. In the second century BCE, Polybius, concerned as he was with 'universal history',[6] was thereby also concerned with imperial succession, adding Rome as the com-pletion of the sequence begun by Herodotus.[7] Polybius also provides a valuable witness to the theory of imperial succession in the late fourth or early third century when he quotes from Demetrius of Phalerum who commented on the fall of the Persian Empire to the Macedonians and foresaw the eventual passing of Macedonia as well (29.21). Although Polybius himself was concerned with the Roman Empire and wished to portray it as the successor and surpasser of previous empires (most immediately and notably, that of Alexander), he also displays knowledge of the longer sequence of succession going back through Persia and Media to Assyria.[8]

4.   The existence of a four-kingdom schema in antiquity was already demonstrated in the work of J.W. Swain, 'The Theory of the Four Monarchies: Opposition History Under the Roman Empire', *CP* 35 (1940), pp. 1-21. A serious limitation of his study, however, is the way in which he overlooks the presence of this schema in Greek sources after Herodotus and Ctesias (p. 7), com-pletely ignoring Polybius. This forces him to make the unlikely hypothesis that Roman historians imported the schema directly from the east without the mediation of Greek sources.

5.   Momigliano, 'Daniel and the Greek Theory', p. 31.

6.   It is unclear whether Polybius's one acknowledged predecessor in writing universal history, Ephorus (mentioned in Polybius, *Histories* 5.33.2), included any reference to the succes-sion: Assyria–Media–Persia. The fragments that survive do not mention either Assyria or Media. His account appears to be centered around the rise of the various Greek city-states, their relations with one another and with the surrounding kingdoms of Persia, Carthage, Egypt, and Macedonia. See G.L. Barber, *The Historian Ephorus* (Chicago: Ares Publishers, 2nd edn, 1993), p. 22.

7.   In fact, Polybius gives us his own version of who he considers to be the empires worthy of mention before Rome: the Persians, Spartans, and Macedonians (1.2) as well as giving the estab-lished schema: Assyria, Media, Persia, Macedonia (38.21). The latter comes from the lips of the Roman general Scipio Aemilianus as he watches Carthage burn and meditates on the passing of all empires which will one day include Rome. The reference to the four empires is preserved only in Appian who cites Polybius in *Libyca* 132. The parallel fragments from Diodorus Siculus 32.24 and Polybius 38.21, which are preserved in the Byzantine compilation of *Excerpta de Sententiis*, do not mention the schema (see A.E. Astin, *Scipio Aemilianus* [Oxford: Clarendon Press, 1967], pp. 282-87). While some scholars have questioned whether the reference to Assyria, Media, Persia, and Macedonia was original to Polybius or added by Appian (see F.W. Walbank, *A Historical Com-mentary on Polybius* [Oxford: Clarendon Press, 1979], III, p. 725; D. Mendels, 'The Five Empires: A Note on a Propagandistic Topos', *American Journal of Philology* 102 [1981], pp. 330-37 [333]), its absence from the mutilated Polybian fragment is not a convincing argument, since several lines are almost wholly missing from that text. It appears that the fragment from Diodorus Siculus does in some respects better preserve the original text of Polybius than does Appian (see Astin, *Scipio Aemilianus*, p. 283), but this does not necessarily mean that a detail omitted by Diodorus but pre-served in Appian was the addition of the latter. Without stronger evidence to the contrary, it should be assumed that Appian is in fact citing Polybius as he claims to do.

8.   The significance of Polybius, both as a witness himself to the knowledge of the theory of imperial succession among Greek historians of the second century and as a witness through his

The invention and subsequent diffusion of this theory among Greek and Roman historiographers (including Aemilius Sura,[9] Diodorus Siculus,[10] Trogus Pompeius,[11] and Dionysius of Halicarnassus[12]) is explained by Momigliano as resulting from the specific Greek interest in political and military phenomena.[13] While admittedly not all Greek historians showed an interest in the succession of empires (most notably Thucydides who focuses on contemporary history and exhibits no awareness of or interest in the rise and fall of previous empires), what is truly significant for

sources to its diffusion in the centuries preceding him, was ignored by Swain. This is a serious drawback to an otherwise excellent article. The result is that, by overlooking the persistence of the theory of imperial succession in the Greek tradition, Swain is forced to turn to the east as the source of the 4+1 schema which appears in imperial Roman propaganda. In this he has been followed not only by classical scholars, but by biblical scholars as well who have turned to the Orient rather than to Greece for the source of Daniel's historical schema (e.g. W. Baumgartner, 'Zu den vier Reichen von Daniel 2', *Theologische Zeitschrift* 1 [1945], pp. 17-22; Noth, 'The Understanding of History', especially pp. 200-201). However, by recognizing the existence of the theory of imperial succession in Greek historians from Herodotus onward, it is much easier to see how the four-kingdom schema (like so many other traditions) would have come to Rome (and Israel) through Greece.

9.   The dating of this obscure Roman historian is difficult. We know of his work, *De Annis Populi Romani*, only through a gloss in Velleius Paterculus 1.6.6. Swain (p. 3) dates the passage to between 189 and 171 BCE since the references to the victories over Carthage, Philip, and Antiochus as the time when Rome succeeded Macedonia as the fifth empire ignores both the Third Punic War and the Third Macedonian War. Momigliano also suggests a date shortly after the Roman victories over Macedonia and Syria, suggesting that Sura may have been a witness to these victories ('The Origins of Universal History', in R. Friedman [ed.], *The Poet and the Historian: Essays in Literary and Historical Biblical Criticism* [Harvard Semitic Studies, 26; Chico: Scholars Press, 1983], pp. 133-55 [140]). D. Mendels takes exception to Swain's argument from silence stating that Aemilius Sura may have been well aware of the later, unmentioned conflicts, but nevertheless saw the earlier victories as the defining moments in Rome's rise to power ('The Five Empires: A Note on a Propagandistic Topos', *American Journal of Philology* 102 [1981], pp. 331-32). Mendels's objection is valid; however, given that we cannot make any certain claims regarding this text, the hypothesis put forward by Swain and developed by Momigliano is quite probable. If true, this would place Aemilius Sura's work about a decade before the book of Daniel, providing yet another second-century witness to the four-kingdom theory (or four plus one) of imperial succession.

10.   Writing around 50 BCE (see *Diodorus of Sicily* [trans. C.H. Oldfather; 12 vols.; LCL; Cambridge, MA: Harvard University Press, 1933], I, pp. vii-xi), Diodorus describes the history of Asia in his second book as the succession of Assyrian, Median, and Persian rule. He cites Herodotus on occasion (2.15.1; 2.32.2; 2.32.3) but above all relies on Ctesias for his account of the kingdoms of Assyria and Media in Book 2, as with Persia in Book 9.

11.   An epitome of his *Historiae Philippicae*, written during the reign of Augustus, is preserved in M. Junius Justinius who wrote in the second or third century CE (see Swain, 'The Theory of the Four Monarchies', pp. 16-17; and Momigliano, 'Universal History', p. 143). In it he follows the familiar sequence of empires from Assyria through Rome. Although he was a Gaul from Gallia Narbonensis and wrote in Latin, as Swain points out 'he learned his history from Greeks' (p. 17).

12.   Dionysius dates his work in 1.3.4 to the counsulship of Claudius Nero and Calpurnius Piso (i.e. 7 BCE; see *The Roman Antiquities of Dionysius of Halicarnassus* [trans. Earnest Cary; 7 vols.; LCL; Cambridge, MA: Harvard University Press, 1937], I, p. 11 n. 3). At 1.1.2 he explicitly mentions the series: Assyria–Media–Persia followed by Macedonia and Rome in 1.1.3. As Cary points out, the introductory survey of empires from Assyria to Macedonia is in imitation of Polybius's introduction (p. xii).

13.   Momigliano, 'Daniel and the Greek Theory', p. 30.

Momigliano's argument is that outside of Greece and Rome only one known writer in antiquity uses this theory as a pattern for history. This evidence leads to the conclusion not only that the theory does in fact have its origin in Greek historiography, but also that this one 'foreign' text employing the pattern is somehow related to the Greek historiographical tradition. That one text is, of course, the book of Daniel.

If most scholars have not recognized this point of contact which is unique to Daniel and the Greco-Roman historiographic tradition, it is due to the fact that the second chapter of Daniel contains, in addition to this four-kingdom schema, a similar schematization of history under the image of four metals of decreasing value. This image may also be Greek in origin, as our first written record of it is in Hesiod[14] who describes the four ages (with an interpolated fifth age of heroes) as four metals of decreasing worth. Furthermore, the four metals of Hesiod—gold, silver, bronze, and iron—correspond exactly to the sequence found in Daniel. Nevertheless, it must be recognized that the meaning behind the imagery of the metals—the declining ages of human history—is incidental to the meaning of the dream vision in Daniel 2. It would be absurd from a Jewish perspective to regard Nebuchadnezzar or the Neo-Babylonian Empire as a golden age from which history steadily progresses downward.[15] Indeed, although this is the very conclusion which the imagery itself would indicate, it is a perspective that is nowhere stated nor implied in the interpretation of the dream vision. There is the statement that the second kingdom, represented by the chest and arms of silver will be inferior to the first (2.39). But the history outlined in this vision does not continue its downward trend from there. Rather, the third kingdom is once again great, ruling over the whole world (2.39), and the fourth even surpasses all the others (2.40). Rather than following the pattern of decline indicated by the metals, the interpretation appears to be making statements about the power of these kingdoms which roughly correspond to the historical reality. The very fact that the imagery of the metals is dropped in

---

14.   Hesiod, *Works and Days* (ed. with prolegomena and commentary by M.L. West; Oxford: Clarendon Press, 1978), pp. 109-201. Although Hesiod provides us with the earliest extant account of four ages (or, more precisely, of four human races) represented by metals of declining value, there is no way of telling whether this was his own invention, or (as seems more likely) he worked from a pre-existing model (A. Momigliano, 'The Origins of Universal History', in Friedman [ed.], *The Poet and the Historian*, pp. 133-55 [134]). M.L. West argues that this 'Myth of Ages' must be supposed to have come to Greece from the east. He finds partial parallels in Iranian (*Denkard, Bahman Yasht*), Indian (*Laws of Manu, Mahâbhârata*), and Mesopotamian (*Sumerian King List*) literature. While these Oriental texts do not combine all the elements found in Hesiod's scheme of metallic ages, there are many striking similarities. And while Hesiod is centuries earlier than those texts which mention metals or four ages, his scheme is 'quite alien to the general Greek view of the past as reflected in the whole corpus of epic and genealogical poetry' (Hesiod, *Works and Days*, p. 176). For a further discussion of some of the 'Oriental forerunners' of Hesiod see Astour, *Hellenosemitica*, pp. 217-20. Hesiod's schema remained influential in the Greek tradition as is evidenced by Plato's adaptation of it in the *Republic* 3.415a-c.

15.   This has led to the hypothesis that behind this dream lies an original dream and interpretation which concerned Nebuchadnezzar and his Babylonian successors (Bickerman, *Four Strange Books*, p. 62). As the symbol of decline within a dynasty and the foretelling of its ultimate collapse, the imagery of the metals makes sense.

Daniel 7 where the four kingdoms are again represented under the image of four beasts indicates that it is secondary to the idea of four successive kingdoms. As Martin Noth has succinctly concluded: 'The four metals as symbols of four consecutive epochs were therefore incorporated in the vision of *Dan*. II only as traditional material, without taking over with it the theory originally linked with this material'.[16]

The conflation of images in ch. 2 of Daniel—the four kingdoms and the four metals—has led scholars to seek the origin of this symbolism in Iranian texts (*Bhaman Yasht*, *Denkard*) where a similar combination of elements is evident. Rather than seeking a single source for the conflated traditions in Daniel 2, however, we should recognize that the theme of four metals is secondary to the theory of four empires and has been added to the latter, perhaps by the author of Daniel himself. The similarity of imagery between ch. 2 of the book of Daniel and the *Bhaman Yasht* and the *Denkard* has obscured the fact that Daniel's schema of four successive empires is entirely absent from these Iranian texts, having its precedent only in the Greek historiographical tradition. However, since recourse is frequently made to the Iranian texts in elucidating the material in Daniel 2, it is necessary to address this position before proceeding with a more detailed examination of Daniel's dependence upon Greek historiography for the four-kingdom outlines of chs. 2 and 7.

a. *The* Bhaman Yasht *and the* Denkard
The position which has found most favor with scholars sees Daniel's plan of history, viewed as four successive kingdoms, originating in Iranian traditions which appear in the *Bhaman Yasht* (*Zand i Wahman Yasn*) and the *Denkard*. In the *Bhaman Yasht*, Zarathustra dreams of a tree with four branches: one of gold, one of silver, one of steel, and one of mixed iron. The branches are interpreted as four future periods which are in turn marked by the reigns of various kings:

> *Ohrmazd* said to *Spitaman Zarduxst*, 'The tree trunk that you have seen, <that is the material world which I, *Ohrmazd*, have created>. Those four branches are the four epochs that will come. The one of gold is that during which I and you converse, and king *Wistasp* accepts the religion and breaks the bodies of the *dews* and <the *dews*, from the condition of being visible>, take to flight and hiding. And the one of silver is the reign <of> *Ardaxsir* the Kayanid king. And the one of steel is the reign <of> *Husraw* of immortal soul, son of *Kawad*. And the one on which iron had been mixed is the evil rule <of> the parted hair *dews* of the seed of *Xesm*, when it will be the end of your tenth century, O *Spitaman Zarduxst*.'[17]

---

16. Noth, 'The Understanding of History', p. 198.
17. *Zand i Wahman Yasn* 1.6-11 (translated in C.G. Cereti, *The Zand i Wahman Yasn: A Zoroastrian Apocalypse* [Rome: Istituto Italiano per il Medio ed Estremo Oriente, 1995], p. 149). The system of transliteration for proper names and terms specific to the Zoroastrian religion is that put forward by D.N. MacKenzie, 'Notes on the Transcription of Pahlavi', *BSOAS* 30 (1967), pp. 17-29. The untranslated *dew* means 'demon'; *Xesm* is 'Wrath', personified here as begetting demons. *Ohrmazd* corresponds to Ahura Mazda, and *Zarduxst* is Zarathustra or Zoroaster.

The combination of kings with the descending metal ages in this text has caught the eye of biblical scholars, as has the description of the fourth metal as 'mixed iron' and the characterization of its kingdom as demonic. The parallels with Daniel are noteworthy, but a key element that is missing is the idea of the succession of empire. The kings mentioned in the Iranian text are in fact all Iranian. There is no explicit mention of any other kingdom. Furthermore, the last two kings mentioned belong to the Sassanian period (226–651 CE),[18] indicating that at least this portion of the *Bahman Yasht* does not predate this era. In fact, the earliest manuscripts of the *Bhaman Yasht* date to the thirteenth century CE.[19] It is an epitome of a *Zand* or commentary on a lost book of the Avesta, the *Vohuman Yasn*, and as such it may contain traditional material from a much earlier age.[20] What must be stressed, however, is the difficulty of recovering any early Avestan material in this rather late, Medieval commentary. The vast majority of its historical references appear to belong to two periods: the Sassanian, when the original *Zand* was written, and the eleventh and twelfth centuries (shortly before the final epitome was composed), when Turkish invaders swept through Iran.[21] We must acknowledge the highly tenuous nature, therefore, of the hypotheses of scholars such as Samuel K. Eddy[22] and David Flusser[23] who attempt to discern an original Hellenistic version behind this text and to posit a direct influence of this reconstructed text on the book of Daniel. Their methodology is flawed to the extent that they reconstruct the 'early form' of the *Bhaman Yasht* based largely on a comparison with Daniel. This makes the discovery of a genetic link between the two texts a foregone conclusion.

Eddy makes much of the reference to 'The Demons with Dishevelled Hair of the Race of Wrath',[24] claiming that this must refer to Alexander and his Macedonian forces. (Is not Alexander pictured with 'madly tousled' hair on his coins and in art?) Actually, the reference is undoubtedly late, since the Iranian kings mentioned

---

18.   The king of the golden period is Vistâsp (contemporary with Zoroaster), that of the silver is Ardakhshîr the first Sassanid who began to reign in 226 CE, and that of the steel is Khûsrô who reigned from 531–579 CE. See *Pahlavi Texts, Part I* (ed. F.M. Müller; trans. E.W. West; The Sacred Books of the East, 5; Oxford: Clarendon Press, 1880), pp. 193, 199.

19.   Eddy, *The King is Dead*, p. 19.

20.   That the text as we now have it is not even the original commentary (*Zand*) of the *Vohuman Yasn* is indicated by the fact that it quotes from this commentary (2.1). We are therefore twice removed from this Avestan text, having only a Medieval epitome of a lost Sassanian commentary of a lost text of the Avesta. See *Pahlavi Texts*, Part I, lii-liii, p. 194 n. 4.

21.   *Pahlavi Texts*, Part I, liv.

22.   Eddy's numerous emendations of the text of the *Bhaman Yasht* reveal his eagerness to assign a Hellenistic date to the text and to associate it with the book of Daniel. At 1.1 he substitutes 'bronze' for 'steel' to provide a closer parallel to the text of Daniel (2.32, 39). Also, in his own sbronze would, as then being plentiful' (p. 344 n. 11). Also at 1.1, and again at 1.5, he gratuitously supplies the word 'clay' based again on Daniel (2.33, 41). He does more than his stated goal of suppressing any late references (such as the identification of the period of iron with the reign of 'Khusro, son of Kevad' [1.5] who reigned in the sixth century CE) in his attempt to approximate the 'original version of Hellenistic date' (p. 343). He goes so far as to suppress any evidence which contradicts his particular interpretation of the text (which is made with an eye on Daniel).

23.   Flusser, 'The Four Empires', pp. 148-75.

24.   Eddy, *The King is Dead*, p. 19.

by name who precede the appearance of these demons are themselves of a late date. Furthermore, the demons are said to come from the east,[25] not the west, suggesting an origin in Turkistan, not Greece. If there is a historical referent behind these demons, it is in all probability the Turks, not Alexander and his men. If one wishes to do some selective pruning of the *Bhaman Yasht* in order to eliminate the late material and thereby obtain the early Avestan core such as Eddy claims to do, it would be wiser to excise this entire passage than to seek to find a reference to the Macedonians in the single detail of 'dishevelled hair'. This one detail onto which Eddy latches, along with all of the surrounding material which he cuts out, can much more simply be explained as referring *in toto* to the Turks who are repeatedly mentioned by name and alluded to throughout the text.[26] It should likewise be noted that the four metals named in the *Bhaman Yasht* do not correspond exactly to those in Daniel 2 (whereas the metals in Hesiod do). The *Bhaman Yasht* has steel instead of the bronze found in Hesiod and Daniel. And while much has also been made of the description of the fourth metal as 'mixed iron' seeing a parallel to Daniel's 'iron mixed with clay', it must be emphasized that there is no reference to clay in the *Bhaman Yasht*. A true parallel only appears when one creatively emends the text as Eddy does.[27] It seems more likely that the 'mixed iron' is simply an inferior alloy to the preceding steel, in keeping with the symbolism of the declining worth of the metals.

In a related text, the *Denkard*, which dates to the ninth century CE,[28] the four periods of Zarathustra's millennium are identified with the same four metals as in the *Bhaman Yasht*. The decreasing value of the metals is more explicitly identified with religious decline:

> The first is that of gold, in which Ohrmazd reveals the religion to Zarduxst. The second is that of silver, in which Wistasp receives the religion from Zarduxst. The third is that of steel, the epoch in which Adurbad i Mahraspandan, the restorer of righteousness was born. The fourth <is that> on which iron was mixed, an epoch in which the dominion of the heretics and of the other evil ones proliferated.[29]

We can notice some variance between this text and the *Bhaman Yasht*. The king Wistasp here appears in the second age of silver rather than the first of gold. Also, the third age is not marked by a king's reign but by Adurbad who was a high priest and prime minister of King Shahpûhar II (309–379 CE).[30] In addition to supporting a Sassanian date for the traditions concerning the four periods of Zarathustra's millennium as found in the *Bhaman Yasht*, this passage also confirms the realization that there is no fundamental connection between these ages and different kingdoms

---

25. *Bahman Yasht* 2.24.

26. *Bahman Yasht* 2.50 where the epithet 'leathern-belted [*sic*] ones' is used to describe the Turks. This identification is made explicit in 3.8.

27. Eddy, *The King is Dead*, p. 344. In his translation of the *Bhaman Yasht*, he quite gratuitously supplies the word 'clay'.

28. *Pahlavi Texts, Part IV* (ed. F.M. Müller; trans. E.W. West; The Sacred Books of the East, 37; Oxford: Clarendon Press, 1892), p. xxxiii.

29. Denkard 9.8.2-5 (translated in Cereti, *Zand i Wahman Yasn*, p. 170).

30. *Pahlavi Texts, Part IV*, p. 10 n. 2.

in the Iranian texts. An age may be distinguished by a king or a priest or demons or Zarathustra himself. Finally, those kings that are in fact mentioned turn out to be invariably Iranian and mostly of the Sassanian period. What is central to the Iranian texts is the notion of four ages to which the declining value of the metals corresponds. What is central to Daniel is the idea of four kingdoms to which the symbolism of four metals is secondary as we have seen.

   The most decisive argument of all for concluding that the four ages described in the *Bhaman Yasht* are not the source of Daniel's four kingdoms is that, even if we admit to Eddy's hypothesized Hellenistic text, the ages or kingdoms described therein begin with Persia in the golden age of Zarathustra. Even if we allow that the references to the Sassanian kings are later 'corrections' by which an original prophecy has been altered to reflect a more recent situation (much in the same way that Daniel's fourth kingdom has been variously identified by interpreters through the ages), the fact remains that the golden age and first kingdom in the 'original' Persian text must have referred to Persia itself. Admitting the possibility of references to Alexander,[31] we still must conclude that Assyria and Media had no role whatsoever in the lost Avestan text upon which the *Bhaman Yasht* comments.

   Flusser follows Eddy in suggesting that the four-empire schema is the creation of Oriental propaganda against Hellenism. He likewise makes the same conjectures that the lost Avestan text spoke of four kings in connection with the four ages and that these four kings represented the four kingdoms of Assyria, Media, Persia, and Macedonia.[32] As we have just seen, there is no real basis for these conjectures in the text itself. If we did not have ch. 2 of the book of Daniel where the four metals do represent these four kingdoms, it would never have occurred to these scholars that this same series of kingdoms must have existed in the lost Persian text. There we may find mention of ages, of millennia, of Persian kings, of demons, but no mention of successive empires, and certainly no equation of pre-Persian Assyria and Media with ages of gold and silver. The *Bhaman Yasht* reflects an original text that was thoroughly centered and focused on Persia whose golden age is identified as the time of Zarathustra.

b. *The Babylonian Dynastic Prophecy*

Another text which has been suggested as bearing upon the origins of the four successive empires of Daniel is the so-called Babylonian Dynastic Prophecy.[33] This Akkadian text was probably written in Babylon during the period of Seleucid control of Babylonia.[34] As it has not been as influential as the aforementioned Iranian

---

   31.   There do in fact appear to be two references to the Macedonian leader at 2.19 where 'Akandgar' is probably a miswriting of Alaksandar (*Pahlavi Texts*, Part I, p. 200) and at 3.34 where it is written 'Alasandar' (*Pahlavi Texts*, Part I, p. 228). The transliterations here follow the table provided in *Pahlavi Texts*, Part I, pp. 435-38.

   32.   Flusser, 'The Four Empires', p. 173.

   33.   Reproduced with a transliteration, translation and brief commentary by A.K. Grayson, *Babylonian Historical-Literary Texts* (Toronto Semitic Texts and Studies, 3; Toronto: University of Toronto Press, 1975), pp. 24-37.

   34.   Grayson, *Babylonian Historical-Literary Texts*, p. 9. The frequent mention of Babylon and its various conquerors and rulers points to the location. If the 'Hanaeans' (iii 9) are to be

texts in the discussion of Daniel's four-kingdom schema, it may be treated more succinctly. In the dynastic prophecy there is in fact mention of different kingdoms following one upon another, but the identity of these kingdoms does not correspond to those in Daniel, nor is it clear that four and only four are intended, as there is no mention of this detail in the extant text. This very fragmentary text consists of four columns—two on each side of a single broken tablet. In the first column, of which only the end of each line is preserved, there is mention of Assyria in l. 10 and Babylon in ll. 13, 20, 23, and 24. It appears from what can be reconstructed and from the context of the rest of the text that this column does make reference to the fall of Assyria to Babylon.[35] After a lacuna, column two begins by mentioning the brief reigns of two kings and continues with the seventeen-year reign of a 're[bel] prince' (ii 11) who, as Grayson rightly points out,[36] must be Nabonidus. There then follows the account of the fall of this king to a 'king of Elam' (ii 17). This is probably a deliberate archaism referring to Cyrus the Persian, just as the next group mentioned, the 'Hanaeans' (iii 9), appears to be an archaizing reference to the Macedonians.[37] The sequence of nations that emerges from this Babylonian text—Assyria, Babylon, Elam, and Hanû—is significantly different from what we find in Daniel. Even if we substitute Persia and Greece for their archaic representatives, the omission of Media from the kingdoms represented makes it highly unlikely that this sequence of rulers has any relation to the kingdoms in Daniel 2 and 7. As Doron Mendels has correctly noted, the series of kings or empires found in various eastern texts is not fixed, while the succession of empires in Greek and Roman historiography follows the same pattern.[38] It is this Greek and Roman pattern, which began with the series of Assyria–Media–Persia as found in Herodotus and Ctesias, and was later expanded to include the kingdom of Alexander, that provides the classical fourfold schema of kingdoms. It is this schema which was taken up by Roman propagandists to produce a 'four-plus-one' plan of history with Rome as the fifth empire. It is this same schema which appears in Daniel ch. 2 where a similar four-plus-one pattern occurs.

c. *The Herodotean Tradition*

We have seen, then, that while the Iranian traditions in the *Bhaman Yasht* and *Denkard* share similarities of symbolism with the dream visions of Daniel 2 and 7, they are ultimately talking about something quite different. In fact, even the parallels on the level of symbolism are imperfect. Hesiod's four metals provide a closer match to those in Daniel. In the final analysis we must also note that these Iranian

---

understood as Alexander's Macedonian army (as appears likely from the context), the history recounted comes down to the Hellenistic period. See p. 26 of Grayson's volume.

35.   Grayson points out the reference to the Assyrian army in line 10 and booty entering Babylon in line 20 (*Babylonian Historical-Literary Texts*, p. 24).

36.   Grayson, *Babylonian Historical-Literary Texts*, p. 25.

37.   Grayson, *Babylonian Historical-Literary Texts*, p. 25 n. 7.

38.   Mendels, 'The Five Empires', pp. 334-35. Among the eastern texts he enumerates are the Babylonian dynastic prophecy, the third *Sibylline Oracle*, Tob. 14, the *Testament of Naphtali*, and Dan. 2, 7, and 8. I shall demonstrate below that the sequence in Daniel is a closer match to the Greek and Roman pattern than is often thought.

texts are very late, written over a thousand years after Daniel. Whatever earlier traditions may be preserved in them cannot be easily extracted, while the majority of historically identifiable elements pertain to the Sassanian period or later. Even if one admits to a direct connection between the book of Daniel and these Iranian texts, the direction in which the common traditions were transmitted would be far from certain.

While the Babylonian dynastic prophecy was probably written in the Seleucid era in Babylon,[39] placing it in roughly the same time period as Daniel, its empires do not match those of Daniel, and its interest is more locally focused on Babylon and the changing rulers over that city rather than the rise and fall of empires. It also shows no evidence of a fourfold structure in its listing of successive rulers over Babylon.

By way of contrast, the Herodotean tradition shares the same interest in the passing of empire from one kingdom to another as does Daniel. The series of kingdoms found in Greek historians beginning with Herodotus corresponds more exactly to the kingdoms in Daniel than do those found in the eastern texts.[40] Herodotus' *Histories* were unquestionably written in the mid-fifth century BCE and were widely read and imitated throughout antiquity, including the Hellenistic period (a point I will address shortly). Subsequent Greek historians, beginning with Ctesias, codified Herodotus's outline of imperial succession from Assyria to Media to Persia, ultimately adding the fourth kingdom of Alexander. The book of Daniel was written in the Hellenistic period in a country under Seleucid-Greek rule at a time when Greek culture and education were being eagerly sought by many of the local elites. The conditions for the assimilation of the Greek theory of imperial succession by a Jewish writer were ideal. Yet the Greek influence in the book of Daniel has not been readily acknowledged.

An immediate objection to the claim that Daniel imported his four-kingdom outline from Greece might be the fact that he refers not to Assyria but Babylonia as the first kingdom in this series. In Daniel 2, when Daniel is interpreting the dream of the statue of four metals, he tells the dreamer, King Nebuchadnezzar of Babylon, that he is the 'head of gold' (2.38), which represents the first kingdom. As is often stated by commentators, the substitution of Babylonia for Assyria makes perfect sense in the context of Jewish history.[41] What is often overlooked, however, is that the substitution also makes sense—or rather, never even happens—from the perspective of Herodotus and the historiographic tradition which proceeds from him. Herodotus never actually mentions a Babylonian empire, but describes Babylon as if it were an Assyrian city. In fact, Babylon is referred to as the new Assyrian

---

39. Grayson, *Babylonian Historical-Literary Texts*, pp. 9, 27.

40. Of course Herodotus does not have a fourth Greek kingdom since he did not live to see it. This was added by his successors in the Greek historiographical tradition after the conquest of Alexander (e.g. Polybius, Diodorus Siculus, Dionysius of Halicarnassus). It may be argued, however, that Herodotus's account of the Greek victories over the Persians already suggests the supplanting of that empire.

41. E.g. Collins, *Daniel*, p. 168.

capital after the fall of Nineveh (1.178). Also, during the campaign of Darius against Babylon, the Persian Zopyrus refers to the city's inhabitants as 'Assyrians' (3.155). By confusing or fusing the two Mesopotamian empires, Herodotus promises to speak of the many kings of Babylon in his History of Assyria (1.184), and he attributes to a certain Queen Nitocris (supposedly an Assyrian queen reigning in Babylon who is as historically elusive as Daniel's Darius the Mede) works of construction which were actually carried out by Nebuchadnezzar (1.185).[42] In effect, the book of Daniel's Nebuchadnezzar, as king of Babylon (Dan. 1.1), would be an Assyrian king by Herodotus's reckoning. For Herodotus, there is in fact no Neo-Babylonian Empire, just the truncated remains of the Assyrian Empire with its capital in Babylon after the fall of Nineveh. The discrepancy which appears to exist between the first kingdom of Daniel and that of Herodotus suddenly vanishes.

Interestingly enough, there is another Jewish text from the Hellenistic period which in all probability knew and drew upon Herodotus: the book of Judith. The arguments put forward by various scholars for such a dependence have already been briefly summarized in Chapter 1. We may now add that in Judith there is a similar historical confusion as in Herodotus. Nebuchadnezzar is referred to as king of the Assyrians (Jdt. 1.1), a seemingly ridiculous error for a Jewish author to make, yet not so strange if we admit the influence of Greek sources. Herodotus has preceded the author of Judith in calling the kings and people of Babylon Assyrians. The reference to Nebuchadnezzar as king of Assyria, along with the many other glaring historical errors in the first part of the book of Judith, have been variously dealt with in the history of scholarship on Judith. Assuming that the book of Judith intended actually to recount history, some scholars have hypothesized textual corruptions or a confused historical knowledge on the part of its author to account for these difficulties.[43] Recognizing the work to be fiction, more recent scholars have suggested that these historical inaccuracies are deliberate fabrications intended to focus the reader's attention beyond a simple (and incorrect) historical reading to a deeper meaning in the text.[44] It certainly would appear that the author has no intention of trying to preserve an accurate historical account, but this in itself would in no way preclude a literary borrowing from Herodotus. The same author who told the story of the 'Jewish Thermopylae' at Bethulia may have also picked up other elements from Herodotus with which to tell this story. Writing on the genre of the Greek novel (a body of literature to which the Hellenistic Jewish novellas like Judith are closely related), John R. Morgan reminds us that this literature was not

---

42. These include changing the course of the Euphrates by cutting channels, and constructing embankments along both sides of the river. See Marincola, *Herodotus*, p. 559 n. 77.

43. For a brief summary of representative treatments see T. Craven, 'Artistry and Faith in the Book of Judith', *Semeia* 8 (1977), pp. 75-95 (77-78).

44. Craven, *Artistry and Faith*, pp. 73-74. C.C. Torrey had earlier stated that the author of Judith 'takes pains to tell his hearers plainly that they are listening to fiction' (*The Apocryphal Literature* [New Haven: Yale University Press, 1945], p. 89). R.H. Pfeiffer had also suggested the possibility that the author of Judith may have 'blundered deliberately to show that his story was fiction' (*History of New Testament Times with an Introduction to the Apocrypha* [New York: Harper & Brothers, 1949], p. 291).

'sealed off from other literature at large, [but drew upon] other genres, like epic or historiography'.[45]

Another example of a literary borrowing from Greek historical sources in the book of Judith may be found in the detail of the five days which the thirsty, besieged inhabitants of Bethulia agree to wait for divine intervention on their behalf before surrendering (Jdt. 7.30). We find inscribed on stone at the temple at Lindos the account of how that city's inhabitants, besieged by Darius with their water supply cut off, agreed to wait five days for help from the gods. In the event that help did not come, they would surrender their city to the Persians. Help arrives in the form of a miraculous cloudburst, and they, like their Jewish counterparts, are ultimately saved from the great invading army. The date of this inscription is 99 BCE, but the story itself is much older. The inscription cites six historians who had earlier recorded these events.[46]

One final example of the possibility of Greek historical sources in the book of Judith can be found in the names of Holofernes, the Assyrian general, and his eunuch, Bagoas. These were the names of two commanders under Artaxerxes III in his campaigns against the west. According to Diodorus Siculus, Holofernes, who was the brother of King Ariarathes of Cappadocia, accompanied Artaxerxes III in his campaign against Egypt (31.19.2-3). Elsewhere Diodorus tells us that Bagoas was the most trusted commander of Artaxerxes in his Egyptian campaign (16.47.4) and that he was also (as in the book of Judith) a eunuch (17.5.3).[47] The appearance of these names in the book of Judith might reflect a familiarity on the part of the author with the campaigns of Artaxerxes III against the west in 353 BCE.[48] However, there is very strong evidence that the book of Judith was written two centuries after this event.[49] Rather than supposing that these names reflect a Persian-period date for the composition of Judith, or that they result from another muddled memory of a two-century-old event, it makes more sense to see yet another literary borrowing from the Greek historians who recorded these events.[50] Greek histories

45.   J.R. Morgan and R. Stoneman (eds.), *Greek Fiction: The Greek Novel in Context* (New York: Routledge, 1994), p. 4.

46.   A translation of the pertinent portion of the text can be found in Hadas, *Hellenistic Culture*, pp. 166-67.

47.   According to Pliny, *Natural History* 13.41, Bagoas (Latin: *Bagous*) was the Persian word for 'eunuch'.

48.   R.H. Pfeiffer, *History of New Testament Times*, p. 294.

49.   The Maccabean date for the book of Judith can no longer be disputed. The parallels with the time and career of Judas Maccabeus are too numerous to be coincidental. As R.H. Pfeiffer has noted: 'It is only after 168–165 that a king (Antiochus Epiphanes) forced the Jews to forsake their God and change their religion: no other historical event could have suggested such fantastic statements as we read in 3.8 and 6.2' (*History of New Testament Times*, p. 294). The full evidence for a Maccabean date can be found on pp. 294-95 of Pfeiffer's study; M.S. Enslin and S. Zeitlin, *The Book of Judith* (JAL, 9; Leiden: E.J. Brill, 1972), pp. 28-30; and G.W.E. Nickelsburg, *Jewish Literature between the Bible and the Mishnah* (Philadelphia: Fortress Press, 1981), pp. 108-109.

50.   It is unfortunately unclear as to what Diodorus's own sources were for this material. There are references to a Holophernes also in Polybius 3.5.2; 32.10; and 33.6. The figure referred to by Polybius, however, is a later Cappadocian prince who usurped the throne with the aid of the

would be readily available to a Hellenized Jewish novelist at this time, just as they clearly were to the Hellenistic Jewish historians of this period.[51] Moreover, 'historical novels',[52] or even pseudo-historical novels such as Judith, illustrate just how blurred the lines could become between history and fiction—how frequently they combined and how freely they could borrow one from the other.[53]

Before returning to the book of Daniel, I would like to cite one other example from the Greek tradition that illustrates once more the influence of the father of history not only upon subsequent historiography, but also upon the nascent novelistic tradition. In Chariton's *Chaereas and Callirhoe*,[54] the Persian beauty Rhodogyne is

Seleucid King Demetrius I in 159/58 BCE (see A. Pietersma, 'Holophernes', in *ABD* III, p. 257). In the first century CE, Appian also recorded this information in his *Syrian Wars* 47. Diodorus also mentions a later Holophernes in 31.19.7. It is also worth noting that the corrupt spelling employed by Diodorus: Ὀλοφέρνης corresponds to the name as we find it in Judith. The more correct spelling: Ὀροφέρνης is found in Polybius. It could be that the author of Judith and Diodorus picked up this variant spelling from the same or a similar source.

51. It is clear that Eupolemus was familiar with Ctesias either directly or through an intermediary. Ctesias invented the fictitious Median king Astibares who reappears in Eupolemus 39.4. It also appears that Eupolemus was familiar with Herodotus from his listing of Egyptian names in 32 (see the discussion in Wacholder, *Eupolemus: A Study of Judaeo-Greek Literature*, p. 164). It has also been strongly argued that Pseudo-Eupolemus was familiar with the work of Berossus who wrote his history of Babylon in Greek at the beginning of the third century BCE (see R. Doran, 'Pseudo-Eupolemus: A New Translation and Introduction', in *OTP*, II, pp. 873-82 [877]). In all likelihood Artapanus most likely knew Manetho (who wrote his Egyptian history in Greek at the beginning of the third century BCE) and probably Hecataeus of Abdera as well. This conclusion can be inferred from the close parallels with Diodorus Siculus whose major source for his Egyptian material was Hecataeus (see J.J. Collins, 'Artapanus: A New Translation and Introduction', in *OTP*, II, pp. 889-903 [894]).

52. The category of 'historical novel' as defined by L.M. Wills (*The Jewish Novel in the Ancient World* [Ithaca, NY: Cornell University Press, 1995], p. 30) consists of novelistic works which cover the recent past, have as their main character a truly historical figure, and were most likely presumed to be factual or true by their readers. These would include Jewish texts such as *3 Maccabees* and the *Tobiad Romance*, and the Christian Acts of the Apostles. A non-Jewish exemplar of a historical novel (although it also took on a Jewish form among its many recensions) is the *Alexander Romance*. While the date of composition of the *Alexander Romance* is uncertain, it is probable that an early form of this *Romance*, which would eventually take on innumerable forms in a multitude of languages, already existed in the third or second century BCE (see R. Stoneman, 'The *Alexander Romance*: From History to Fiction', in Morgan and Stoneman [eds.], *Greek Fiction*, pp. 117-29 [118]; R. Stoneman [trans., with an introduction and notes], *The Greek Alexander Romance* [New York: Penguin Books, 1991], p. 17; R.H. Pfeiffer, *History of New Testament Times*, p. 108).

53. Preceding both the book of Judith and the *Alexander Romance* is Xenophon's *Cyropaedia* which may be the first exemplar of what we might call the genre of historical fiction. As John R. Morgan has suggested, the fact that three later novelists were called Xenophon (Xenophon of Ephesus, Xenophon of Cyprus, and Xenophon of Antioch) may indicate the use of a pseudonym intended to situate them in the literary tradition of their fourth-century BCE namesake (Morgan and Stoneman [eds.], *Greek Fiction*, p. 5).

54. As with the Jewish novellas, the dating of the Greek novels is notoriously difficult. The discovery of fragments of *Chaereas and Callirhoe* in Egypt in the first part of the twentieth century led some scholars to date this novel around the middle of the second century CE. See W.E. Blake

presented as the daughter of Zopyrus and the wife of Megabyzus. The appearance of these two 'Persian'[55] male names in tandem would sound very familiar to one well-acquainted with Herodotus' *Histories*. In fact, the names appear as a father and son pair in Herodotus 3.153 as distinguished Persians (Megabyzus was one of the seven conspirators who killed the usurper Magus, and his son Zopyrus the self-mutilated hero of the siege of Babylon). A second father–son pair in this line is presented in 3.160 bearing the same names. It is more than a coincidence that Chariton's narrative, set to a large extent in the ambit of the Persian Empire,[56] should reproduce the same pair of names as we find in Herodotus's account of the Persian Empire. The very choice of the Persian Empire and the court of the Persian king as settings for Chariton's work of fiction would seem to be based on a knowledge of the works of Herodotus and Ctesias, drawing inspiration from their vivid accounts. The reproduction of a pair of names known from Herodotus verifies this suspicion, indicating that his *Histories* were in fact used as a quarry of material providing elements of setting, style, plot, and detail which could be rearranged by novel writers. So, Chariton could find there a couple of good 'Persian' names to enhance the color of his narrative, the author of Judith could find the gripping story of Thermopylae, and the author of Daniel could find the idea of the succession of empires.

Returning to Daniel's succession of kingdoms, a second consideration which favors a direct link to Herodotus and the Greek historiographic tradition is the inclusion of Media among the four kingdoms.[57] Given that the Medes never conquered nor ruled over Judea, the inclusion of Media only makes sense if we consider foreign sources for Daniel's four kingdoms.[58] The sequence Assyria–Media–Persia

(trans.), *Chariton's Chaereas and Callirhoe* (Ann Arbor: University of Michigan Press, 1939), p. v. See also B. Egger, 'Looking at Chariton's Callirhoe', in Morgan and Stoneman (eds.), *Greek Fiction*, pp. 31-48 (31). However, the geographical and social background of one of the story's main locations—Miletus—seems to fit that area of Asia Minor during the early Roman Empire. Therefore, scholars such as B.P. Reardon (*Collected Ancient Greek Novels* [Berkeley: University of California Press, 1989], pp. 17-18) place *Chaereas and Callirhoe* in the mid-first century CE. In either case, *Chaereas and Callirhoe* would be the earliest extant Greek novel.

55. As D. Asheri notes, the name Zopyrus (Ζώπυρος) is a perfectly good Greek name meaning 'one who inflames' or 'who is in flames'. It may be a Graecized form of Shâpôr, or Shahpûre in Pahlavi (David Asheri, *Erodoto: Le Storie: Libro III: La Persia* [Milan: Fondazione Lorenzo Valla, 1990], p. 357).

56. Books 4–8 of Chaereas and Callirhoe involve the Persian king Artaxerxes, his court (in Babylon), and his campaign against the revolting Egyptians.

57. While it is not made explicit that the second kingdom is Media in the interpretations of the visions in chs. 2 and 7, the Medes are explicitly mentioned in the interpretation of the vision in ch. 8. Also, the overall structuring of the book of Daniel as a series of events and visions taking place in the reigns of successive Babylonian, Median, and Persian kings makes this identification virtually certain. A discussion of the many views which have been proposed for identifying Daniel's four kingdoms can be found in H.H. Rowley, *Darius the Mede and the Four World Empires in the Book of Daniel: A Historical Study of Contemporary Theories* (Cardiff: University of Wales Press Board, 1935), pp. 61-173.

58. A certain case can be made that the inclusion of Media is based upon biblical prophecies which foretold the fall of Babylon at the hands of the Medes. The pertinent texts are Isa. 13.17 and

is well known among Greek historians beginning with Herodotus and appears to derive ultimately from the Persian sources on which Herodotus based his account (1.95).[59] While Herodotus is the first writer whom we know to have written this succession of empires, it is not inconceivable that Daniel may have picked up this idea elsewhere, even perhaps from the same original Persian sources as Herodotus. Still, the fact that Daniel completes the sequence with a fourth kingdom—that of Greece—indicates that he wrote after Alexander and followed in the same tradition as Herodotus and other Greek and Roman historians after him (e.g. Polybius, Diodorus Siculus, and Dionysius of Halicarnassus) who extended the series into their own time to include Macedonia (and ultimately Rome). This makes an un-mediated Persian source seem far less likely. We may also add that the works of Greek literature were more likely to have been accessible to a Jew in Seleucid Pales-tine than would be the distant court records of a long-defunct Persian Empire.

The third consideration I would like to make in favor of Daniel's borrowing from Herodotus is his reference to four kings of Persia (Dan. 11.1).[60] Granted, four is a highly symbolic number that is very common in apocalyptic literature; neverthe-less, its use in reference to the kings of Persia does not easily lend itself to typical apocalyptic interpretations. No details at all are given about the first three kings, in contrast to the descriptions of each of the four beasts in ch. 7. There is not even so much as an accompanying reference to the global aspect symbolized by this num-ber (such as 'the four winds of heaven' found in 7.2 and 8.8). Furthermore, if the similarly symbolic number ten can be used in ch. 7 in reference to the kings of the fourth kingdom preceding Antiochus IV (the little horn),[61] why not use it as a more accurate reflection of the actual eleven Persian kings from Cyrus to Darius III? An

---

Jer. 51.11, 28. Especially given Daniel's interest in the prophet Jeremiah evidenced in ch. 9 of Daniel, the possibility that he preserved a historical fiction to prove correct Jeremiah's prophecy cannot be overlooked. Nevertheless, the focus in these passages from Isaiah and Jeremiah is on the punishment and destruction of Babylon. No mention or hint is made of a Median kingdom which would replace it. Media is simply the anticipated instrument of its destruction. It should also be noted that ch. 14 of the book of Tobit does not refer to a Median empire succeeding Assyria, but merely refers to the destruction of the city of Nineveh at the hands of the Medes.

59.   As has often been noted by commentators, the pattern of Assyria–Media–Persia reflects a Persian understanding of historical events. The Persians would have seen their neighbors the Medes as the conquerors of Assyria who in turn were conquered by Persia. Babylonians (and Jews) would rather emphasize the Chaldean role in overthrowing Assyria. Although the pattern which includes Media suggests a Persian perspective, it must be reiterated that it was the Greek historians, begin-ning with Herodotus and Ctesias, who inherited this view and codified it in their written works. It is through these Greek historians that this scheme of history was transmitted.

60.   The insistence on 'four' as being the number of Persian kings is reinforced in the vision in Dan. 7.6 where Persia is symbolized as a leopard with four wings and four heads. The heads in particular are indicative of individual kings in apocalyptic symbolism (see, e.g., Rev. 13.1-3; *4 Ezra* 12.22-23).

61.   Various identifications have been proposed for these ten kings. Most scholars hold them to be the successive rulers of the Seleucid dynasty (see Collins, *Daniel*, p. 320) although there were only seven Seleucid kings between Alexander and Antiochus IV. That number can be increased by including Alexander and regents or claimants such as Heliodorus, but it appears more likely that ten is simply a round, symbolic number.

answer suggests itself if we once again posit the influence of Herodotus whose *Histories* deal with the four Persian kings from Cyrus to Xerxes I. While scholars have proposed alternative identifications for the four Persian kings in Daniel, these proposals generally have little to recommend them. The most widely supported identification is that of the four Persian kings mentioned in the Bible: Cyrus, Darius, Xerxes, and Artaxerxes (Ezra 4.5-7).[62] There is, however, no compelling argument to favor this identification. The four kings mentioned in Ezra are presented neither as consecutive (which they were not) nor as exhaustive. The Jews, who were ruled by the Persians for two centuries, were well aware that there were other Persian kings interspersed between the reigns of these kings. Furthermore, it seems to be the case that more than one Persian king may be indicated by some of these names. At the very least it would appear that two kings named Darius are alluded to in Ezra–Nehemiah (Ezra 4.5 and Neh. 12.22). Therefore, characterizing the Persian Empire as marked by the reigns of precisely four kings makes little sense from a Jewish perspective. From a Greek literary perspective the characterization does make sense, however. In Herodotus there are four and only four Persian kings who rule consecutively. Within the world of his *Histories* these four kings do make up the Persian Empire. The link between Daniel and Herodotus becomes even stronger when we consider the characterization of the fourth and 'final' Persian king. This fourth king who stands alone from the nondescript three who precede him is described as exceedingly rich, and he undertakes a campaign in which he musters all the forces of the earth against Greece. The characterization so perfectly matches that of Xerxes in Herodotus's *Histories* that commentators from antiquity already made the connection. I will now take a closer look at the passage from Daniel that provides us with this description of the fourth Persian king.

Daniel 11.2b presents a difficult Hebrew text.[63] Here I give the rendering of the NRSV which I believe accurately reflects the meaning of the original Hebrew:

> Three more kings shall arise in Persia. The fourth shall be far richer than all of them, and when he has become strong through his riches, he shall stir up all against the kingdom of Greece.

There are two elements brought into relief in this succinct description of the fourth Persian king: (1) his surpassing wealth, and (2) his mustering of the entire world to war against Greece. These elements correspond exactly with the characterization of Xerxes in Herodotus. Herodotus frequently makes note of the great wealth of

---

62. Among proponents of this view, J.A. Montgomery (*A Critical and Exegetical Commentary on the Book of Daniel* [ICC; Edinburgh: T. & T. Clark, 1927], p. 423) identifies the fourth king as Darius III, while L.F. Hartman and A.A. Di Lella (*The Book of Daniel* [AB, 23; New York: Doubleday, 1964], p. 288) identify the fourth king as Darius II, both basing their identifications on the reference to Darius in Neh. 12.22. It is clear, however, that the Darius mentioned in Ezra 4.5 must be Darius I since he appears between Cyrus and Ahasuerus (Xerxes). If the combined work of Ezra–Nehemiah thus mentions at least two kings named Darius (Darius I in Ezra 4.5 and either Darius II or Darius III in Neh. 12.22), this brings the total of Persian rulers named in the Bible to more than four. This makes the biblical text an unlikely source for Daniel's four Persian kings.

63. See the Appendix for a discussion of the difficulties in translating this passage.

Xerxes and of his vast provisions.[64] He also describes quite vividly the great mustering of forces by Xerxes from all of Asia over a period of four years (7.19-21). The clarity of the allusion did not escape ancient commentators like St Jerome and Porphyry who identified the fourth Persian king as Xerxes.[65] It misses the point somewhat to state as Montgomery does that the Jewish tradition could not have had any memory of Xerxes' wars with Greece.[66] There need not have been any Jewish memory of the Greek campaign of Xerxes; just as there was almost certainly no Jewish memory of Median hegemony, nor of a Persian empire marked by precisely four kings, nor a confused memory which conflated Assyrian and Babylonian rule. The unlikelihood of finding any of these traditions within Judaism, coupled with the fact that they all appear in Herodotus, makes the direct influence of Greek historiography on the book of Daniel all the more probable.

2. *Daniel 11: Greek History Told as Prophecy*

Along with the historical overviews of the four kingdoms in Daniel chs. 2 and 7, there is another key passage in the book of Daniel that strongly suggests a source in Greek historiography. This is the detailed, symbolic rendering of Seleucid and Ptolemaic history in ch. 11.[67] The political events described therein concerning the Ptolemaic and Seleucid dynasties do not even mention the Jews or their land until vv. 16 and 20 (and these are just passing references which are not developed).

64. A characteristic passage is the encounter between Xerxes and the Lydian, Pythius (8.27-29). The great wealth of Pythius is enumerated, yet he can only be called the wealthiest man in the world, *after* Xerxes.

65. Jerome (*Commentariorum in Danielem* 3.11.2b), however, interpreted the text to mean there would be four kings after the first for a total of five: Cyrus, Cambyses, Pseudo-Smerdis, Darius, and Xerxes. His rival, Porphyry, likewise identified the same four successors of Cyrus. Based on the image of Persia as a leopard with four heads and four wings in ch. 7, it makes more sense to understand ch. 11 as referring to a total of four kings. It is significant, however, that both Jerome and Porphyry were able to identify Daniel's fourth Persian king as Xerxes based on the brief description which so closely matches what we know from Herodotus. See Bickerman, *Four Strange Books*, p. 114; and Montgomery, *A Critical and Exegetical Commentary*, p. 423.

66. Montgomery, *A Critical and Exegetical Commentary*, p. 423. It is likewise a mistake to assume that the fourth king necessarily represents the last king of the Persian empire (Collins, *Daniel*, p. 377). The description simply does not fit Darius III who was defeated by Alexander. It should also be noted that there is no expressed relationship or conflict between the powerful king of v. 3 (Alexander) and the wealthy campaigner of v. 2 (Xerxes). The account simply moves from the most representative king of the Persian empire to the most representative of the Greek. In a similar fashion to Xerxes' representation of Persia, Nebuchadnezzar was alluded to as representing Babylon (Dan. 7.4 recalls the portrayal of Nebuchadnezzar in Dan. 4—see also 2.37), although he was neither the first nor last king of this empire.

67. This largely 'non-Jewish' history may have been derived from some Greek historical account. The poor quality of the Hebrew in Dan. 11 has long been noted by scholars who hypothesize the use of a source written in a language other than Hebrew. See Collins, *Daniel*, p. 377, who also refers to the earlier studies of G.A. Barton ('The Composition of the Book of Daniel', *JBL* 17 [1898], pp. 62-86) and J.C.H. Lebram ('König Antiochus im Buch Daniel', *VT* 25 [1975], pp. 737-72).

The main concern of the author, which is expounded in vv. 21-45, is the action of Antiochus IV against the 'holy covenant' (11.30). Yet this persecution of the Jewish religion is not viewed as an isolated moment in history, but as the culmination of a long string of interrelated events. It is the fourth king of Persia who attacks Greece (11.2),[68] setting the stage for Greek retaliation with the appearance of a powerful king, an obvious reference to Alexander (11.3). The breakup and division of his kingdom (11.4) occasions the political maneuvering and military expeditions of those to whom it has been partitioned (11.5-30). It is in the course of these military ventures that the Jewish homeland itself is overrun (11.16) and levied for taxes (11.20). Finally, coming to the period of greatest interest to the author of Daniel (that of Antiochus IV), the growing hostility and action against 'the holy covenant' by the Seleucid king is described in direct relation to his ongoing wars with the Ptolemaic kingdom. So, it is after Antiochus returns from his first Egyptian campaign with great riches that he turns his attention against 'the holy covenant' (11.28). Again, after his humiliating forced retreat from his second Egyptian campaign, due to the intervention of Rome ('ships of Kittim', 11.30), he is enraged and takes action against the holy covenant.[69]

The meandering way in which Daniel leads up to the main moment of historical interest for him is reminiscent of Herodotus's leading up to the Persian War by going back to the time of Croesus. A broader context is used to situate the current events in a historical chain of cause and effect. It is in a complex web of political, military, economic, and psychological factors extending over space (including the empires of Syria, Egypt, and Rome) and time (dating back to the Persian empire) that the current crisis in the reign of Antiochus IV is situated and understood in Daniel ch. 11. This wider focus, which includes nations and events that do not

---

68. It is interesting to note the negative portrayal of the Persian empire in ch. 11 of Daniel. Not only does the divine messenger of Daniel's vision (who is elsewhere identified as Gabriel—9.21) state that the prince of the kingdom of Persia impeded him for twenty-one days from coming in answer to Daniel's prayer (11.13), he also says that he must soon fight the prince of Persia again (11.20). It is because Gabriel is absent fighting the prince of Persia that the prince of Greece is free to make an appearance on the scene (11.20). This portrayal of Persia as an enemy of the Jewish people is in stark contrast with the glowing description of Cyrus as God's anointed in Isa. 45.1. This might be considered yet another indication of Greek historiographic sources behind the accounts in Dan. 7–12, but it must be remembered that not all Jews during the long period of Persian rule would share the same enthusiasm for Persia as expressed in Isaiah at the moment of their liberation from exile.

69. The psychological motive expressed here in Daniel for the persecution of the Jews by Antiochus closely matches the description given in Polybius. Daniel states that when ships of the Kittim come against Antiochus, he will be disheartened (niphal נכאה), turn back (שוב), and express indignation (זעם). Polybius in 29.27 says that after the intervention of the Roman commander, Popilius Laenas, Antiochus led his army back to Syria, distressed (βαρυνόμενος) and complaining (στένων). The other Jewish texts which tell of Antiochus's Egyptian invasion, 1 and 2 Maccabees, do not match the profile of Antiochus which we find here in Polybius and Daniel. Furthermore, they each recount only one of Antiochus's two campaigns (although 2 Maccabees alludes to the other), while Daniel, like Polybius, describes both (Dan. 11.25, 29; Polybius 28.18-23; 29.26-27). While Polybius, who wrote a few decades after Daniel, cannot be a source for him, they may be working out of a common tradition.

immediately impact the Jewish people, is a marked departure from earlier Israelite historiography. Worthy of special notice is the intervention of Rome as the most immediate cause of Antiochus's retreat and subsequent action against Jerusalem. This observation of Daniel fits in well with contemporary Greek historiography. Shortly after the book of Daniel was written, Polybius would expound his thesis on the interdependence of historical events based on the ubiquitous political and military influence of Rome (1.1.5; 3.1.4-5). So too, Daniel has his eye on a broad international scene, giving a thorough treatment of the extended human causes which have led up to a key historical moment. At the same time, Daniel does not lose sight of the ultimate divine causation of 'what is to happen' (10.14). In this he is remarkably similar to Herodotus who deftly combines statements on the inevitability of events ('what had to be' and 'what was going to happen'[70]) with unmistakably free human choices and actions. This relationship between human and divine causation in the theological histories which Daniel and Herodotus weave will be discussed in detail in the following chapters.

In Daniel 11, the human causes of the religious persecution under Antiochus IV lie in the broad unfolding of political and military events in the world at large. There is less focus on the local and immediate causes which one finds in 1 and 2 Maccabees. Instead of narrating the intrigues among the various competitors for the Jewish high priesthood, Daniel looks to the world at large with its competing kings and nations. The focus is broader, and many of the details we know of from other sources fade into the background or disappear. This corresponds to the method of universal historiography which one finds in Polybius, where many events are omitted or briefly reported in order to treat 'each event on a proper scale' (29.12.6), for it is the big picture that concerns the universal historian (29.12.11). This universal perspective of Daniel also hearkens back to the *Histories* of Herodotus, which recount barbarian as well as Greek deeds in a great interlocking composition. The book of Daniel, then, incorporates aspects of universal history into its account, revealing a similar focus and method as one finds in the contemporary Greek historian, Polybius. The ultimate unifying factor for Daniel, however, is not the Roman Empire, but the universal sovereignty of God in ordering the course of history, both giving and taking away human kingship (7.26-27).

The history that is told in Daniel 11 is, as we have seen, to a large extent non-Jewish. It describes the fortunes of the Seleucid and Ptolemaic kingdoms, their origins (beginning with a glance back to Persian times), and their interactions with each other, the Romans, and ultimately the Jews in the time of Antiochus IV. This long historical survey of political and military events on an international scale is recounted by Daniel not as conventional historiography, however, but as prophecy. We are not told that these events occurred, but that they will occur. The whole passage begins with the statement: 'Three more kings shall arise in Persia' (11.2). Towards the end of this chapter, it appears that a true prophecy is attempted since the details of Antiochus IV's death in Dan. 11.40-45 do not match what we know

70. J. Gould (*Herodotus* [New York: St Martin's Press, 1989], pp. 73-78) gives a detailed discussion on the occurrence of these phrases in Herodotus and their meaning.

from other sources concerning his demise. This is immediately followed by the eschatological prophecy of 12.1-3. The conventional way to interpret this entire section of the book of Daniel has been to focus on the final 'actual' prophecies and see the initial *ex eventu* prophecies in 11.2-39 as a way of establishing the seer's credentials.

Without venturing to speculate how impressed a second-century BCE Jewish reader would be by these 'predictions' (we know that Josephus was duly impressed over two centuries later), I want to suggest that the primary purpose of this historical review in the form of prophecy is to interpret history, not simply to vouch for the visionary. We have already noted how for Daniel, as also for Herodotus, the concept of 'what must happen' plays an important role. By speaking of history as prophecy foretold by God, Daniel is adding a divine element of causation to the tangled web of human machinations that culminate in a moment of historical crisis for the Jews. Of course, aside from ch. 9 of Daniel where the traditional position that Israel is suffering this historical moment on account of its sins is presented, there is no real answer to the question of why these things must happen. They are simply foretold—preordained—but so too is their end foretold. The message of hope which this understanding of history would give to the Jews of Daniel's time is essentially the same as the advice which Solon gave to Croesus: 'Look to the end, no matter what it is you are considering' (1.32). The fortunes of people both good and bad may rise and fall in the course of history, but in the end one can count on a kind of divine retribution or justice to prevail. The arrogant and menacing king, whether Croesus, Cambyses, Xerxes, or Antiochus, will be brought low.

As mentioned, the content of the history told in ch. 11 largely pertains to the 'Greek' world (i.e. the Ptolemaic and Seleucid kingdoms with reference to Rome as well). To this observation I would like now to add that the peculiar mode of recounting the same history in ch. 11—as prophecy—may be Greek as well. Elias Bickerman noted how Greek dramatists from the time of Aeschylus's *Persians* (472 BCE) 'used the device of re-telling history as if it were the future'.[71] One example he gives is from Aristophanes' *The Knights*, written in 424 BCE. Aristophanes has Bakis, a famous, ancient seer predict the successive reigns in Athens of an oakum seller (Eucrates), a sheep seller (Lysicles), and a leather seller (Cleon). The latter was in fact in power at the time that the play was written. There then follows an actual 'prophecy' which tells of Athens next being ruled by a sausage seller. The final prediction, like Daniel's final prophecy in ch. 11 concerning Antiochus's demise, can be distinguished from the actual history by the fact that it was never realized. Bickerman claims that Porphyry was so easily able to decipher the book of Daniel and correctly situate it in the Maccabean period (anticipating modern biblical scholarship by quite some time) because he was familiar with the 'vaticination style of Daniel [which] was Greek'.[72]

---

71. Bickerman, *Four Strange Books*, p. 117.
72. Bickerman, *Four Strange Books*, p. 117.

3. *Herodotus in the Hellenistic Period*

So far we have seen that there are several elements in Daniel's overview of history as four successive kingdoms which can best be understood as being derived from concepts and descriptions set down by Herodotus. Similarly, we have seen how the detailed historical information in ch. 11 evidences a genuine concern for events which, although distant in time and space, are causally related to the immediate crisis at hand. This broad sweep of interrelated political and military events in Daniel is comparable to the Greek historiographical tradition beginning with Herodotus. We have also noted the fact that Greek culture had an increasingly profound impact upon Judaism in the Hellenistic period—an impact witnessed not only in Jewish literature from the Diaspora, but from Palestine as well. With regard to the impact of Greek culture on Judaism, what now remains to be demonstrated more particularly is the position that Herodotus's *Histories* held within that culture. By examining the diffusion and enduring influence of the *Histories* in the centuries following Alexander, I will argue that it was a text which the average educated Greek in the Hellenistic period would most likely know—a text which inspired imitators as well as critics. If, then, the *Histories* were the common patrimony of educated Greeks during this period, one can make the same conclusion about Jews who had received a Greek education.

Herodotus wrote his *Histories* in the third quarter of the fifth century BCE. His most immediate followers in history writing were also at times his sharpest critics. Writing his *History of the Peloponnesian War* at the end of the fifth century, Thucydides implicitly criticizes Herodotus's work as unreliable by correcting him (without mentioning him by name) in several places.[73] Although, as M.I. Finley has correctly observed, we can never be certain that the many discrepancies in details between Herodotus and Thucydides reflect conscious corrections on the part of the latter,[74] there are instances where it is apparent that Thucydides refers to his predecessor. Such is the case in the so-called methodological chapter (1.20) where he refers to incorrect assumptions made by Greeks in general. The two examples he gives—(1) the belief that the kings of Sparta were each entitled to two votes, and (2) that the Spartans had a battalion called Πιτανάτης—are both found in Herodotus at 6.57 and 9.53 respectively. As Finley notes, 'it is hard to imagine that there was a "general belief" '[75] in such matters. Thucydides undoubtedly gleaned these 'general Greek assumptions' from Herodotus's *Histories*, implicitly criticizing its accuracy.

In addition to correcting Herodotus's errors in details, Thucydides regarded the very method employed by Herodotus of inquiring into distant events and reporting what was told to him as unreliable. He considered it impossible to acquire precise knowledge about the past (1.1). For Thucydides an accurate account could only

---

73. A. Lesky, *A History of Greek Literature* (trans. J. Willis and C. de Heer; New York: Thomas Y. Crowell Company, 1966), p. 472.
74. Thucydides, *History of the Peloponnesian War* (trans. R. Warner with an introduction and notes by M.I. Finley; Baltimore: Penguin Books, 1972), p. 15.
75. Thucydides, *History of the Peloponnesian War*, p. 15.

be had of events to which one was contemporary. The second-hand reports of distant times and places which fill Herodotus's work had no place under the stricter standards of historical reliability erected by Thucydides. Although, as we have mentioned, Thucydides never explicitly criticizes Herodotus, his method and standards of historical reliability paved the way for a negative judgment of Herodotus's work.

Shortly after Thucydides, in the early fourth century, Ctesias began a long tradition of explicitly criticizing Herodotus. In his *Persika*, Ctesias claimed to correct the many mistakes of Herodotus in his account of the Persian War. In spite of Ctesias's own soon-acquired reputation as an unreliable historian, Herodotus's *Histories* were already viewed with suspicion by the next generation of historians. Yet, in spite of the negative appraisals which would hound his work throughout antiquity,[76] the fact remains that both Thucydides and Ctesias were very familiar with and influenced by Herodotus's *Histories*, as were his later critics. The very fact that such vehement attacks against him were even written, such as Plutarch's *On the Malice of Herodotus*,[77] suggests that his work did enjoy a continual, wide audience and influence, otherwise there would be no need to so passionately refute it.

One way of understanding the strange admixture of Herodotus's often-dubious reputation and his continuing appeal and authority in antiquity has been to view his work from the two perspectives of history and style. Thus, while his accuracy and veracity are often questioned by his harshest detractors, his eloquent style is praised by his defenders as a model to be imitated. Foremost among those who praised his style where his compatriot, Dionysius of Halicarnassus, in the first century BCE and Lucian in the second century CE. The latter writes:

> I wish it were possible to imitate Herodotus's other qualities too. I do not mean all and everyone (this would be too much to pray for) but just one of them—whether the beauty of his diction, the careful arrangement of his words, the aptness of his native Ionic, his extraordinary power of thought, or the countless jewels which he has wrought into a unity beyond hope of imitation.[78]

Oswyn Murray, in a very significant article on the reputation of Herodotus in the Hellenistic world, goes beyond the qualified admission that Herodotus continued to be read in this period for his style while being scorned as a historian. He contends that 'such grudging admissions scarcely do justice to the central position of

---

76. A good summary of the ongoing fortunes of Herodotus's work not only in antiquity but also up to the modern age can be found in A. Momigliano, 'The Place of Herodotus in the History of Historiography', in *idem*, *Studies in Historiography* (London: Weidenfeld & Nicolson, 1966), pp. 127-42.

77. Among the titles of lost works which attacked Herodotus, Momigliano cites: *On Herodotus's Thefts* by Valerius Pollio, *On Herodotus's Lies* by Aelius Harpocration, and *Against Herodotus* by Libanius. See Momigliano, 'The Place of Herodotus', p. 133. For details, see W. Schmid, *Geschichte der griechischen Literatur: Die griechische Literatur in der Zeit der attischen Hegemonie vor dem Eingreifen der Sophistik* (Munich: Beck, 1934), pp. 665-70.

78. Lucian, *Herodotus or Aëtion* 1, in *Lucian* (trans. K. Kilburn; 8 vols.; LCL; New York: Putnam's, 1921-67), VI, p. 143.

Herodotus as one of the most widely read authors throughout antiquity'.[79] Supporting this claim, Murray provides the numerical argument of papyrus fragments of Herodotus from Greco-Roman Egypt. According to his count, Herodotus ranks ninth among all authors represented in this corpus and stands alongside Thucydides as one of the most widely attested historians in this period.[80] Of course the number of surviving fragments is not an exact means of gauging the number of manuscripts that once existed, but the original number of copies of Herodotus was clearly quite large. Murray also points to the poetry in the Hellenistic period as a witness to the continued popularity of Herodotus. Without attempting to give an exhaustive list of poets whose writings show the influence of Herodotus, Murray cites as examples Callimachus, Apollonius Rhodius, and the unknown author of the tragedy of Gyges of Lydia who faithfully transformed the story told by Herodotus.[81] Another bit of physical evidence which Murray provides for the positive reputation of Herodotus in the Hellenistic world can be found in the honorific statues of him which stood not only in his native Halicarnassus, but also in the library of the kings of Pergamon.[82]

It becomes apparent that Herodotus, like any truly great figure, inspired both ardent admirers and harsh critics. The fact is that he was not and could not be ignored. His *Histories* were read and studied by those who vilified him as well as by historians who used him as a source or who imitated his method and style. In the fourth century BCE, the historian Theopompus produced an epitome of Herodotus in two books. At about the same time Ephorus wrote his history using Herodotus among his sources. The many instances of Herodotean influence evidenced in Ephorus have been duly noted by Jacoby.[83] Even among the detractors of Herodotus, such as Hecataeus of Abdera, there was obvious imitation. While he accuses Herodotus of telling tall tales (παραδοξολογεῖν) and inventing stories (μύθους πλάττειν),[84] his own account of Egyptian history, religion, and customs is largely based upon that of Herodotus.[85]

It cannot be denied, then, that Herodotus continued to be read widely well into the Hellenistic period and beyond. Writing in the first century CE, Quintilian lists

79. O. Murray, 'Herodotus and Hellenistic Culture', *CQ* 22 (1972), pp. 200-13 (202).

80. Murray, 'Herodotus and Hellenistic Culture', p. 202-203.

81. Murray, 'Herodotus and Hellenistic Culture', pp. 203-204.

82. Murray, 'Herodotus and Hellenistic Culture', p. 204.

83. F. Jacoby, 'Herodotos', in W. Kroll (ed.), *Paulys Real-Encyclopädie der classischen Altertumswissenschaft: Supplement* (15 vols. [to the Supplement]; Stuttgart: J.B. Metzler, 1894–1963), II, pp. 205-520 [510-12]. Jacoby follows J. Bauer in recognizing that Diodorus XI-XVI is largely excerpted from Ephorus (J. Bauer, *Die Benutzung Herodots durch Ephoros bei Diodor* [Leipzig: Teubner, 1879]). From the close similarities between passages in this section of Diodorus and Herodotus (e.g. Herodotus 8.13 and Diodorus 11.13.1; Herodotus 7.6-9 and Diodorus 11.14.2-4) it becomes apparent that Diodorus's source, Ephorus, used Herodotus himself as a source.

84. Diodorus Siculus 1.69.7. The work of Hecataeus, who was a historian of the late fourth or early third century BCE writing under the patronage of Ptolemy I Soter, forms the basis for much of Diodorus's Book 1 which deals with Egypt (see Diodorus 1.46.8).

85. Murray, 'Herodotus and Hellenistic Culture', p. 207.

Herodotus prominently among authors to be studied.[86] The *Histories* had a secure place in the curricula of the Greek and Roman worlds. We have seen how Herodotus's work was used both by later poets as well as historians. It was also noted earlier how the *Histories* were used by later fiction writers—both Jewish, like the author of Judith, and Greek, like Chariton. It even became the object of parody at the hands of Lucian who, while an admirer of Herodotus's style, had no qualms about poking fun at the *Histories* in his own *True History*.[87] It is now worth mentioning one more piece of Hellenistic Jewish literature in this context in order to strengthen the claim that Herodotus was read not only by Greeks in the Hellenistic period, but by Jews as well.

The text to which I refer is the *Exagoge* of Ezekiel. Like so much of the Hellenistic-Jewish literature, its date and provenance are difficult to pin down. And like so much of this same literature, it is often simply assumed with a minimum of argumentation that it was written in Alexandria.[88] With regard to its date, we at least have firm *termini* to situate the *Exagoge* between the translation of the LXX (third century BCE), which Ezekiel used, and Alexander Polyhistor (first century BCE), who used him.[89] Without entering into the arguments over provenance or a more precise dating, we can for our purposes broadly state with certainty that Ezekiel was a Jewish author of the Hellenistic period. The work which Ezekiel wrote takes that most Jewish of stories—the Exodus—and transforms it into a very Greek tragedy. The 269 extant verses of the *Exagoge* reveal a dramatic structure which is heavily influenced by the fifth-century tragedian Euripides.[90] Many scholars have also suggested an awareness of the works of Sophocles and Aeschylus.[91] With respect to Herodotus, the possibility that Ezekiel was familiar with the *Histories* has been raised by Howard Jacobson. He first suggests the influence of the *Histories* on the *Exagoge* in the similarities between the dream sequences in each of these works involving the fall of one person or dynasty which is then replaced by another (an element common to Daniel as well).[92] Later on in his work, he pinpoints three

86. Quintilian, *Institutio Oratoria* 10.1.73.

87. Among the many allusions to Herodotus in Lucian's *True History*, there are the accounts of giant ants and dog-faced men (*True History* 1.16). See Herodotus 3.102 and 4.191.

88. H. Jacobson, *The Exagoge of Ezekiel* (Cambridge: Cambridge University Press, 1983), p. 13. See Jacobson's n. 1 for an extensive list of scholars supporting an Alexandrian origin.

89. Jacobson, *The Exagoge*, p. 6.

90. Jacobson, *The Exagoge*, p. 23.

91. Jacobson, *The Exagoge*, p. 24.

92. Jacobson, *The Exagoge*, pp. 96-97. Jacobson finds the closest parallel to the *Exagoge* in the dream of Cambyses at 3.30. He notes similarities in the language used (e.g. the verb δοκέω which, however, he admits is not rare in the narration of dreams) and in the content. In the *Histories*, Cambyses dreams that a messenger from Persia informed him that Smerdis sat on the royal throne with his head reaching to heaven. In the *Exagoge*, Moses dreams of a great throne on top of Mt Sinai which reaches to heaven and which he is invited to ascend (*The Exagoge*, pp. 68-75). One might easily argue that the images of the 'throne' and 'reaching to heaven' are generic enough, but Jacobson reinforces his argument for Ezekiel's familiarity with Herodotus with further parallels (the themes of coronation and universal rule) in the dreams of Xerxes (7.19). He argues that one who had turned 'the tale of the Exodus into a Greek drama after the fashion of the *Persae*' might

sections of the *Histories* (the crossing of the Hellespont, and the scenes surrounding Thermopylae and Salamis) which had an effect on Ezekiel's own themes and conceptions.[93] To cite examples just from the first of these three sections, Jacobson claims that Ezekiel would have seen in the crossing of the Hellespont a 'fascinating analogue to the crossing of the Red Sea, the traversing on foot of a body of water by a large mass of men'. One telling argument for Herodotean influence in Ezekiel can be found at the points where the *Exagoge* diverges from the biblical text. Ezekiel's account of the splitting of the Red Sea (224-28), for instance, indicates that Moses struck the sea with his rod. There is no mention of striking the sea in the biblical account (Exod. 14.21). Jacobson suggests that the shift may have been prompted as an antithetical parallel with Xerxes who had the Hellespont scourged (7.35),[94] although he does not rule out some biblical precedent for this development.[95] Among the verbal parallels which Jacobson considers significant is the use of the adjective ἁλμυρός ('briny') to describe both the Hellespont in Herodotus (7.35) and the Red Sea in Ezekiel (229). The term is not found in the biblical account in Exodus 14. Likewise, the Bible makes no mention of foot soldiers (πεζός) among the pursuing Egyptian force, while Ezekiel (198) uses the same term employed by Herodotus of Xerxes' army (7.41). These few examples from Jacobson's broader treatment of Ezekiel's *Exagoge* should be sufficient to demonstrate the likelihood of a general knowledge of Herodotus's *Histories* in the Hellenistic period among Jews possessing a Greek education.

Taken together, the evidence of abundant copies of Herodotus's work, the demonstrable influence of the *Histories* on poets, historians, and fiction writers of the Hellenistic period, and even the testimony of Herodotus's many critics, all bear witness to the enduring popularity and influence which his *Histories* had even centuries after his death. The reputation of Herodotus in antiquity was certainly not as negatively one-sided as one might be led to believe by his detractors. Rather, we must agree with the judgment of Oswyn Murray and affirm 'the central position of Herodotus as one of the most widely read authors throughout antiquity'.[96]

---

naturally turn to Herodotus for more information on the Persian Wars. I would rather argue that an author so clearly familiar with Greek tragedy as is Ezekiel would certainly have also read and studied Herodotus in the course of his education.

93. Jacobson, *The Exagoge*, pp. 138-40.

94. Jacobson, *The Exagoge*, p. 138.

95. E.g. Zech. 10.11, which may refer to the striking of the Red Sea. Another possibility is conflation with the similar accounts of the prophets Elijah and Elisha crossing the Jordan. This they accomplish by striking the river with a mantle, causing it to part for them (2 Kgs 2.8, 14). See Jacobson, *The Exagoge*, p. 142.

96. Murray, 'Herodotus and Hellenistic Culture', p. 202.

Chapter 3

THE HUMAN IN HISTORY

Having noted the likelihood of Herodotean influence on the book of Daniel, I now turn to a more focused reading of Daniel and Herodotus. In order to understand better and appreciate Daniel's theology of history, I will in this chapter examine his characterization of human agents in history alongside the similar portrayal which we find in Herodotus. In the following chapter, I will continue by exploring the divine role in history in each of these works. This close examination of the human and the divine agents in these two texts will then lead to a unified picture of history in Daniel in my final chapter. For Daniel's view of history, like that of Herodotus, is based upon parallel planes of causation—one that is human and one divine.

Turning to our texts, we may note that neither the *Histories* of Herodotus nor the book of Daniel is composed in such a way that the modern reader is left without questions regarding their unity and structure. While it is generally recognized that Herodotus is the single author of the *Histories*, the variety of the *logoi* he weaves together and the disparity in length between them raises the issue not only of sources but also of the theme and purpose of the work. What is one to make, for example, of the lengthy digression on Egypt in the second book of the *Histories*? Do Herodotus's many excursions into the fabulous and curious phenomena of distant lands relate to his (central?) theme of conflict between Asia and Europe which begins for him with Croesus and culminates in Xerxes? If these questions prove difficult to answer, the situation with the book of Daniel is even more complex. We do not know who the author was, and indeed there are clear indications of multiple authors and stages of composition as witnessed by the two languages employed in the book (three if one includes the Greek deuterocanonical accretions[1])

---

1.   In addition to the deuterocanonical material found in the LXX, there are several texts among the Dead Sea Scrolls that appear to have some relationship to the biblical book of Daniel. The *Prayer of Nabonidus* (4QPrNab [= 4Q242]) and '4QHistorical Text' (4Q248) may be sources that were used by the biblical author, while Pseudo-Daniel (4Qpseudo-Daniel [= 4Q243-244-245 = 4QpsDan[a, b, c]) and the so-called 'Aramaic Apocalypse' (4Q246) may have themselves been influenced by Daniel. See J.J. Collins, 'New Light on the Book of Daniel from the Dead Sea Scrolls', in F. García Martínez and E. Noort (eds.), *Perspectives in the Study of the Old Testament and Early Judaism: A Symposium in Honour of Adam S. Van der Woude on the Occasion of His 70th Birthday* (Leiden: E.J. Brill, 1998), pp. 180-96 (180). Collins cautiously notes: 'Whether in fact there is any direct influence in any of these cases, however, is still debatable'.

and by the shift in genre and voice between the first and second halves of the book.[2] This is all further complicated by the fact that the break in language between Aramaic (2.4b–7.28) and Hebrew (1.1–2.4a; 8.1–12.13) does not correspond to the change from court tales told in the third person (chs. 1–6) to first person apocalyptic visions (chs. 7–12). Yet this collection of tales and visions is held together by more than just the name of Daniel (who is in fact noticeably absent from the tale in ch. 3), just as there is more connecting the varied *logoi* of the *Histories* than the fact that Herodotus so personally recounts them. I believe it is sometimes a fault of readers to strain to see more structure and unity in a text than is actually present. Nevertheless, I will venture to maintain that the book of Daniel is more than a random hodgepodge of disparate material carelessly slapped together into an anthology of 'Danielica'. There are themes and structures which span the entire book of Daniel, providing continuity between court tale and vision.

What, then, is the connection between court tales and visions? Why were these later visions attached to the earlier court tales? The pseudepigraphic impulse of apocalyptic literature provides only a partial answer. There is perhaps in Daniel this desire to lend an air of authority and legitimacy to prophetic announcements by associating them with a famous figure of old. The process of biblical canonization (which was already underway in the second century BCE) increased the value of the established tradition. Thus the other great apocalyptic collection from this period— the book of Enoch—finds its spokesperson in the ancient patriarch who walked with God and mysteriously disappeared from the earth (Gen. 5.24). 'Gaps' in the stories of ancient heroes such as Enoch[3] provided the opportunity both to flesh out these old tales with new narratives and also to give an instant mantle of authority to new pronouncements. All of this, however, does not explain the book of Daniel. While there may be some connection between the Daniel of the Aramaic court tales and the ancient figure of Daniel noted for his wisdom and justice in the book of Ezekiel (14.14, 20; 28.3) and in Ugaritic myth,[4] a simple identification of the two

2. Other indications of a complex composition history include the fact that each court tale is a self-contained unit. While there are references that tie later episodes to earlier scenes (particularly in ch. 5), each chapter presents a complete story in itself, at times duplicating earlier material (e.g. Daniel is introduced to Nebuchadnezzar for a second time in 2.25 although from 1.19-21 he would seem already to be a well-known person at the royal court). The tale of the three youths in ch. 3 makes no mention of Daniel, although he is associated with them in chs. 1 and 2. These three characters disappear entirely from the book after ch. 3. Furthermore, the dual name Daniel-Belteshazzar may indicate that traditions about two separate characters have been combined. It is worth noting that in the entire book of Daniel, six out of the ten occurrences of the name Belteshazzar occur in ch. 4. This suggests the possibility that an original Belteshazzar narrative centered around the episode in Dan. 4.

3. The wide range of biblical heroes who become 'authors' of these pseudepigraphical works can be seen from a brief glance at Charlesworth's *OTP*. Among the alleged authors of these works are: Adam, Enoch, Shem, Abraham, Jacob, Joseph, Moses, Solomon, Elijah, Isaiah, Ezekiel, Zephaniah, Job, Ezra, and Baruch.

4. The figure of Dn'il from the story of *Aqhat* (the extant fragments of which date to the thirteenth or fourteenth century BCE) was a king who was noted for his justice in hearing the cases of the widow and orphan (*2 Aqhat* V.7-8). See Hartman and Di Lella, *Book of Daniel*, p. 7.

figures does not work. An ancient Canaanite king from the second millennium BCE cannot be easily transformed into a Jewish exile living over 700 years later. Pseudepigraphic works such as 1 Enoch, *4 Ezra*, and 2 Baruch did not so radically transform or transport their main characters. The Daniel who appears as a wise, young courtier in Babylon does not seem to have been a well-established figure in the Jewish tradition at the time the apocalyptic visions were ascribed to him. There is no indication that these tales had an authoritative status before the composition of the visions which were attached to them.

Why, then, does the visionary of the Maccabean age associate himself with the wise Jewish exile? The connection, I believe, is in the historical understanding expressed in the prayer of Daniel ch. 9. There Jeremiah's prophecy of a 70-year exile is reinterpreted to mean an exile lasting 70 weeks (i.e. weeks of years) or 490 years. The present period of persecution under Antiochus IV is seen as the continuation of the period of exile. Furthermore, the 'wisdom circle' of the *maskilim* to which the final dream vision makes repeated reference (Dan. 11.33, 35; 12.3, 10) and to which the author of Daniel most likely belongs[5] finds an appropriate spokesperson in the Daniel of the folk-tales who was wiser than all the sages of Babylon (Dan. 1.20). The period of exile, determined not so much by physical location but by the persistence of foreign domination, began with Nebuchadnezzar of Babylon and continued until Antiochus IV of Syria. Thus the focus on the successive reigns of these foreign kings and their kingdoms is a major structuring device throughout the book of Daniel as a whole. Daniel is very much concerned with this prolonged exile of domination by foreign kings; therefore he combines his prophecies concerning the end of these kingdoms with the stories relating to the beginning of this foreign rule. Meanwhile, the *maskilim*, the wise Jews who remain faithful to their God, provide the counterpoint to these foreign kings in both court tale and apocalypse.[6] The roles of these two classes of people—the rulers and the wise—in the book of Daniel once again reminds us of a similar focus in the *Histories* of Herodotus. In each of these works, it is these two categories of people who play a prominent role throughout and move history forward on the human level. Therefore I will now move on to a consideration of these two main human forces in history—the king and the sage—as they are portrayed in the book of Daniel and the *Histories* of Herodotus.

1. *The King in Daniel*

It comes as no surprise that kings and other classes of rulers should hold such a prominent place in history or historical tales whether ancient or modern. Not only do the leaders of nations and empires direct the course of events to a significant

---

5.   Collins, *Daniel*, p. 66.

6.   In pre-exilic history it was the prophet who served as counterpoint to Israel's king (e.g. Samuel and Saul, Elijah and Ahab. The post-exilic setting provides both a new type of ruler (the foreign king) and a new type of critic and advisor (the wise).

degree, they also possess the means to create official accounts and propaganda relating to their deeds. The biblical books of Kings and Chronicles systematically treat of the successive monarchs in Israel and Judah, mentioning their prominent deeds and judging each according to religious criteria. Reference to a more complete account in the Book of the Annals of the Kings of Judah (or Israel) is frequently made (e.g. 1 Kgs 14.19, 29). Although kings are by no means the only actors in Israelite and Judean history (there are accounts of prophets, commanders, other individuals, and the nation as a whole), the king as the Lord's anointed is a central figure throughout these books.

What makes the book of Daniel's structural composition unique against this background of Israelite historiography is that its series of kings (which provides the structural unity as we pass from tale to tale and from vision to vision) is no longer Israelite or Judean but foreign. Beginning with Nebuchadnezzar, the king of Babylon, we pass through the successive reigns of Belshazzar, Darius the Mede, and Cyrus the Persian in the court tales. The dream visions, which begin in ch. 7, repeat part of this cycle, returning to the time of Belshazzar of Babylon and continuing once again with Darius and Cyrus. The content of the visions also refers to kings and kingdoms as we have seen. In addition to the Babylonian, Median, and Persian kingdoms, whose rulers give structural unity to the book of Daniel, there is added in the visions a fourth kingdom, which is to be identified with 'Greece' from the clear allusions to Alexander and Antiochus IV in chs. 7, 8, and 11. It is these foreign kings and kingdoms that structure and dominate the landscape of Daniel. Let us turn now to the individual episodes in which they are involved.

a. *The Kings in the Court Tales*
The first and most important of the kings in the court tales of Daniel is Nebuchadnezzar who appears in chs. 1–4. The introductory first chapter sets the exilic stage by speaking of his siege of Jerusalem. It is worth noting, however, that it is the Lord who controls the action of this scene by delivering over to Nebuchadnezzar Jehoiakim, king of Judah, along with the vessels of the temple (1.2). This recalls the similar narrative in 2 Kgs 24.1-4 where the impending fall of Judah and Jehoiakim is described as the work of YHWH who is pictured as loosing the invading armies against Judah (2 Kgs 24.2). The description in Daniel, which has Nebuchadnezzar deport Jehoiakim and 'some of the vessels of the house of God' (מקצת כלי בית־האלהים), is even more closely tied to the account in 2 Chron. 36.6-7. Chronicles, like Daniel, speaks both of Jehoiakim's deportation and of the confiscation of 'some of the vessels of the house of YHWH' (מכלי בית יהוה) at this time. The second book of Kings, in contrast, mentions only the deportation of Jehoiakim's son, Jehoiachin, and the removal and destruction of *all* of the temple vessels in his time (2 Kgs 24.13-15).

The book of Daniel, then, begins its story where the Deuteronomistic History leaves off, mentioning the deportation of the Judean king and the removal of the temple vessels at the hands of Nebuchadnezzar. Daniel also fills in the exilic 'gap' in the work of the Chronicler, which jumps from the beginning of the exile to the decree of Cyrus.[7] The initial description of Nebuchadnezzar in the book of Daniel also follows the established pattern of describing foreign kings as instruments of God in punishing Israel, with little character or personality of their own.[8] In the ensuing story in Daniel 1, the king plays only a minor role as Daniel and his companions are introduced into his service. The introductory chapter of Daniel firmly connects the book to the Israelite historiography that has preceded it, but it just barely prepares us for the up-close look at the foreign king and his court in the following chapters.

As we progress through the court tales, the role and characterization of Nebuchadnezzar expands from this unassuming beginning. In ch. 2 we hear of the king's dream, which troubled him and kept him from sleeping. He summons the various categories of wise men and presents to them the startling ultimatum: tell him his dream and its meaning and be rewarded, or else face utter destruction. The king proves intransigent to their pleading that his demand is impossible, finally becoming angry and ordering the execution of all the sages in Babylon. When Daniel finally comes forward and tells both the dream and its interpretation, Nebuchadnezzar bows down and worships him and orders sacrifice to be offered to him. He confesses that Daniel's God is supreme, promotes Daniel to high offices, and offers him gifts. While Nebuchadnezzar wields the power to kill or reward his sages, it is still Daniel's God who reveals the dream and its meaning to Daniel, thus securing his safety and advancement while eliciting the king's confession.

In this chapter, the character of Nebuchadnezzar takes on a new depth which was previously unknown in the Hebrew Scriptures.[9] He is no longer depicted as simply the conqueror of Jerusalem, but now as a troubled dreamer seeking insight into his dream. Although his volatile temper leads him to order the death of all the sages in Babylon, thus threatening Daniel and his companions, he is not portrayed as the direct adversary of the Jews. His quarrel is with the wise men of Babylon for failing to interpret his dream. His tempestuous nature merely provides the occasion for Daniel to demonstrate the superiority of the wisdom that comes from his God compared to that of the Babylonian wise men. His confession that Daniel's God is the 'God of gods and Lord of kings' (2.47) is a curious statement to find on the lips of the destroyer of Jerusalem and its temple. Curious too is this phrase for its departure from the symmetrical, standard formula: 'God of gods and Lord of lords'

---

7. This decree is cited in 2 Chron. 36.22-23 immediately after the account of the fall of Judah, and it is repeated in Ezra 1.1-4. Neither in the books of Chronicles nor in Ezra–Nehemiah, which picks up the story where Chronicles leaves off, is there an account of the exilic period.

8. The book of Judges presents a series of such foreign kings who are described as no more than instruments of God's punishment (Judg. 3.8, 12; 4.2; etc.). The same may be said of the 'anonymous' king of Assyria who captured Samaria in 2 Kgs 17.6-7, and of Nebuchadnezzar in the accounts of 2 Kings and 2 Chronicles mentioned above. This monochromatic description of the foreign king as the scourge of God can also be found in the prophets (e.g. Isa. 7.17-20).

9. The accounts of Nebuchadnezzar's campaign against Jerusalem found in 2 Kgs 24–25 and 2 Chron. 36 provide no description or characterization of Nebuchadnezzar, nor do they have him speak a word. Jer. 27–28 speaks of Nebuchadnezzar simply as the instrument of God to whom rule of the nations has been given.

which one finds in Deut. 10.17 and Ps. 136.2-3. This modified phrase in the mouth of the most notorious of foreign kings accentuates the mastery of God in heaven over the earthly king. In this tale, it is not merely Daniel who proves superior to the Babylonian wise men, but it is especially God who proves superior to the Babylonian king. It is also significant in this context that the interpretation of the king's dream foretells the very downfall of his kingdom, which will ultimately be replaced by a kingdom set up by the God of heaven (2.44).[10] The foreign king in ch. 2 has been transformed from God's instrument to God's rival. In this rivalry Nebuchadnezzar appears ultimately impotent. He must admit that Daniel's God is his superior as 'Lord of kings'.

The mercurial disposition of Nebuchadnezzar which appears in ch. 2 is amplified in Daniel 3. If he became enraged and very angry (בנס וקצף שגיא) with the wise men in 2.12, his anger and wrath (רגז וחמה) toward the three youths in 3.13 advance to the point where he is so filled with wrath (התמלי חמא) in 3.19 that his face becomes visibly distorted. At the other extreme, the prostration before Daniel and confession of his God in ch. 2 is surpassed by the direct praising of God by Nebuchadnezzar in ch. 3, along with the royal decree prohibiting anyone to speak ill of the God of Shadrach, Meshach, and Abednego on pain of death and destruction of property. The confrontation between the earthly king and the God in heaven that was implicit in the tale in ch. 2 is made explicit in ch. 3. First, Nebuchadnezzar throws down the gauntlet by erecting a golden statue in the plain of Dura, ordering that everyone should worship the idol which he has erected. From the Jewish perspective, the worship of idols is seen as the ultimate affront to God. When the three Jewish youths refuse to worship the statue, Nebuchadnezzar's direct challenge to them—'who is the god that will deliver you out of my hands?'—is answered unmistakably by the ordeal in the fiery furnace. The story ends with Nebuchadnezzar confessing that the God of Shadrach, Meshach, and Abednego is without peer.

In ch. 4, Nebuchadnezzar actually becomes the main character of the story. Most of the account is narrated in the first person by Nebuchadnezzar himself. Daniel (or, as he is predominantly called in this chapter, Belteshazzar) once again arrives on the scene in order to provide the interpretation of the king's dream, but once the interpretation is given he quickly fades into the background. There are no honors, praise or promotions heaped upon him this time. Rather, the story ends as it began, with Nebuchadnezzar alone on stage. The conflict in ch. 4 is familiar enough from the preceding tales: a great king is confronted with a greater God. While glorying in his accomplishments, Nebuchadnezzar is stricken by God with a type of madness, being forced to live like a savage beast without reason. After seven years of this divine castigation, his reason returns and, in yet another hymn of praise, he

10.   The enthusiastic response of Nebuchadnezzar seems to ignore the rather ominous meaning conveyed by his dream. This has led scholars such as Bickerman to suggest that an original Babylonian prophecy in the time of Nebuchadnezzar stands behind the traditions preserved in Dan. 2. Bickerman suggests that the prophecy originally referred to the king and his successors within the Babylonian dynasty. See Bickerman, *Four Strange Books*, pp. 62-63.

acknowledges the God who 'is able to bring low those who walk in pride' (4.34). The conversion of Nebuchadnezzar is completed in this highly personal tale told in his own voice. There appears to be a discernible historical background to this story which relates not to Nebuchadnezzar but to the last king of Babylon, Nabonidus.[11] The book of Daniel adapts the tradition to the more famous and familiar Nebuchadnezzar, the powerful king *par excellence* and arch-fiend of Israelite history. The humbling and conversion of this king by God powerfully affirms the message 'that the Most High is sovereign over the kingdom of mortals' (4.17).

Chapter 5, the story of the mysterious writing on the wall, introduces us to a new Babylonian king, Belshazzar. Many of the elements in this story are familiar from the preceding chapters (especially ch. 2). We have again what amounts to a court contest involving a difficult interpretation in which Daniel outshines his peers and earns rewards and a promotion. The king once again is reliant upon the Jewish exile to provide an interpretation for him, and once again he is ultimately powerless with regard to the divine decrees foretelling the end of his rule. Belshazzar, however, is not simply a carbon copy of Nebuchadnezzar. His offense is even more directly aimed at the God of the Jews than was Nebuchadnezzar's idol in ch. 3 or his boasting in ch. 4. Belshazzar's action is a direct affront to the temple in Jerusalem (and its God) by sacrilegiously using its vessels for his banquet. Whereas Nebuchadnezzar expressed his rage and anger to the extreme, Belshazzar's characteristic emotion is fear to such a degree that his face turns white, his knees knock and he loses continence. Most significant of all is the fact that for Belshazzar there is no conversion and confession of God. He rewards Daniel for providing the interpretation, but fails to take the further step of acknowledging his God. As Daniel makes explicit in his words to the king:

> O king, the Most High God gave your father Nebuchadnezzar kingship, greatness, glory, and majesty. And because of the greatness that he gave him, all peoples, nations, and languages trembled and feared before him. He killed those he wanted to kill, kept alive those he wanted to keep alive, honored those he wanted to honor, and degraded those he wanted to degrade. But when his heart was lifted up and his spirit was hardened so that he acted proudly, he was deposed from his kingly throne, and his glory was stripped from him. He was driven from human society, and his mind was made like that of an animal. His dwelling was with the wild asses, he was fed grass like oxen, and his body was bathed with the dew of heaven, until he learned that the Most High God has sovereignty over the kingdom of mortals, and sets over it whomever he will. And you, Belshazzar his son, have not humbled your heart, even though you knew all this! You have exalted yourself against the Lord of heaven! The vessels of his temple have been brought in before you, and you and your lords, your wives and your concubines have been drinking wine from

---

11.   Elements of this tradition are also preserved in the fragmentary text from Qumran: 'The Prayer of Nabonidus' (4Q242). See J.T. Milik, '"Prière de Nabonide" et autres écrits d'un cycle de Daniel', *Revue Biblique* 63 (1956), pp. 407-15. Babylonian records tell of an absence of Nabonidus from Babylon at the oasis of Tema (see *ANET*, pp. 305-307). This absence from the city, during which time his son Belshazzar governed as regent, may be behind the account in Dan. 4.25 which reports Nebuchadnezzar as being 'driven away from human society.'

them. You have praised the gods of silver and gold, of bronze, iron, wood, and stone, which do not see or hear or know; but the God in whose power is your very breath, and to whom belong all your ways, you have not honored. (5.18-23)

The final king in the court tales, the historically elusive Darius the Mede, presents us with yet another very different type of monarch. From the outset this king is well-disposed towards Daniel. Daniel has no need of a promotion from him for some display of wisdom, for he is the most illustrious of Darius's three supervisors over the entire kingdom from the very outset of the story. Even after Darius is foolishly manipulated by the jealous supervisors and satraps to entrap Daniel (by signing an irrevocable decree forbidding all petitions for thirty days except to the king), he works all day to try to find a way to save Daniel from his own decree. But under the new 'Mede and Persian law' (6.13, 16) the king, benevolent though he may be, is himself subject to the force of his own irrevocable decrees, over which he has no power. Forced against his will to consign Daniel to the lion's den, his final recourse is a prayer to Daniel's God: 'May your God, whom you faithfully serve, deliver you!' (6.17). Being unable to eat or sleep out of his concern for Daniel, the king hurries to the lion's den the next morning to see if Daniel's God has in fact saved him. The king rejoices when he finds this to be the case, and he promptly releases Daniel and throws his accusers and their families to the lions, which immediately kill them. The king then issues another decree, this time commanding that the God of Daniel be feared by all throughout his dominion.

The overall impression one obtains of the kings in the court tales, from the benevolent and well-meaning Darius to the thoroughly wicked Belshazzar (along with the rather enigmatic Nebuchadnezzar), is that they are ultimately not the ones who control history. In spite of their very real power exercised in rewarding and punishing, menacing, and decreeing, we are repeatedly reminded by word and example that God is the 'Lord of kings' who possesses an everlasting kingdom. This is proclaimed by Daniel as well as by the kings themselves. In contrast, the earthly kings who have the appearance of dominion and power spend sleepless nights worrying, and tremble in fear before ominous signs. They are dependent upon others to interpret their troubling dreams, and become mere pawns in the hands of jealous and manipulative ministers. This portrait of the king that the book of Daniel presents is familiar to the reader of Herodotus. There too, the great kings, who would appear to be in a position of supreme power, fall prey to the workings of fate and divine envy. As we shall soon see, they are troubled by dreams, oracles and portents, and they are also reliant upon (and at times manipulated by) their counselors and ministers. While the detailed picture of the foreign king which we find in Daniel is a new element in the story of Israel and Judah, the judgment upon their role in history is familiar. They are subject to the ultimate king and authority. Their exercise of dominion is contingent upon God's will and purpose.

b. *The King in the Dream Visions*
Although ch. 7 is a continuation of the Aramaic portion of the book of Daniel, it does not follow as a continuous narrative. Whereas ch. 6 concluded with mention

of the reigns of Darius and Cyrus, ch. 7 takes us back in time to the reign of Belshazzar once more. But this king is not the subject of the chapter. His name is merely used in a standard formula dating Daniel's vision to a year in the king's reign. Rather, ch. 7 presents us with the initial dream vision of Daniel told in the first person, much in the same way that Nebuchadnezzar related his own dream vision in ch. 4. The role of the interpreter passes from Daniel, who is now the recipient of the vision, to one of the attendant 'angels' present in the vision. While kings are thus absent from the scene relating the vision and its interpretation, the content of the dream itself pertains directly to kings and kingdoms.

The content is substantially the same as that of the vision of Nebuchadnezzar in ch. 2. Four successive kingdoms are represented,[12] now under the appearance of various beasts. Among the innovations in ch. 7 with regard to ch. 2 is the added detail concerning the fourth kingdom in general and its 'final' king in particular. The interpretation of the vision in ch. 2 began with the identification of the single king, Nebuchadnezzar, as the head of gold, continuing with descriptions of three kingdoms not specifically named. Chapter 7 initially speaks of four kings (מלכין) in 7.17, not four kingdoms (מלכות) as we found in ch. 2. This quickly changes as Daniel inquires further about the fourth beast and is told that it is a fourth kingdom, different from the other kingdoms (7.23).[13] The beast's ten horns represent ten kings (7.24), but it is the small eleventh horn that represents the king with which the vision is primarily concerned. This king (who is to be identified with Antiochus IV) is described at some length in vv. 25-26:

> He shall speak words against the Most High,
>> shall wear out the holy ones of the Most High,
>> and shall attempt to change the sacred seasons and the law;
> and they shall be given into his power
>> for a time, two times, and half a time.
> Then the court shall sit in judgment,
>> and his dominion shall be taken away,
>> to be consumed and totally destroyed.

---

12.   Some have suggested that the four kingdoms in Dan. 7 are not successive but concurrent. See, e.g., I. Fröhlich (*Time and Times and Half a Time* [JSOTSup, 19; Sheffield: Academic Press, 1996], pp. 73-76) who follows K. Hanhart ('The Four Beasts of Daniel's Vision in the Light of Rev. 13.2', *NTS* 27 [1981], pp. 576-83) in offering such a synchronic interpretation. They propose that the kingdoms referred to are those of Egypt, Parthia, Rome and Syria. While it is true that the imagery and interpretation in Dan. 7 do not explicitly state that one kingdom follows another (whereas Dan. 2 does clearly indicate succession), the imagery does favor an identification with the four successive kingdoms referred to in Dan. 2 and throughout the book (e.g. the description of the first beast is strongly reminiscent of the description of Nebuchadnezzar in ch. 4, while the four-headed, four-winged leopard matches the four kings of Persia in ch. 11).

13.   The fluidity of the terminology in speaking alternately of kings and kingdoms reinforces the idea that for Daniel each kingdom is often identified with a characteristic king. Aside from ch. 5 which speaks of Belshazzar (who was not in fact a king), there is one king for each kingdom in the court tales: Nebuchadnezzar of Babylon, Darius the Mede, and Cyrus the Persian. In the dream visions it is Antiochus IV who becomes the representative king of the Greek kingdom.

The king is marked by his blasphemous arrogance in speaking against God and presuming to change the sacred seasons and the law. While scholars debate as to the meaning of the phrase 'holy ones of the Most High',[14] what is clear is that the king's temporary success against them (just like his final demise) finds its ultimate cause beyond his control. In spite of his efforts, the king does not acquire dominion over the holy ones by himself; rather, they are given into his power (7.25). The next verse makes it clear that the giving and taking of dominion belongs to the judgment of the divine court (7.26). So, although ch. 7 introduces us to a new genre, in which Daniel himself relates his apocalyptic visions bearing on a new historical crisis in the time of Antiochus IV, the understanding of this new king's role in the unfolding of history is substantially the same as that of the kings in the court tales. His power is seen as entirely contingent upon the divine disposition.

Chapter 8 contains yet another vision, this time of just two beasts: a ram and a goat. Again, kingdoms are represented by these animals, namely Medo-Persia[15] and Greece (8.20-21). Also, once more, the horns on the animal representing Greece stand for individual kings. This time the first great horn is a clear reference to Alexander, just as the four that sprout in its place must be the Diadochi and their respective kingdoms. Once again, however, it is the final little horn representing Antiochus that receives the greatest attention. The characterization of this final king reaches even greater depth than in ch. 7:

> At the end of their rule,
>> when the transgressions have reached their full measure,
> a king of bold countenance shall arise,
>> skilled in intrigue.
> He shall grow strong in power,
>> shall cause fearful destruction,
>> and shall succeed in what he does.
> He shall destroy the powerful
>> and the people of the holy ones.
> By his cunning
>> he shall make deceit prosper under his hand,
>> and in his own mind he shall be great.

14.   The Aramaic קדישי עליונין may refer to angelic beings (see, e.g., M. Noth, 'The Holy Ones of the Most High', in *idem*, *The Laws in the Pentateuch and Other Studies*, pp. 215-28 [first published in *Norsk Teologisk Tidsskrift* 56 [1955] [= Festschrift Sigmund Mowinckel], pp. 146-57), to the Jewish people (see, e.g., Hartman and Di Lella, *The Book of Daniel*, pp. 91-92), or to a sect within Judaism to which Daniel belonged (see, e.g., C.H.W. Brekelmans, 'The Saints of the Most High and Their Kingdom', *OTS* 14 [1965], pp. 305-29). I prefer the identification with the whole of the Jewish people since this would be the appropriate counterpart to the other nations symbolized by the four beasts. We may add that a choice between angelic and human beings is not strictly necessary. Since human events are mirrored in Daniel by their divine counterparts (e.g. the angelic confrontations involving the 'princes' of Persia and Greece in ch. 10), the holy ones of the Most High may refer simultaneously to the Jewish people and their angelic representatives.

15.   The representation of Media and Persia as a single beast with two horns points to the close relationship between these two kingdoms. Herodotus likewise indicates the close relationship between Media and Persia, especially in the person of Cyrus who was born of a Median mother and a Persian father, and who is even called 'King of the Medes' (1.206).

Without warning he shall destroy many
  and shall even rise up against the Prince of princes.
But he shall be broken, and not by human hands. (Dan. 8.23-25)

Brought into particular relief here is the intrigue, cunning, and deceit of this king in addition to the more typical kingly characteristics of a 'bold countenance' (עַז פָּנִים) and the power to cause destruction and achieve his goals. The phrase מֵבִין חִידוֹת (here translated 'skilled in intrigue') literally means 'one who understands riddles or enigmas'. חִידוֹת refer to obscure utterances needing interpretation.[16] The king before us in this chapter is thus contrasted with the kings of the court tales who could not understand their mysterious dream visions or the strange writing on the wall. This king possesses a certain wisdom that was formerly reserved only to Daniel in this book. In 5.12, in fact, Daniel's wisdom was described as the ability to solve riddles (אֲחִידָן). The Aramaic word used in ch. 5 corresponds exactly to the Hebrew word in ch. 8, each being based upon the root חוד.

The word translated as 'cunning' in 8.25 (שֵׂכֶל), like the understanding (בִּין) upon which the participle מֵבִין is built, is basically a positive quality meaning good sense, prudence, or insight.[17] Thus, the king in ch. 8 not only has the ability to understand obscure utterances like Daniel did, but he also has the discretion to act in an intelligent manner, like Daniel.[18] With the attribution of this wisdom to Antiochus, which includes both an interpretive and a practical dimension, he appears with characteristics typical of both king and sage. One finds a certain overlap of these two categories in Herodotus as well, most notably in the persons of Croesus (1.89, 207; 3.36) and Demaratus (7.3, 235). Yet, neither of them is particularly wise as king; they become wise advisors to others only after they themselves have been deposed from ruling. In Daniel 8, however, the wisdom of the sage and the power of the king are united to deadly effect. The king uses his wisdom for evil ends to advance deceit or treachery (מִרְמָה). His cunning combined with his power enables him to succeed even to the point of destroying 'the people of the holy ones'.[19] Thus, while this latest king described in ch. 8 possesses some of the positive qualities of the sage, they are used for ever greater acts of destruction, permitting him to succeed against God's holy people for a time and even to oppose the Prince of princes. Still, his ultimate destruction is once again assured by divine, not human, forces.

---

16. See BDB, p. 295, which also cites Num. 12.8 contrasting God's speaking to Moses 'face to face' and 'clearly' with the more general mode of divine revelation in 'riddles' (חִידוֹת) which come through visions and dreams.

17. BDB, p. 968.

18. The prudence and discretion of Daniel is emphasized in his going to inquire of Arioch the reason for the king's decree in 2.14.

19. R.H. Charles (*A Critical and Exegetical Commentary on the Book of Daniel* [Oxford: Clarendon Press, 1929], p. 219) suggests that this final phrase results from confusion with the following verse and so omits it. This results in eliminating the reference to the king's prevailing over the 'people of the holy ones'. I believe the unanimous witness of the versions to the text of MT warrants a bit more restraint in emending the text. Furthermore, the parallelism between vv. 24 and 25 supports the inclusion of the phrase. In v. 24 the king destroys first the powerful (עֲצוּמִים) and then the people of the holy ones (עַם־קְדֹשִׁים). A similar progression takes place in v. 25 where the king moves successively against many (רַבִּים) and then the prince of princes (שַׂר־שָׂרִים).

Aside from dating their contents to the reigns of Darius and Cyrus, chs. 9 and 10 tell us little about kings. With ch. 11 a new historical survey is undertaken, beginning with the four kings of Persia and culminating once more in the 'final' Greek king. We have already seen how the four Persian kings of Daniel 11 correspond to the four Persian kings from Herodotus's *Histories*, the fourth king in particular being identified with Xerxes, the wealthy campaigner against Greece. Alexander is then described as a 'warrior king' (מלך גבור) who will acquire great dominion, but whose kingdom will nevertheless be broken and divided. The sudden destruction of Alexander's kingdom, brought about by his premature death at the height of his power (see also Dan. 8.8), seems to provide for Daniel a historical precedent for his prophecies concerning the sudden and immanent end of the current kingdom. The mutability of human fortunes is brought into relief by his quick survey of the recent past. Of course the fleeting nature of the prosperity of the wicked is a familiar theme from Israel's wisdom literature (e.g. Ps. 37; Prov. 11.18). Still, the particular example of Alexander's dramatic rise and fall highlights for Daniel the application of this traditional wisdom to the foreign monarch. Alexander's significance for Daniel is made clear by the attention devoted to him in ch. 8 where he and Antiochus IV are the only Greek kings to be described.[20] The meteoric rise and fall of this most powerful of earthly kings provides from history the pattern for Daniel's prophecy.

Returning to ch. 11, Daniel continues with a rather lengthy description of the dealings between the 'king of the south' and the 'king of the north'. That these titles refer collectively to the kings of the Ptolemaic and Seleucid dynasties is made clear from the historical allusions.[21] The accuracy of the historical references also compels us to consider to what extent Daniel is reporting historical evidence available to him, and to what extent he is creating and shaping the material he presents.[22] The poor quality of the Hebrew in ch. 11 has led some scholars to propose that a non-Hebrew historical text was used by Daniel and influenced his style in this chapter.[23] The account of events before the time of Antiochus IV is rather matter of

20. The sprouting of the little horn out of the fourth beast in ch. 7 and out of the he-goat in ch. 8 points to the close relationship Daniel sees between the powerful founder of the Greek empire and Antiochus IV. Alexander is seen as the evil root out of which Antiochus grows.

21. To cite just a few of the many allusions, Dan. 11.5 speaks of the king of the south growing strong, but one of his officers growing stronger still and ruling a larger kingdom. The reference is to the rise of Ptolemy I Soter who obtained control of Egypt after Alexander's death. Seleucus I Nicator fought with Ptolemy against Antigonus before he could secure his own larger kingdom. See Montgomery, *A Critical and Exegetical Commentary*, p. 427. Dan.11.6 speaks of the daughter of the king of the south coming to the king of the north. Again the allusion can be seen clearly as referring to the wedding of Antiochus II Theos with Berenice, daughter of Ptolemy II. See Collins, *Daniel*, p. 378.

22. A similar question has been raised with the *Histories* of Herodotus. In response to works which have stressed the literary structure and themes of the *Histories*, some scholars, such as K.H. Waters, have pointed to the objectivity with which Herodotus reports on kings and tyrants. Waters rejects the existence of any moral, political, philosophical, or religious scheme which Herodotus imposed upon his treatment of these characters. See K.H. Waters, *Herodotus on Tyrants and Despots* (Historia, 15; Wiesbaden: Franz Steiner Verlag, 1971), p. 7.

23. G.A. Barton ('The Composition of the Book of Daniel', *JBL* 17 [1898], pp. 62-86 [62-66]) was the first to suggest this. He has been followed in more recent years by Collins (*Daniel*, p. 377).

fact, with little description or emphasis upon the character of the kings involved.[24] The message one is left with is that the various attempts by these kings to extend their power through war or alliance do not come to any lasting fruition. The history of the kings of the north and the south before the time of Antiochus IV is one of repeated failure. One need only note the numerous references in this chapter to various failures (often following quickly upon initial successes) to see that there is an underlying pattern to the history in this chapter (see e.g. 11.6, 11, 12, 14, 15, 17, 18, 19, 20). This quick run through Seleucid and Ptolemaic history illustrates the words of Croesus to Cyrus that 'human life is like a revolving wheel and never allows the same people to continue long in prosperity' (Herodotus 1.207). The great reversal of fortune witnessed in the swift rise and fall of Alexander is constantly repeated on a lesser scale among the successors to his divided kingdom.

The detailed descriptions of Antiochus IV that begin in v. 21 and continue to the end of the chapter are by now familiar from chs. 7 and 8. His cunning and deceit are noted in vv. 21, 23, and 27. His arrogance and rage against the 'holy covenant' (11.28, 30) is once again a dominant theme. Verse 24, however, introduces us to a new aspect of Antiochus's character: his lavishness. The scattering of plunder, spoil, and wealth described in this verse matches the lavishness of Antiochus as described in Greek and Jewish historians (Polybius 26.10; 1 Macc. 3.30; Josephus *Ant.* 12.7.2). Likewise we have already noted in the previous chapter how the psychological profile of Antiochus, after Rome had abruptly ended his second Egyptian campaign, is remarkably similar to the description given by Polybius.[25] We must conclude that the descriptions of kings (particularly Antiochus IV) in the dream visions of Daniel have a certain objective basis in the broader historical record. Daniel bases the theological assertion that the will of God ultimately prevails over the machinations of kings on a fair amount of historical observation.

We can see, then, that throughout the dream visions of Daniel, the portrayals of various kings stay close to the historical record. If the court tales provided improbable stories of Nebuchadnezzar and introduced fictitious characters such as Darius the Mede, the dream visions mirror the historical evidence concerning Xerxes, Alexander, the Ptolemaic and Seleucid dynasties, and above all Antiochus IV. This does not prevent Daniel from presenting some general themes regarding kings and

---

24.   The one exception occurs in the description of Ptolemy IV Philopater (11.11-12) who is described as being enraged (יתמרמר), the same term used of Alexander in the vision in ch. 8. Philopater is also characterized as having an exalted heart (ירום לבבו) after his victory at Raphia over Antiochus III. While rage and *hubris* are common traits of kings throughout the book of Daniel, they are not indiscriminately applied to all of them. It would seem, then, that such particular character descriptions as one finds in 11.11-12 with regard to Ptolemy IV have their origin either in Daniel's own experience and recollection (the battle of Raphia occurred some 50 years before the book of Daniel), or they must be traced to the historical sources available to Daniel. It is interesting to note that negative traditions concerning Ptolemy IV appear in other Hellenistic Jewish literature (*3 Maccabees*) and in Greek historians (Polybius 14.12.3-4). The similarity of these Greek texts to Daniel once again points to the probability that Daniel used Greek sources for much of his historical data.

25.   See p. 44 n. 69.

kingdoms in the second half of the book. Rather, the motifs of the sudden rise and fall of kingdoms, the inability of kings to achieve any lasting success, and the ultimate retribution that befalls the arrogant are all based upon historical observation. It is upon this historical foundation that the prophecies concerning Daniel's final king, Antiochus IV, are constructed.

2. *The King in Herodotus*

The *Histories* of Herodotus contain literally a cast of thousands. Among the many characters we meet in the course of his narrative, the number of kings and tyrants is likewise impressive. The lengthy list of Greek tyrants in the study of K.H. Waters[26] gives one a sampling of the total number of monarchs encountered in Herodotus. It is not, however, among the local Greek rulers, nor even in every foreign king, that we find the counterpart to the foreign kings in Daniel. Rather, it is with the Great Kings—the rulers of the Persian Empire—that an analogy may be made with the kings in Daniel. This series of kings in Daniel begins with Nebuchadnezzar who is given dominion over the whole earth (Dan. 2.37-38) and continues with the successors to his empire down to Antiochus IV. In fact, Nebuchadnezzar is referred to as 'the king of kings' in Dan. 2.37. This was the self-designation of the kings of Persia (see Ezra 7.12),[27] corresponding to the Greek expression for the Persian monarch: 'the Great King'. It is these empire rulers, these great kings, who are of primary concern to both Daniel and Herodotus. In addition to the four Persian kings of the *Histories*, I feel it is necessary to include in this study the first foreign king on whom Herodotus focuses his attention: Croesus. This is not only due to the central role assigned to him by Herodotus as the initiator of injury against the Greeks, who begins the great conflict between east and west (1.5-6), nor simply because of his close association with the Persians. It is also based upon his dual role as king and (after his deposition by Cyrus) as wise advisor.

a. *Croesus*
The Croesus *logos* spans several chapters in Herodotus (1.6-92), beginning with his family history and including digressions on the Athenians and the Spartans. The core of this section, which deals directly with Croesus, tells of his rapid subjugation of the Greeks in Asia, his encounter with the Athenian sage, Solon, and his subsequent misfortune and downfall. His reasons for attacking the Greek cities of Asia Minor are not spelled out. We are simply told that he did so on various grounds, bringing charges that were sometimes greater ($\mu\acute{\epsilon}\zeta$ova) and sometimes trivial ($\phi\alpha\hat{\upsilon}\lambda\alpha$) against the cities he attacked (1.26). The impression is of one who will use

26. He lists over fifty Greek tyrants in his Appendix to Part I. Waters, *Herodotus on Tyrants*, pp. 42-44.

27. As Joseph Blenkinsopp points out in his commentary on this passage from Ezra, the title 'king of kings' was taken over by the Persians from Mesopotamian protocol (J. Blenkinsopp, *Ezra–Nehemiah: A Commentary* [OTL; Philadelphia: Westminster Press, 1988], p. 147). Nebuchadnezzar, then, actually did precede the kings of Persia in laying claim to this title.

any pretext to satisfy his ambitious nature while seeking to maintain the appearance of propriety. Croesus is not exactly a ruthless conqueror, but an opportunistic expansionist.

We gain a deeper look into the mind of Croesus in his dialogue with Solon (1.29-33). Here we begin to see a fatal flaw of this would-be empire builder. He is hospitable enough in welcoming Solon to Sardis, but ends up sending him away rudely when he does not find the wisdom of Solon to his liking. Solon had refused to flatter the king by numbering him among the happiest of people. Such a judgment Solon reserves for those who have completed their lives in happiness. That Croesus considers himself to be the happiest of men is suggested by Herodotus as the cause for the divine retribution (νέμεσις) that soon befalls him: 'After Solon's departure a great nemesis fell upon Croesus from God, presumably because he supposed himself the happiest of men' (1.34).[28] This is the lone occurrence of the word νέμεσις in Herodotus, although the concept of divine jealousy acting against arrogant and overreaching humans is a recurring theme. It is not simply the wealth or prosperity of Croesus that evokes the divine retribution according to Herodotus. It is the very attitude of Croesus with regard to his good fortune, supposing himself great and worthy of admiration and praise from others. Thus he becomes upset when Solon does not share his estimation of himself. The focus on the internal disposition of Croesus as the motive for divine retribution is very similar to the focus in Dan. 4.27 where divine punishment falls upon Nebuchadnezzar not for any of his deeds but for his boasting of them.[29] The connection in the narrative between the arrogance of Croesus (brought out in the exchange with Solon) and the tragedy that soon befalls him (beginning with the death of his son) is made clear by Herodotus's not-so-subtle suggestion in 1.34 which includes his singular use of the word νέμεσις.

It is also noteworthy that the punishment coming upon Croesus is foretold to him in a dream, just as Nebuchadnezzar's castigation was predicted in his dream. This makes it clear that the punishment is of divine origin and not merely a coincidence of circumstances. The dream of Croesus also concerns the future of his dynasty, as do the later dreams of Astyages (1.107-108) and Cyrus (1.209).[30] These dynastic dreams in Herodotus find a close parallel in the dynastic dreams of Daniel 2 and 7. This will be discussed in depth in the following chapter on the divine in history. We may conclude our discussion about Croesus by stating that the crowning mistake of this tragic character is his rashly supposing himself the happiest of men. It is a particular variety of arrogance or ὕβρις. It is this interior disposition or attitude that especially provokes the anger of God, unleashing the force of divine retribution or νέμεσις.

---

28. My translation.

29. Here, as elsewhere, I follow the versification of MT. Many English translations number this verse as 4.30.

30. See R. Bichler, 'Die "Reichsträume" bei Herodot: Eine Studie zu Herodots schöpferischer Leistung und ihre quellenkritische Konsequenz', *Chiron* 15 (1985), pp. 125-47.

b. *Cyrus*

The four Persian kings who appear in the *Histories*—Cyrus, Cambyses, Darius, and Xerxes—are each formed from a different mold.[31] This tends to affirm Waters' basic thesis on the historical objectivity of Herodotus in reporting on kings without imposing a predetermined scheme upon them. Yet the diversity of characterization does not negate the many similarities found among Herodotus's Persian kings. We might compare this situation to the book of Daniel where we found Nebuchadnezzar, Belshazzar, and Darius to be dissimilar in many ways, yet each one's story reaffirmed the same underlying motif of God's sovereignty over human kings who are ultimately powerless. So also with Herodotus, it may be that he is constructing his account around the historical evidence available to him; nevertheless, his treatment of these four very different kings reveals some common threads and recurring themes.

Herodotus begins the *logos* of Cyrus, the first Persian king, by telling of the attempt on his life as a baby by his grandfather, Astyages. This was done in response to the latter's two troubling dreams and the interpretation of the Magi who informed him that his daughter's son would usurp his throne (1.108). Cyrus is saved from this attempt and adopted by a herdsman and his wife. His true identity comes to light, however, when at the age of ten while playing at 'kings' with the other village boys, he displays the demeanor of a true king and not the son of a slave. He demands the obedience of his companions who have chosen him 'king' and he furiously whips his one playmate who refuses to obey. When brought before Astyages to explain his actions, Cyrus's self-assured response is further evidence of his noble nature. This episode from the childhood of Cyrus conveys the message that the king is king by nature; it is something one is born to, not something one becomes.[32] The qualities of leadership and self-assuredness, as well as the capacity for cruel brutality, are inborn in Cyrus. These qualities will mature as Cyrus grows into the consummate military commander. They will also prove to be his downfall in his final campaign against the Massagetae.

Back when Cyrus was first introduced in the Croesus *logos*, his skill as a military commander was immediately brought into relief. He succeeded against the formidable Lydian cavalry by means of a clever stratagem, using camels to drive off the Lydian horses (1.80). Thus it is not sheer strength of arms by which Cyrus succeeds, but through cunning as well.[33] He shows magnanimity in sparing Croesus

31. Herodotus himself quotes the Persian saying on the different manner of rule of the first three kings: 'Darius was a tradesman, Cambyses a tyrant, and Cyrus a father—the first being out for profit wherever he could get it, the second harsh and careless of his subjects' interests, and the third, Cyrus, in the kindness of his heart always occupied with plans for their well-being' (3.89). His portrait of the Persian monarchs is not limited, however, to this simple plan.

32. In a similar way, the story of the revolt of the Scythian slaves (4.3-4) shows how the slaves are such by nature. When they see their masters confronting them not with arms but with whips, they remember that they are but slaves and ceased resistance.

33. This combination of power and cunning is not quite the same as that which we saw in Dan. 8. Here it is skillful military tactics; in Dan. 8 it seems to refer rather to diplomatic maneuvering and manipulation. Also we must note that (as is typically the case in Herodotus) the stratagem employed is not Cyrus' own idea, but comes from a wise advisor.

from the pyre, but above all it is his own fear of retribution (τίσις) and realization of the instability of human affairs that prompt him to spare Croesus (1.86). From Croesus's example, Cyrus gains enough insight and wisdom (at least for the moment) to avoid making the same mistake of arrogant presumption which would call down upon himself retribution. He not only spares Croesus, he even makes him his advisor. In an ironic twist, however, it will later be the advice of Croesus that ultimately brings about the end of Cyrus as he crosses one boundary too many in his expansion of empire. Cyrus, made over-confident by his many successes, finally comes to his end with the head of his corpse stuffed into a skin filled with human blood. He has received the retribution promised to him in a warning by the queen of the Massagetae for his bloodthirsty ways (1.212). Henry Immerwahr, in his landmark monograph on Herodotus, sees a close correspondence between the accounts of Cyrus's rise to kingship and his demise.[34] The conditions of his accession, beginning with the dynastic dreams of his mother and his survival as an infant of the attempt on his life, instill in Cyrus 'his belief in his superhuman origin' (1.204). Herodotus cites this belief and Cyrus's previous successes as the two main reasons behind his fateful decision to attack the Massagetae. It is this *hubris* of the king in imagining himself more than human that guarantees a tragic end for him.

c. *Cambyses*

In spite of his unseemly demise in Herodotus's account,[35] Cyrus on the whole comes across in a better light than some of the other kings of Persia. The contrast is sharpest with his immediate successor, Cambyses. Cambyses is introduced as the successor of Cyrus at the beginning of the second book of the *Histories*, but (after a long digression on Egypt) his story does not begin until book three. After conquering Egypt, the cruelty of Cambyses is immediately seen in the public humiliation of Psammenitus, the Egyptian king. He is forced by Cambyses to witness the degradation of his daughter and son (3.14). Nevertheless, just as Cyrus relented and spared Croesus from the pyre, Cambyses also felt 'some pity' (οἶκτον τινά) at the reaction of Psammenitus and spared him further disgraces.[36] After this brief moment of limited pity, Cambyses proceeds to offend both Persians and Egyptians by his desecration and sacrilegious burning of the corpse of Amasis (3.16). This violation of customs or laws (νόμοι) is a key feature in the portrait of Cambyses.[37]

---

34. H.R. Immerwahr, *Form and Thought in Herodotus* (ed. W. Morris; Philological Monographs, 23; Cleveland: Press of Western Reserve University, 1966), p. 165.

35. Herodotus himself admits to knowing other accounts of the death of Cyrus (1.214). He claims to record what he considers to be the most likely account. Still, the fact that he chooses to relate an indecorous episode when more irenic traditions may have been known by him (such as the version told by Xenophon in *The Education of Cyrus* 8.7) indicates that Herodotus may have considered it to be the most plausible account precisely because it was an appropriate retribution for the warring expansionist.

36. The presence of Croesus at this scene further ties it to the account of his own deliverance from the pyre. The open weeping of Croesus and the Persians who witnessed the humiliation and response of Psammenitus also stands in contrast to the qualified 'some pity' which Cambyses felt.

37. Immerwahr's portrait of Cambyses focuses on the two traits of destroying customs and destroying his own dynasty (*Form and Thought*, p. 169).

The rage and madness of Cambyses come to full light in his disastrous campaign against the Ethiopians (3.25). His rash and unthinking action in continuing to march on Ethiopia without having made provisions for the long trek leads to his troops' turning to cannibalism. Only upon hearing of this does Cambyses come to his senses and retreat. Upon his return to Memphis, he kills the Egyptians who were celebrating the apparition of their god, the calf, Apis (3.27). He stabs Apis in the thigh, and scourges the Egyptian priests (3.29). Herodotus tells us that the Egyptians claim this last outrage was the cause of Cambyses' passing from a state of simply lacking sense to one of complete madness. His evil act is thus punished with a madness that causes him to perpetrate more evil acts. Among these are the murder of his brother, Smerdis (3.30), and the murder of his sister whom he had married (3.31-32). The further atrocities of the mad Cambyses are presented in 3.33-37.

The retribution that finally overtakes Cambyses is his own death by an accidentally self-inflicted wound to his thigh (3.64). That this wound was in the same spot where he had stabbed the calf Apis points to the direct relationship between the sacrilegious assault on the Egyptian god and his own demise. If Cyrus was the insatiable conqueror whose final retribution was to be sated with blood, Cambyses is the violator of νόμοι whose own sacrilegious acts work to bring about his downfall. This is so not only in the case of the self-inflicted wound, but also in having had his brother killed, for Smerdis (by Cambyses' own account in 3.65) was the one man who could have helped him against the plotting of the Magi.

The account of Cambyses in the *Histories* shows striking similarities to the descriptions of Antiochus IV in Daniel.[38] To be sure, both kings had a particular reputation for madness, and this may be part of a more general historical opinion not limited to Daniel and Herodotus. With regard to Antiochus IV, Polybius informs us of the madness that was attributed to him (Polybius, 31.9). Likewise, the second book of Maccabees tells us of Antiochus becoming like a wild beast in his rage against Jerusalem (2 Macc. 5.11).[39] The book of Daniel, however, is more one-sided

---

38. Many of these similarities have been noted by J.C.H. Lebram in his article, 'König Antiochus im Buch Daniel', *VT* 25 (1975), pp. 737-72. Rather than making the connection directly with Herodotus, however, Lebram suggests that the portrait of Antiochus in Daniel is based upon Egyptian traditions concerning Cambyses (pp. 769-70). M. Delcor ('L'Histoire selon le Livre de Daniel', in A.S. Van der Woude [ed.], *The Book of Daniel in the Light of New Findings* [Leuven: Leuven University Press, 1993], pp. 365-86) correctly points out the unequal value of the parallels drawn by Lebram (p. 369). In particular, Lebram's claim that Dan. 8.9-12 is based on traditions about the impious King Cambyses appears to be unwarranted. Everything in this passage can be explained based on the actions of Antiochus himself without recourse to Cambyses. Such is not the case, however, with the account of the death of Antiochus in Dan. 11. There we find details concerning Antiochus that do not match the historical record, but do correspond to Herodotus's account of Cambyses.

39. The undeniable influence of Greek historiography on 2 Maccabees is yet another question, which I shall not delve into here. Given, however, the context of the present passage concerning Antiochus's sacking of Jerusalem, it is worth noting briefly that the description of his arrogance and pride in terms of his plans to make the land navigable and the sea passable on foot (2 Macc. 5.21) calls to mind the manifestation of Xerxes' *hubris* in his bridging of the Hellespont and cutting of a canal through Mt Athos.

in emphasizing the impetuous rage on which this king acted (Dan. 11.30, 44) than are the other Jewish accounts in 1 and 2 Maccabees.[40] This matches the portrayal of Cambyses who acts not on reason, but out of impulsive anger. Furthermore, both kings are conspicuous for their violations of customs or laws, including the chief crime attributed to each of them: sacrilege. Each profanes the god or temple of an occupied people, an act which is explicitly seen to be the cause of divine retribution, both by Daniel and by Herodotus. We also find in both Daniel and Herodotus that the king commits his sacrilegious act upon returning from an unfortunate military campaign that did not achieve its goal (Antiochus from his second Egyptian campaign; Cambyses from Ethiopia). This element of rage induced by military failure is not shared by the other Jewish accounts of Antiochus's desecration of the Jerusalem temple.

Admittedly, these similarities between the Cambyses of Herodotus and the Antiochus of Daniel are to a certain extent due to the similarity between the objective historical evidence concerning these two kings. This in itself indicates that Daniel had his eye on historical sources which were independent of the Jewish traditions preserved in 1 and 2 Maccabees. Still, it is good to bear in mind that the image of Antiochus IV as a raging madman was not necessarily the predominant perception in antiquity. Polybius's own objectivity has been called into question in regard to his negative portrayal of Antiochus.[41] The most authoritative modern study of Antiochus IV concludes that he was an above-average Seleucid monarch whose various projects and policies were carefully thought out.[42] This matches the impression one gets of Antiochus from the letter preserved in 2 Maccabees 9, or from the comment of the king in 1 Macc. 6.12 that he was good and beloved (χρηστὸς καὶ ἀγαπώμενος) in his rule. No such hints at another side of Antiochus appear in Daniel, however. The unmitigated indignation (11.30) and rage (11.44) which Daniel ascribes to his archfiend, who sacrilegiously transgresses the laws and customs not only of the Jews (7.25; 11.31, 36) but of his own people as well (11.37-38), may derive from a characterization based on Cambyses.[43] Daniel may have noticed

---

40.   The first book of Maccabees tells of Antiochus sacking Jerusalem and its temple in the context of his successful (first) campaign against Egypt, not after a failed venture. His insolence and arrogance displayed in this account are no more than what is typical of the victorious conqueror. First Maccabees also describes Antiochus' prohibitions against the Jewish religion as part of a practical program of unification of customs which was directed to his entire kingdom, not a persecution specifically aimed at the Jews. Second Maccabees presents more of a mixed picture. There are passages highlighting extreme cruelty and mad rage, such as the martyrdom of the woman and her seven sons (ch. 7) and the final murderous threats of Antiochus before his death (9.4-7). On the other hand, 2 Maccabees also contains the account of Antiochus' death-bed conversion (9.11-17) and preserves what appears to be an authentic letter of the king which presents a much more benign picture (9.19-27).

41.   Otto Mørkholm, *Antiochus IV of Syria* (Classica et Medievalia Dissertationes, 8; Copenhagen: Gyldendalske Boghandel, 1966), p. 184.

42.   Mørkholm, *Antiochus IV*, pp. 186-91.

43.   The total disregard which Daniel reports Antiochus as having not only for the God of the Jews, but for the gods of his ancestors as well, finds a very close similarity in Cambyses who violates not only Egyptian religious customs, but Persian religious practice also (3.16).

the parallels between the historical Antiochus and the Cambyses of Herodotus's narrative, and then carried over additional characteristics from the latter to his description of the former. The possibility of such a borrowing is heightened by the final parallel I would like to consider.

The most remarkable similarity between Daniel's Antiochus and Herodotus's Cambyses may be seen in the death scenes of each. Cambyses, after hearing rumors about the revolt of the Magi, hurries back from Egypt only to die of his self-inflicted wound in Ecbatana in Syria[44] while bemoaning the fact that he had rashly killed the one man who may have helped him: his brother, Smerdis. According to Dan. 11.44-45, Antiochus, after hearing alarming reports from the east and north, rushes back from Egypt only to come to his end between the sea and the holy mountain with no one to help him. Here Daniel not only stands apart from the otherwise unanimous tradition,[45] which locates the death of Antiochus IV in the east, but he matches detail for detail the account of Herodotus on the death of Cambyses. Both kings were campaigning in Egypt. Here it may also be noted that this is the third Egyptian campaign of Antiochus according to Daniel, whereas historically there were only two. Daniel invents a third campaign, deliberately situating Antiochus in Egypt before his death. Both kings hear rumors from the east that greatly trouble them and cause them to hurry back. Both kings die in the province of Syria before they reach their destination. Both die with no one to help them. Both Daniel and Herodotus saw this as a fitting end for these perpetrators of sacrilege whose attacks on religion brought down upon them divine retribution. The connection between their sacrilegious act and their death is also made explicit in each account. Herodotus has Cambyses die by a wound in the exact same spot where he had sacrilegiously assaulted Apis, and Daniel has Antiochus die in view of the holy temple mount which he had desecrated. As mentioned before, it is with this account of Antiochus's death that Daniel 11 departs from what had been an impeccable historical account. The fact that the invented elements concerning the death of Antiochus perfectly match Herodotus's narrative of Cambyses' death strongly suggests that Daniel drew inspiration for his account from that of Herodotus.

---

44. The location and even the existence of an Ecbatana in Syria is disputed (see Asheri, *Erodoto: Le Storie: Libro III: La Persia*, p. 285). Nevertheless, Herodotus's account which places the death of Cambyses in the province of Syria matches the account of Daniel which locates Antiochus's death in this same province. Daniel at least is historically mistaken in that Polybius 31.9, 1 Macc. 6.1-17, and 2 Macc. 9.1-29 all situate his death in Persia under somewhat similar circumstances. One intriguing possible identification for the location of Ecbatana in Syria would be Pliny's 'Acbatana' located on Mt Carmel (*Natural History* 5.75). This would make the references to the sea and the mountain in Daniel an even closer parallel to Herodotus. It must be kept in mind, however, that Daniel's holy mountain is undoubtedly the temple mount in Jerusalem.

45. 1 Macc. 6.1-16 places his death in Persia while retreating from his failed attempt to take the city of Elymais and rob its temple. 2 Macc. 9.1-28 gives a similar report, except that the city named is Persepolis, and Antiochus arrives as far as Ecbatana in his retreat. Polybius (33.9) specifies that it was the sanctuary of Artemis in Elymais that Antiochus was attempting to rob, and that during his retreat he died at Tabae in Persia. Josephus (*Ant.* 12.9.1) had at hand both 1 Maccabees and Polybius (whom he cites) in composing a similar account.

d. *Darius*

The Darius *logos* occupies a central place in the *Histories*, covering much of Books 3-4. Darius himself is in many ways the most favorably depicted of the Persian kings in Herodotus, just as Darius the Mede is the most sympathetic of the foreign kings in whose court Daniel serves.[46] It was by Darius's counsel and decisive action that the usurper Magi were overthrown. He then secures the throne for himself by his persuasive speech in favor of monarchy and the clever ploy of his servant Oebares to insure that Darius is chosen to be king. His trickery involved in securing the kingdom is not presented in a negative light.[47] Rather, in his first act as king, Darius good-naturedly erects a monument giving due recognition to his horse and Oebares for their role in winning him the throne. He displays a certain balance of justice and compassion in condemning Intaphrenes (one of the seven conspirators against the Magi) for his disrespect toward the king, while acquitting the innocent parties and granting mercy to Intaphrenes' wife for her wise answer. He honors and rewards Zopyrus for his heroic self-sacrifice in the siege of Babylon. He is merciful to his Eretrian prisoners, forgetting the anger he had born against the inhabitants of that city for burning Sardis (6.119).

In spite of the many positive portrayals of Darius, there is a down side to his character as well. The Persian saying quoted by Herodotus in 3.89 characterizes Darius as ruling avariciously in the manner of a tradesman or shopkeeper (κάπη-λος). This is corroborated by the tribute lists which Herodotus reports in the following chapters. In addition to being overly concerned with money, Darius disregards the wise advice of his brother, Artabanus, who encouraged him to abandon his plan for invading Scythia. He reacts cruelly to the request of Oeobazus that one of his three sons be excused from the Scythian campaign. His Scythian campaign itself is a failure, although he at least succeeds in successfully retreating (thus showing more sense than his predecessor Cambyses did in his obstinate march on Ethiopia).[48]

---

46. It is not my intention to delve fully into the complex issue of possible identifications or explanations for Daniel's curious figure, Darius the Mede. It may be the case, as suggested by Brian Colless ('Cyrus the Persian as Darius the Mede in the Book of Daniel', *JSOT* 56 [1992], pp. 113-26) that we have here an example of another doubly named person in the book of Daniel, and that Darius the Mede is to be identified with Cyrus the Persian. This is plausible if we read the 'and' in Dan. 6.29 as being explicative, thus identifying the two characters. By using the double name, the book of Daniel could then preserve the historical reality of Babylon falling to Cyrus (also mentioned in Herodotus), while at the same time keeping the schema of a Median kingdom between those of Babylon and Persia. The choice of the name of Darius for this Mede may reflect Daniel's interest in the personality or qualities of Darius Hystaspes as seen in Herodotus. The variety of kings in both the *Histories* and Daniel allows us insight into their manifold limitations.

47. Immerwahr (*Form and Thought*, p. 172) notes that the pictures of Darius as 'usurper' and 'legitimate monarch' are for the most part favorable, whereas in the accounts of his campaigns we encounter a less sympathetic figure. The positive portrayal in his accession is reinforced by the divine confirmation of his kingship. This can be seen both in the prophetic dream of Cyrus that foretold Darius's future rule (1.209) and in the miraculous thunder and lightning as a sign from heaven that accompanies his winning the contest for the kingship (3.86).

48. In addition to comparing favorably to his predecessor, Cambyses, Darius also fares well in a comparison with his successor, Xerxes. As Immerwahr points out (*Form and Thought*, p. 174),

While displaying a certain amount of sense, Darius is not above being manipulated by his inner circle. Herodotus tells us of the great influence which the doctor Democedes had over Darius. Democedes used his power on more than one occasion to influence the king to release prisoners (3.132). Being held at Susa himself against his will, Democedes finally tricks Darius into letting him return to Greece as part of a spying expedition. In the course of the expedition he then makes his escape (3.133-37). Another example of Darius being hoodwinked by his ministers may be found in the story of the Ionian, Histiaeus. Darius had initially made Histiaeus one of his counselors in order to retain him at his court, thus being able to keep a closer eye on this potential rebel. In spite of his initial caution, Darius is later tricked by Histiaeus into letting him return to his country during the Ionian revolt (5.106-107). In much the same way, Daniel's Darius the Mede is also manipulated by his ministers. He is tricked into promulgating a decree that he will later regret. In the *Histories* as in Daniel, even the king who (relatively speaking) appears in a favorable light is ultimately seen as ineffectual. Subject to the machinations of those around him, even the 'good' king makes bad decisions and is unable to carry out his own designs. Darius passes from the scene quietly at the beginning of Book VII, his elaborate plans for vengeance upon Athens and the suppression of the revolt in Egypt left unfulfilled.

e. *Xerxes*

If the Darius *logos* is at the center of the *Histories*, the Xerxes *logos* is at its climax. The conflict between east and west, Asia and Europe, reaches its culmination in the great campaign of Xerxes against Greece. Yet the king who is at the center of this conflict initially shows no interest in the campaign planned by his father. In the story which leads up to the decision to invade Greece, we see most clearly how the Great King is not the author or director of these events, but rather how he is subject to other forces in history, both human and divine. Herodotus states that Xerxes was persuaded to undertake the invasion of Greece from the double pressure of Onomacritus's oracles on the one hand, and the advice of the Pisistratidae and Aleuadae on the other (7.6-7). Later, when he heeds better advice and changes his mind about invading Greece, he is once more 'forced' into taking up the cause by a dream from God. According to his own words, the dream will not allow him to act as he would have liked (7.14-15). So at the very beginning of the Xerxes *logos* we find the Great King impelled to act against his own will by pressure from various counselors, but above all by the weight of divine oracles and dreams.

Xerxes is a complex character in the *Histories*, vacillating between various positions, alternately showing good and bad sense. His initial pleasure at the generosity of Pythius the Lydian (7.29) is replaced by rage when the latter asks for the release of the eldest of his five sons from the Greek expedition (7.39). His anger at the

---

this can be seen especially in the wisdom and moderation displayed in the advisor scenes. Darius is more likely to listen to good advice graciously, as he does when Gobryas counsels a retreat from Scythia (4.134). Xerxes, in contrast, reacts violently to suggestions of caution by Artabanus in deciding on war against Greece (7.11), although he later changes his mind.

destruction of his bridge over the Hellespont leads him to the bizarre act of having its waters whipped (7.35). Later, however, Herodotus hints at Xerxes' repentance for this act (7.54). After reviewing his troops, Xerxes makes the same mistake as Croesus in declaring himself happy. Yet, immediately after this arrogant pronouncement, he corrects himself to a certain degree by weeping and waxing philosophical on the brevity of human life (7.45-46).[49] The sharp contrast between the king's rapidly shifting moods in this latter episode is duly noted by Artabanus.

Xerxes is not a thoroughly demonized king like Antiochus IV in the book of Daniel, but more along the lines of the hot-tempered, self-satisfied Nebuchadnezzar. He is not without his good qualities, but his overconfidence, ostentation, and rage are sufficient to ensure the failure of his campaign. In the significant exchange with Demaratus, Xerxes is unable to understand or be persuaded by the truth of Demaratus's statements that the Spartans will bravely fight against any odds for their law (7.101-105). Convinced of the invincibility of his army, he fails to perceive how the natural elements of earth and sea are fighting against him (7.48-49). He also undertakes unnecessary displays of power along his route. Herodotus comments on his arrogance (μεγαλοφροσύνη)[50] in having a canal cut across Mt Athos (7.24). Xerxes unwisely gives vent to his anger in desecrating the dead Spartan king Leonidas. In listening to his advisors, he is more inclined to follow the bad advice of Mardonius than the good advice of Artabanus and Demaratus. He is blinded by his own great power to the fact that there are other and greater forces in history with which he must contend.

To sum up the role and characterization of kings in the book of Daniel and the *Histories* of Herodotus, we may state that both works contain a critical appraisal of the king's power. Kings may very well consider themselves great, or happy, or blessed (a point particularly emphasized in the accounts of Nebuchadnezzar, Croesus, and Xerxes), but this is a mistaken judgment. By exalting themselves, they effectively set themselves up as rivals to God, becoming the target of divine envy. Their eagerness to acquire power and dominion also leads them to cause injury to others. The crimes they commit in their aggressive expansion leave them subject to the law of retribution. While thinking themselves to be great, kings depend upon counselors who often fail them (e.g. Croesus's fatal advice to Cyrus; Nebuchadnezzar's inept Chaldeans), or who even deceive and manipulate them (as with Darius in both works). Ultimately the king is subject to the destiny or fate that is divinely decreed and revealed to them through dreams and oracles. The content of these

49.   Although Xerxes' broadened perspective here is an improvement, his tears are somewhat misplaced, as Artabanus points out to him. The shortness of human life is the least of human sorrows. Rather, the misfortunes that often trouble humans make life seem long even as they look forward to death.

50.   The noun μεγαλοφροσύνη here, like the verbal form φρονέειν μέγα in 7.10e, is obviously used in a negative sense. It is not high-mindedness or magnanimity, but considering oneself great. In this Xerxes errs grievously. Thus, even his generosity is turned into the vice of μεγαλοφροσύνη as witnessed in the episode where he turns on Pythius the Lydian. We see there that the previous generosity of Xerxes to Pythius was made in order that the Lydian could not boast of being more generous than himself (7.39).

dreams, which so often trouble them, frequently pertains to the end of their rule and the establishment of a new dynasty in their place. The severe limitations of kings and of their dominion can thus be seen as a prominent theme in both Daniel and Herodotus.

3. *The Sage*

The less-than-idealistic portrayal of kings in Daniel and Herodotus opens the door to new human agents who might effectively direct the course of historical events. In Israel, this counterpart to the king in the 'classical' histories was the prophet who defiantly stood up to the king in proclaiming the word of YHWH. In the post-exilic period, the role of the prophet gradually changed and subsided. There was no longer a king in Judah for the prophet to exhort and admonish. Furthermore, the word of YHWH, which the prophets proclaimed, was finding a new expression in the formation of a written canon of Scriptures. As this written corpus took on increased importance, so did the role of learned interpreters of its meaning. Scholars, scribes, and sages emerged as an increasingly important class in preserving, transmitting, and interpreting the written words of YHWH. Historically, the position of this group *vis-à-vis* the king had been decidedly less polemical than that of the classical prophets. This may be due to the fact that the origins of these didactic traditions were closely connected to the royal court.[51]

The book of Daniel presents us with a picture of the wisdom guild in its relation to the royal court. Chapter 1 introduces us to young men of nobility from among the Jewish exiles who are selected for training to enter the king's service. They are instructed in the language and literature of the Chaldeans,[52] after which they enter the king's court and respond to all his inquiries with wisdom and insight. Daniel is the most prominent of the four youths mentioned in ch. 1, and it is he who will dominate the ensuing folk-tales. The one tale in which he is absent—the tale of the fiery furnace in ch. 3—does not involve a test or display of wisdom on the part of its three protagonists, therefore we can omit it in our discussion of the sage in the book of Daniel and focus on the one true wise man throughout the book: Daniel himself.

a. *Daniel the Sage in the Court Tales*
After the introductory chapter, which situates Daniel in the court of the foreign king, there are five distinct court tales in the following chapters. As we have already noted, Daniel is absent from the tale in ch. 3. Chapter 6, like ch. 3, is a tale of divine deliverance from mortal danger in which Daniel's role is decidedly passive. It is in

---

51. See G. von Rad, *Wisdom in Israel* (London: SCM Press, 1972), p. 15. R.E. Murphy (*The Tree of Life: An Exploration of Biblical Wisdom Literature* [Grand Rapids: Eerdmans, 2nd edn, 1996], pp. 3-4) rightly situates the primary locus of wisdom traditions within the family or clan, without denying the role of trained scribes of the court or temple in shaping and transmitting these traditions.

52. 'Chaldeans' here may refer not only to the ethnic group, but the guild of sages as well. Such is clearly the meaning of the term in passages such as Dan. 2.2-4.

the remaining chapters—two, four, and five—that we primarily see the wisdom of Daniel displayed in the court of the king.

In ch. 2, Daniel is among the wise men of Babylon who are to be killed by decree of Nebuchadnezzar in his rage against the Chaldeans for their failure to interpret his dream. In order to avoid this fate, Daniel first inquires of Arioch, the king's officer entrusted with carrying out the execution, the reason for this decree. The text of Dan. 2.14 emphasizes the discretion and prudence of Daniel in speaking with Arioch.[53] Once Daniel finds out the motive behind the decree, he goes to the king to ask for time to give the interpretation of his dream. Having taken these practical steps, Daniel then goes home and instructs his companions to pray to God concerning this matter. Then, during the night, the mystery is revealed to Daniel in a vision. Thus, while acting with prudence and practicality, the wisdom that ultimately saves Daniel and his companions is not his discretion or cunning, nor is it any innate quality in him. Rather, it is something received in a revelation from God. The nature of this wisdom is not like the practical advice to be found in proverbs. It is a mantic wisdom that is able to divulge the divine message concealed in enigmatic dreams and visions. If Daniel is deemed wise, his wisdom lies in his relationship to the God who reveals such mysteries (2.28).

The words of Daniel make explicit the connection between this type of wisdom and the divine. In both his hymn of praise to God and in his speech before the king, Daniel clearly states that wisdom is not a human, but a divine quality. Thus, after the king's dream has been revealed to him, Daniel acknowledges in his hymn that wisdom and power[54] belong to God (2.20), and that it is God who gives wisdom to the wise (2.21). From these more general statements Daniel moves on to affirm that it is God who has given him both wisdom and power by revealing to him the king's dream (2.23). When he appears before Nebuchadnezzar, Daniel begins his speech by stating that none of the various categories of sages in the Babylonian court can reveal to the king the mystery of his dream (2.27). No human has this wisdom; it is a quality reserved to God alone (2.28). Daniel protests that in and of himself he is no wiser than any other living being (2.30). The Aramaic phrase used in this verse כל־חייא includes all natural life. Wisdom, then, is not attributed to any living creature, but only to the one who lives forever (חי עלמא) whom Nebuchadnezzar will acknowledge in 4.31.

Moving on to Daniel 4, we find Daniel (as noted previously) in a decidedly supporting role in this chapter while Nebuchadnezzar takes over center stage. The somewhat peripheral position that Daniel occupies in ch. 4 is deserving of at least one brief note in regard to his wisdom. When he is summoned once more before

53. The Aramaic phrase התיב עטא וטעם is the lone instance where the more traditional type of wisdom, consisting in the ability to turn a good phrase, is attributed to Daniel. It recalls the Hebrew construction in Prov. 26.16: משיבי טעם. The wisdom that will distinguish Daniel in chs. 2, 4, and 5, however, is the ability to interpret dreams and mysterious writing.

54. The combination of the two elements of wisdom and power reinforces the observation that there are these two main categories with which the book of Daniel deals: the wise and the powerful. In human terms this translates into the sage and the king, but Daniel acknowledges that both receive whatever wisdom or power they have from God.

Nebuchadnezzar in order to interpret yet another mysterious dream, the king expresses his confidence that Daniel will succeed in interpreting his dream after the other sages had failed. This confidence is based upon the king's own recognition that in Daniel is 'the spirit of the holy God' (רוח אלהין קדישין, 4.5, 6). The source of Daniel's wisdom is here acknowledged by the king, just as it was by Daniel himself in ch. 2. No practical wisdom, political savvy, or cunning is needed on Daniel's part, since his life is not threatened as it was in ch. 2. Rather, Daniel enjoys the king's confidence and favor from the outset, and the only wisdom he manifests here is the mantic wisdom by which the dream is successfully interpreted.

Chapter 5 repeats the assessment of Daniel's wisdom as being due to the spirit of the holy God in him (5.11). This time the appraisal is not given by Daniel or the king, but by Belshazzar's queen as she informs him of the one who might solve the riddle of the writing on the wall. The divine quality of the wisdom to be found in Daniel is further emphasized by the simile in which the queen states that Daniel's wisdom is 'like the wisdom of God' (כחכמת־אלהין, 5.11). The nature of this wisdom is summarized in the following verse as the ability to interpret dreams, to solve riddles, and to 'loosen knots'—that is to say 'solve problems'. As in chs. 2 and 4, the wisdom displayed by Daniel is one of interpretation and revelation. It is not the practical, proverbial wisdom that instructs one how to live. Its sole purpose is to make known the meaning of a mysterious message from God which has come to the king either in a dream (chs. 2 and 4) or through writing on the wall (ch. 5).

Before giving the interpretation to the writing on the wall, however, Daniel launches upon a brief lecture to the impious King Belshazzar. The content of this preliminary speech also pertains to wisdom, only now it is the practical wisdom which one might encounter in the book of Proverbs or on the lips of Solon. Daniel reprimands Belshazzar for failing to learn from the example of his father, Nebuchadnezzar. The lesson is that power comes from God who gave dominion to Nebuchadnezzar. But God does not tolerate a haughty heart or impious spirit. Rather, he abases those who display such *hubris*. Thus, Nebuchadnezzar was castigated until he learned to acknowledge God's sovereignty over human kingdoms. This is a lesson that Belshazzar did not learn, for he failed to humble his heart. The message of humility before God is a traditional wisdom motif, both in Israel and in Greece. Such is the gist of Artabanus's advice to Xerxes when he warns him that 'it is the great ones that God smites with his thunder' and that 'God tolerates pride (φρονέειν μέγα) in none but Himself' (7.10e). The arrogance or presumption, which Artabanus cautions against, corresponds to the exalted heart which Daniel denounces.[55]

---

55. The phrase that describes Belshazzar's exalting his heart (רם לבבה) in Dan. 5.20 is perhaps the closest possible Aramaic equivalent to the Greek expression φρονέειν μέγα. The Aramaic noun לבב refers to the mind or seat of thought as does the Greek verb φρονέω. Likewise the Aramaic verb רם and the Greek adjective μέγα both refer to height or greatness. The arrogance and presumption expressed in the accompanying Aramaic phrase ורוחה תקפת להזדה ('and his spirit was hardened so that he acted proudly') adds a further parallel to the presumptuous conceit implied by φρονέειν μέγα.

b. *Daniel the Seer in the Dream Visions*

In the second half of the book of Daniel, the account changes dramatically from stories told about Daniel to visions narrated by Daniel. As Daniel moves from the role of leading character to that of narrator, the focus shifts from him personally to the content of the visions he relates. Nevertheless, there are some significant points of characterization that are related by the text. Most notably, it is now Daniel who is filled with fear and terror by dream visions (7.1, 15, 28; 8.17) just as Nebuchadnezzar had been in chs. 2 and 4. Daniel, who was wiser than all the sages of Babylon, is left unable to understand the visions he sees (8.27; 12.8). He becomes weak and ill (8.27); he is left powerless and changes color (10.8), reminiscent of Belshazzar upon seeing the writing on the wall. In a word, Daniel, when confronted with puzzling divine revelations, is left in the same state of fear and powerless confusion that the foreign kings were when they were the recipients of such mysteries.

The tables have turned somewhat in the second half of the book, and now Daniel finds himself in need of an interpreter. But a human interpreter is no longer sufficient. Rather, Daniel approaches an angelic being in his first vision to inquire as to its meaning (7.16). In Daniel's next vision, Gabriel is explicitly named as the one sent to explain his vision to him (8.16). Likewise, Gabriel is sent to Daniel with a divine message in response to his prayer in ch. 9 (v. 21). It appears that Gabriel is understood to be the messenger again in chs. 10–12, although he is not named. The removal of the task of interpretation to the level of the divine further highlights the distance between the wisdom and power that are found with God and the helpless confusion that is the lot of humans. The sage is now left in the same impotent state as the king, lacking both wisdom and power. The angelic interpreter provides an added degree of separation between the divine and human levels, thus amplifying the transcendence of God and emphasizing the verdict of the court tales that wisdom and power belong to God alone.

c. *The Wise Advisor in Herodotus*

The number of characters in the *Histories* who dispense advice or counsel of one sort or another is as impressive as the number of kings and tyrants. Richard Lattimore provided a helpful list and analysis of these persons in his important article on wise advisors in Herodotus.[56] He divided wise advisors into two main groups: tragic warners and practical advisors. It is the former category that resonates the most with Daniel who interpreted foreboding dreams and signs for the foreign kings, in whose courts he served, and warned them of impending judgment. Among these tragic warners, it is above all Solon in his dialogue with Croesus, and Artabanus in his exchanges with Xerxes, who pronounce the central motifs of wisdom in Herodotus. In the key *logoi* involving these characters (which frame much of the *Histories*), the recurring themes of the fickleness of fate, and the dangers of presumption and arousing divine envy are brought to the fore.

Solon is a rather independent figure in the *Histories*. He is described as one of the various Greek sages (σοφισταί) who paid a visit to Croesus at his capital of Sardis

---

56.   R. Lattimore, 'The Wise Adviser in Herodotus', *CP* 34 (1939), pp. 24-35.

(1.29). He has no official connection with the Lydian court, being Croesus's guest, not his servant. His credentials for dispensing wisdom lie in his having written a code of laws for the Athenians at their request and the experience gained through his subsequent travels.[57] In fact, his broad experience of the human condition is the necessary prerequisite for answering Croesus's question concerning who is the happiest of people. In Solon's speech (1.32), he calculates for Croesus the number of days in a human life, reminding him of the uncertainty and chance which govern them.[58] Given such uncertainty, only the one who has happily concluded the many days of life is to be considered happy. His speech also opens and closes with reference to God as the agent by which the prosperous or happy often suffer a reversal of fortune. The wisdom of Solon, then, while not being based upon any divine revelation, points to a divine factor in the reversals of fortune witnessed through human observation. Since God does bring about such reversals in the course of human events, the sage's advice is to look to the end to see who is truly happy. A true verdict cannot be given until the end of whatever it is one is considering has taken place.

The experiential wisdom of Solon differs considerably from the mantic wisdom of Daniel, who interpreted dreams and visions of judgment from God. Nevertheless, although the nature of their wisdom is substantially different, the content is fundamentally the same. Both deal with reversals of fortune brought about by God as a type of judgment or retribution against the presumptuous. This can be seen more clearly in the words of Solon if we situate them in their context as a warning to the arrogant King Croesus. Similarly, the dreams and writing interpreted by Daniel were warnings of impending divine judgment against arrogant kings. Furthermore, the practical conclusion of Solon's advice to Croesus is to look to the end. This might be seen as a major theme of the book of Daniel, as it points to a coming great reversal against the powers of arrogant kingdoms to be accomplished by God.

Artabanus is the tragic warner *par excellence* in Herodotus. According to Lattimore, he epitomizes the characteristics of the warner in that 'he is in general pessimistic, negative, unheeded, and right'.[59] Artabanus belongs to the close inner circle of the king's confidants, being the brother of Darius and uncle of Xerxes. Thus, he is of noble blood like Daniel, but of the same family as the king he advises, not a foreigner. The wisdom of his words to Xerxes, like that of Solon's to Croesus, is based upon his own experience of human affairs. In counseling Xerxes, he bases his advice on his previous experiences with Darius (7.10c). As was the case with

57. Croesus, in his address to Solon, also associates the travels of Solon with his pursuit of knowledge (1.30).

58. The length of human life is a point which is belabored by Solon in his speech. He is not content to give its reckoning according to years, but breaks this down into days (being sure to account for intercalary months). This tends to emphasize the length rather than the brevity of human life (contrast with Xerxes in 7.46) by figuring it to be the rather large number of 26,250 days. The point is that human life is sufficiently long for any number of calamities to occur. The judgment is repeated by Artabanus who 'corrects' Xerxes' weeping over the brevity of life by pointing out that misfortunes can make it seem overly long (7.46).

59. Lattimore, 'Wise Adviser', p. 24.

Solon, it is practical knowledge garnered from lived experience, not mantic wisdom, that is his forte. Artabanus has no skill in interpreting oracles or dreams. In fact, he dismisses dreams as being of no consequence, doubting that they could come from God (7.16b). The only divinely inspired counsel that does in fact come to Artabanus is a deceptive dream in which God tricks him into going against his previous good advice and threatens him with punishment for trying to avert what must be.[60]

As for the personality of Artabanus, he is motivated by a concern for the well-being of the king, counseling him accordingly. There are no mischievous or self-serving motives as one finds with Mardonius who counsels war in the hope of becoming governor of Greece (7.6). Moreover, Artabanus is humble in regard to his own advice, using the same disclaimer as Daniel does (Dan. 2.30) in stating that 'no special wisdom of his own' (οὐδεμιῆ σοφίη οἰκηίη, 7.10c) stands behind his words. He is not referring, as Daniel was, to wisdom as a divine gift, but rather as the fruit of experience and the observation of human events. He believes his counsel is valid and wise because he has first-hand experience of similar circumstances in Darius's Scythian campaign. Although there is no divine authority behind the wisdom of Artabanus, the words he speaks bear witness to a divine reality. Even more insistently than Solon, Artabanus points to the divine jealousy of human greatness that is the underlying cause behind disastrous reversals of fortune. The wise course in which he counsels Xerxes is one of caution and restraint, for 'God tolerates pride (φρονέειν μέγα) in none but Himself' (7.10e).

While Solon and Artabanus spell out the *Histories*' main themes of wisdom in their extended speeches, there are yet other wise counselors who deserve mention. Among these we must note Croesus for the curious double life he leads. His early career, as an arrogant king who would not heed the sage warning of Solon, is transformed after his deposition by Cyrus into a career as a counselor to the king who defeated him. François Hartog, in his insightful study, has shown how royalty in Herodotus has 'something barbarian about it'.[61] As long as Croesus is a king, he cannot be wise, for the king or tyrant by nature is driven by *hubris*. And, as we have just seen from the speech of Artabanus, *hubris* is the very antithesis of wisdom. In his speech advocating an end to monarchy, Otanes identified the twin vices of *hubris* and envy (φθόνος) as the root of all evil in the king (3.80). Stripped of his rule, the king is freed to some degree from these two forces. Whereas a reigning king could never be truly wise, being governed by *hubris* and envy, a former king such as Croesus is able to dispense sound judgment and wise advice to some

---

60. The deceptive dream is modeled after the lying dream of Agamemnon in Book 2 of the *Iliad*. There the divinely sent dream deceptively foretold victory in order to draw Agamemnon into battle. In the *Histories*, as in the Iliad, the divinity encourages the king through a dream to enter into a conflict with the intention of bringing ruin, not victory, to him. This dream, which visits both Xerxes and Artabanus in the *Histories*, will be discussed in greater detail in the following chapter as a manifestation of the divine in history.

61. F. Hartog, *The Mirror of Herodotus* (trans. J. Lloyd; Berkeley: University of California Press, 1988), p. 330.

degree. This he does for both Cyrus and Cambyses, although, as we have seen in the episode with the Massagetae, his advice is not always sagacious.

I would like to mention one final wise advisor in Herodotus from a somewhat different mold. This is the Athenian commander, Themistocles. He does not serve as a tragic warner like Solon, Artabanus, or even (at times) Croesus. Rather he belongs strictly to Lattimore's second category: the practical advisor. What is significant in a comparison with the book of Daniel is the fact that Themistocles' wisdom or practical advice consists primarily in the correct interpretation of an oracle. This is a most unusual circumstance in the *Histories*, where oracles, dreams, and portents are so often misinterpreted. In 7.143 Themistocles correctly interprets the Delphic oracle as foretelling an Athenian victory at sea and he counsels his countrymen to prepare accordingly. This is the exact opposite of what the professional interpreters understood by the prophecy. Thinking the oracle to foretell an Athenian defeat at Salamis, they counsel avoiding a naval battle and abandoning their country. The contrast between the professional class of interpreters who fail to deliver the correct interpretation of a divine message and the single true interpreter who stands apart from them is reminiscent of the contrast expressed between Daniel and the various classes of professional diviners (Dan. 2.10; 4.4; 5.7).[62]

In the case of Themistocles, the correct interpretation of the oracle and the practical advice that flows from this interpretation go hand in hand. We may note that in Daniel no practical advice follows the correct interpretation. The divine message is an immutable judgment that cannot be altered. It cannot be overturned, and it would appear to require no human assistance. While the Delphic oracle also announces what must be, or what will in fact happen, it works more closely with human choices, whether by conditional prophecies (e.g. if Croesus attacked the Persians, he would destroy a great empire), or by suggesting a course of action (e.g. Croesus should find out which of the Greek states is the most powerful and come to an understanding with it). So, while the oracle foretold Athenian victory at Salamis, the Athenians must cooperate with the oracle's cryptic advice to achieve that end. Reserving further discussion of divine oracles for the following chapter, we may state for the moment that the wisdom of Daniel, like that of Themistocles, consists in correctly interpreting the divine message. The practical counsel that accompanies this interpretation in Herodotus is absent from the book of Daniel.

To sum up the role of human agents in history according to the *Histories* of Herodotus and the book of Daniel, both emphasize the ultimate inability of the 'Great King' to achieve his purposes. Although he is seemingly the one with the most power, he is thwarted by divine forces which work to bring down the mighty. He is also subject to human forces, being dependent upon advisors whose advice may be bad or even deceitful. The role of the sage is heightened at the expense of the king. Although the wisdom in Daniel is primarily mantic, while that in Herodotus is for the most part practical, there are indications of both in each of these works. In the *Histories*, as in the book of Daniel, it belongs to the wise to correctly

---

62. One minor difference is that the professional groups in Daniel are unable to proffer any interpretation, while the professional interpreters in Herodotus offer an incorrect one.

interpret dreams and oracles that pertain to the course of future events. In both works we encounter crafty advisors who can trick the king into unwittingly doing what they want. But the truly wise person is the one who understands the role of the divine in history. Solon and Artabanus, like Daniel, understand that there is a divine force in history working against the powerful and arrogant. The one who is wise shuns *hubris* which brings upon oneself divine retribution, but this is a lesson which kings such as Croesus, Cambyses, Xerxes, Nebuchadnezzar, Belshazzar, and Antiochus either do not learn, or else they learn it only after their power has been taken from them.

Chapter 4

THE DIVINE IN HISTORY

The *Histories* of Herodotus, as I have indicated above in Chapter 2, had a profound influence on successive generations of history writers, as well as on poets and novelists. I have also briefly touched upon the earlier traditions of Greek epic and tragedy that undoubtedly influenced Herodotus. Among these influences, the pride of place certainly belongs to Homer. In the *Histories* there are not only the many direct references to the Homeric epic works,[1] but also scenes which reveal themselves as based upon Homeric precedents.[2] When we compare the *Iliad* to the *Histories*, we can see that the theme of a great conflict between Europe and Asia and the extended length of both works both point to the possibility that Herodotus was composing his own prose epic based upon his poetic predecessor. Indeed, the very introduction of Herodotus's work parallels the beginning of the *Iliad*.[3] As Homer began his work by asking what god it was that set the Greeks and Trojans in conflict, Herodotus begins his by identifying not the god but the man whom he knows to have initiated the conflict between east and west. Ultimately, we may state that both works have as a primary concern the giving of due glory (κλέος) to great deeds that have been accomplished.[4]

If Herodotus is deeply indebted to Homer, there are ways in which he seeks to distinguish and distance himself from the poet as well. While later generations

1.   The most noteworthy of these centers around the story of the rape of Helen leading to the Trojan War (1.3-4; 2.113-20). In his rather lengthy analysis of this episode in Book 2, Herodotus quotes directly from Homer three times (*Iliad* 6.289-92; *Odyssey* 4.227-30, 351-52) in support of his argument that Homer knew of the tradition whereby Paris and Helen went to Egypt, but chose not to report it. Thus Herodotus is even able to use Homer in his own argument against Homer.

2,   For example, the lying dream of Xerxes in Book 7, which is based upon the dream of Agamemnon in Book 2 of the *Iliad*.

3.   See T. Krischer, 'Herodots Prooimion', *Hermes* 93 (1965), pp. 159-67. He analyzes Herodotus's opening sentence in terms of a prose imitation of Homer's proem design. Krischer sees in the Homeric pattern three main elements: invocation of the Muse, exposition of the theme, and allocation of guilt or blame. The *Iliad* and the *Histories* share a common theme in that they each tell of a war between Greeks and barbarians. They each likewise ask the question: 'Who was responsible?' Since the *Histories* were written in prose, it would make little sense to call upon the goddess to sing. Herodotus's counterpart to this Homeric element is to set forth himself as the one who is describing the results of his inquiries.

4.   Herodotus, of course, explicitly states as much in his proem. For the 'glories of men' (κλέα ἀνδρῶν) as the subject of epic poetry, see G. Nagy, 'Herodotus the *Logios*', *Arethusa* 20 (1987), pp. 175-84. A key passage from Homer that is also pointed out by J. Marincola (*Herodotus*, p. xvi) is *Iliad* 9.189 where Achilles takes pleasure in singing of the κλέα ἀνδρῶν.

often dismissed Herodotus as a teller of tall tales, Herodotus himself pronounces the same verdict at times on Homer.[5] Herodotus, the historian, bases what he writes (or so he claims) on what he has either seen himself or heard through his various inquiries. Removed from his narrative, then, are the scenes of Olympus so prevalent in Homer. Herodotus has no accounts of divine beings interacting among themselves. Rather, he displays a skeptical attitude about what can be known of the divine world.[6] Yet, the *Histories* are certainly not lacking in references to or suggestions of divine intervention in the course of human history. He has in fact been criticized at times for writing too theological a history.[7] The divine factor in Herodotus is experienced for the most part indirectly, however. Oracles, dreams, portents, and ominous signs are the indirect means by which the divine agent in history is revealed. Unlikely coincidences and unusual acts of nature also reveal a divine influence.

The book of Daniel also reveals a perspective in which the divine in history is most certainly affirmed, but it is manifested in rather mysterious ways. One senses a distance from the days of old, when God spoke to Moses face to face, or even from the days of the classical prophets who forcefully proclaimed the word of YHWH. The book of Daniel reveals a God who speaks exclusively in obscure riddles that require someone who can provide an interpretation. The divine message is communicated primarily through symbolic dream visions (to which we may add the miraculous writing on the wall in ch. 5 and the symbolic interpretation of scripture in ch. 9). While there is certainly a precedent for the revelation of the divine word to the prophets through symbolic visions (especially in Ezekiel and Zechariah), the wise exile (particularly in the court tales) is not the bearer of the divine word in the same way as the prophets before him were. Although the prophets expressed the divine message in language that was often highly symbolic, their relationship with the word was more direct, being its recipients and not simply its interpreters. Daniel, as we have seen, interprets the dreams and signs that come to others in chs. 2, 4, and 6. When he himself receives visions in chs. 7, 8, and 10–12, he also needs an angelic interpreter at this point. Thus there is introduced an intermediary between Daniel and God.[8]

---

5.   In addition to disputing Homer's telling of the abduction of Helen and the Trojan War, Herodotus also explicitly criticizes Homer as the likely inventor of the idea of the river called Ocean encircling the earth (2.24).

6.   See especially 2.3 where Herodotus chooses not to report what the Egyptian priests told him of divine matters (τὰ...θεῖα). This silence may be motivated by a desire not to reveal sacred mysteries, but his following explanatory statement (νομίζων πάντας ἀνθρώπους ἴσον περὶ αὐτῶν ἐπίστασθαι) seems to suggest that all humans are equally limited in their knowledge of the divine (W.W. How and J. Wells, *A Commentary on Herodotus* [Oxford: Clarendon Press, 1928], I, p. 157). The use of ἴσον in the sense of 'just as much', that is, 'just as little' comes across in the translation of de Sélincourt: 'for I do not think that any one nation knows much more about such things than any other'. This is corroborated in 9.65 where Herodotus questions whether one may rightly have an opinion concerning divine matters (although he does go on to express his own view, given this proviso).

7.   Marincola, *Herodotus*, p. xxiv.

8.   One can compare the interpretation given of symbolic images in Jer. 1.11-14. There the prophet is also the recipient of enigmatic imagery from God, but it is God directly who speaks the interpretation to Jeremiah as well. There is not the added element of a third party to mediate the

The divine communications that do take place, both in the dreams of the foreign king and in the visions of Daniel, ultimately deal with the role of the divine in history. At the center of the book of Daniel is the question of theodicy. The author attempts to explain and justify the ways of God in a historical context in which God is seemingly absent. The rule of foreign powers over the Jewish people had been tolerable, if not ideal, when those powers were relatively benign, but with the persecution of the Jewish religion under Antiochus IV the question of the role of God in this new historical moment is brought to the fore.[9] Yet, the answer given in Daniel is that God is still very much at work in history, although this divine action may be mysterious and difficult to perceive. Over and over again we are reminded through the dream visions that the rulers of this earth are ultimately subject to God who both establishes and removes them.

1. *The Divine in Daniel*

As we saw in the previous chapter, God in the book of Daniel is mainly characterized by the two attributes of wisdom and power. These traits, which one usually associates with the sage and the king, are described as belonging to God alone. These qualities are freely bestowed upon whomever God so desires. Not only is the rule of the king seen as entirely dependent upon the will of God, but the wisdom of the sage is a direct result of the divine disposition as well. Thus it becomes clear that it is neither the king nor the sage but God who ultimately has control over the course of history. Yet the mode in which the divine dominion over historical events is exercised is more oblique than that which one encounters in the earlier biblical writings. The clear hand of divine retribution seen throughout the Deuteronomistic History fades into the background in Daniel. Only in ch. 9 do we receive a hint that the current distress of Daniel's people is a divine punishment for their sins. The successive rule of foreign powers is described as part of God's preordained plan in history, but we are not told why. While we are told why God removes these foreign kings from their positions of power (5.20, 22-23), we are not given insight into the divine mind to perceive why God established these kings and kingdoms in the first place (2.37; 5.18).[10] The ways of God remain very mysterious from a human

message. Likewise, the meaning of the many symbolic visions and actions of Ezekiel are revealed to the prophet directly by God. The notable exception is the extended vision of the new temple beginning with Ezek. 40. There a man with a measuring rod is introduced who accompanies Ezekiel on his tour of the new temple, occasionally explaining to him its various features (Ezek. 40.45-46; 41.22; 42.13-14). Even so, this man's presence does not prevent Ezekiel from being directly addressed by God (43.6-7) regarding the purpose of the vision. More comparable to the position of Daniel is that of Zechariah who speaks to the angel (המלאך) to receive the interpretation of his visions in chs. 1–6.

9.   A second wave of Jewish apocalyptic theodicy would appear over two centuries later when another historical crisis—the fall of Jerusalem and destruction of the temple at the hands of the Romans—would spawn works such as *4 Ezra* and *2 Baruch*.

10.   It may very well be that the perspective of ch. 9 (which perceives the persistence of foreign rule as an extension of the period of exile as a punishment for sin) and the perspective of the

perspective. The God of Israel also appears increasingly remote, as intermediary divine beings (One like a Son of Man, Gabriel, Michael) enter into the historical melee on God's behalf.

As the divine activity becomes more remote and elusive in the book of Daniel, so too does the divine message, concealed in symbolic dreams and mysterious writings that require interpretation.[11] This interpretation comes either through God's human agent, Daniel, or through an angelic being. Divine manifestations through dreams and angels are well-attested throughout the Hebrew Scriptures; there is certainly no need to postulate any dependence upon Greek sources on this count. Nevertheless, the distinctive manner in which these elements are employed in the book of Daniel gives us cause once more to investigate similar patterns in the *Histories* of Herodotus. The many striking parallels on both the thematic and the formal levels warrant further investigation. It is to this investigation that I now turn.

a. *Dreams and Signs*

In the book of Daniel, there are a total of four dream visions which are recounted: two of Nebuchadnezzar (chs. 2 and 4) and two of Daniel (chs. 7 and 8). In addition to these dreams, we may also include the appearance of a human hand writing on the wall (ch. 5), the mission of the angel Gabriel in response to Daniel's prayer (ch. 9), and the waking vision of Daniel (chs. 10–12) as means by which a divine message is communicated in the book of Daniel.

In examining kings and sages in the previous chapter I have already noted in passing the dreams of Nebuchadnezzar found in chs. 2 and 4. There are several similarities between these chapters and the Joseph Cycle in Genesis, which also recounts the prophetic dreamings of a foreign king that are successfully interpreted by a Hebrew who thereby rises to a prominent position.[12] The similarities are most striking when one compares Daniel 2 with Genesis 41. P.R. Davies[13] has noted the following similarities: (1) the king has a dream (Gen. 41.1; Dan. 2.1); (2) The dream disturbs the king (Gen. 41.8; Dan. 2.1); (3) the king's sages cannot interpret the dream (Gen. 41.8; Dan. 2.10-11); (4) a member of the court presents an unknown Hebrew captive (Gen. 41.9-13; Dan. 2.25); (5) the hero has confidence that God will reveal to him the dream (Gen. 41.16; Dan. 2.27-30); (6) the hero affirms that God has revealed the future to the king (Gen. 41.25, 28; Dan. 2.45); (7) the hero

Deuteronomistic History (which views Nebuchadnezzar as God's appointed instrument in carrying out punishment) are presumed throughout the dream visions. The book of Daniel should not be isolated from the rest of Israelite and Jewish tradition. If my claim that Daniel was familiar with Greek historiographical traditions is valid, it may be argued *a fortiori* that he was thoroughly acquainted with those of his own people. While emphasizing this continuity with earlier traditions, I wish to point out that Daniel presents us with a marked development as well.

    11.   There is of course a significant precedent for the revelation of future events through the interpretation of dreams in the Joseph Cycle in Genesis. The similarities and differences between the story of Joseph and the tales of Daniel will be examined in detail below.

    12.   For a discussion of the difficulties regarding the Joseph story in comparison to the court legend genre as found in Daniel and Esther, see Wills, *The Jew in the Court*, pp. 52-55.

    13.   P.R. Davies, 'Daniel Chapter Two', *JTS* 27 (1976), pp. 392-401.

succeeds and is promoted (Gen. 41.39-40; Dan. 2.48). To this impressive list G.G. Labonté[14] has added two more details: (1) both accounts open with a temporal note (Gen. 41.1; Dan. 2.1); (2) in both accounts the king recognizes the presence of the divine with the hero (Gen. 41.38; Dan. 2.46).[15] If we consider Daniel 4 as well in this comparison, we may add the seven years of castigation prophesied for Nebuchadnezzar (Dan. 4.13) as a counterpart to the seven years of famine that will come upon Egypt (Gen. 41.30).

The many similarities in these passages from Genesis and Daniel concerning the interpretation of the foreign king's dream fall within an even larger category of parallels between the court tales of Daniel and the biblical story of Joseph in general.[16] These similarities have caused some scholars to reconsider long-standing theories about the dating of the Joseph story in Genesis and its relationship to Jewish novelistic literature (Daniel, Tobit, Esther) of the post-exilic period.[17] While the problems surrounding the story of Joseph fall outside the scope of this study, it is reasonable to conclude, given the evidence cited above, that Daniel 1–6 as a whole (and ch. 2 in particular) are modeled to some extent on the biblical account of Joseph. The strong connection that can be seen between the stories of Daniel and Joseph reminds us once again that the book of Daniel is deeply rooted in earlier biblical traditions. It is equally important to keep in mind, however, that 'the influence of Genesis is only one factor among many in the shaping of the tales'.[18]

Given that the point of comparison in the present study is the work of Herodotus, it is the differences between Daniel and Joseph that most concern me here. So, while the similarities between the book of Daniel and the story of Joseph are impressive, two significant differences should be pointed out. Although in both cases the dreams foretell future events, the dreams of Pharaoh in Genesis are precautionary warnings inviting a human response to anticipate and avert a disaster. They foretell what will happen, and their successful interpretation enables Pharaoh to plan for the upcoming famine. In this they resemble the Delphic Oracle in Herodotus when it likewise at times invites a prudent course of action. Joseph, like Themistocles, not only successfully interprets the dreams, but also suggests what should be done to meet the coming crisis. The dreams of Nebuchadnezzar do not lend themselves to such possibilities of a human response. They are, rather, divine judgments that cannot be thwarted. The four kingdoms will be destroyed (ch. 2),

---

14. G.G. Labonté, 'Genèse 41 et Daniel 2: Question d'Origine', in Van der Woude (ed.), *The Book of Daniel*, pp. 271-84 (277).

15. While Pharaoh explicitly acknowledges that the Spirit of God is in Joseph, Nebuchadnezzar's recognition of the divine in Daniel is expressed through his prostration before him. The same affirmation that the Spirit of God is in Daniel appears later in Dan. 5.11.

16. Collins (*Daniel*, p. 39) has listed many of these similarities which extend even to the level of phrases and expressions. He notes, for example, the similar expressions describing the appearance of Daniel (Dan. 1.4) and Joseph (Gen. 39.6), as well as the common root words behind the Aramaic of Daniel and the Hebrew of Genesis for many key terms.

17. Wills, *The Jewish Novel*, pp. 160-61.

18. Collins, *Daniel*, p. 40.

and Nebuchadnezzar will be punished for his arrogance (ch. 4).[19] This concept of an unalterable decree is also found in the Delphic Oracle. Such is the case with the oracle's words to Gyges that the Heraclids would have their revenge on him in the fifth generation (1.13). So the fifth in his line, Croesus, is doomed to defeat in spite of his every effort to solicit favor from Delphi and the gods. No human response or initiative can mitigate the foretold disaster.

The unalterable nature of the events foretold in the dream visions in Daniel is, I believe, directly related to the historical crisis in which they were written. The oppression and persecution, which foreign rule has now become for Daniel's people, is too severe. A more conditional prophecy that would allow for the possibility of repentance or rehabilitation of the foreign kingdoms is unimaginable. Daniel, it seems, cannot bear the thought of God having a change of heart such as we find in the book of Jonah when the people of Nineveh repented. The period of 'exile' must end for Daniel's people, and this means that the foreign kingdoms must definitively be destroyed. The burning desire for a sure future that cannot be thwarted by any human action is emphasized in the extended vision of chs. 10–12 where we are told that the vision is אמת, that is 'true' or 'certain' (10.1).

In addition to being definitive pronouncements of judgment that cannot be altered or overturned, there is yet another difference between the dreams in Daniel and those in the story of Joseph. The dreams in the book of Daniel (both Nebuchadnezzar's dreams in chs. 2 and 4, and Daniel's dreams in the latter half of the book) are consistently of a particular type. They are all dynastic dreams dealing with the rise and fall of kings and kingdoms. It is in this that they share a common perspective with most of the dreams recounted in the *Histories*. Their subject matter pertains to the historical categories of rule and succession. Nebuchadnezzar's dream in ch. 2, like that of Daniel in ch. 7, deals with the fall of the Babylonian Empire and the successive rise and fall of Media, Persia, and Greece. Nebuchadnezzar's dream in ch. 4 is more limited in scope, focusing on the temporary removal of the king from the exercise of rule. As the dream is realized, a voice from heaven declares to Nebuchadnezzar that his kingdom is passing away from him (4.28). His kingdom, however, will be returned to him after he has learned through his chastisement that the Most High rules (4.22). Daniel's dream in ch. 8 envisions the passing of the kingdom of the Medes and Persians (the ram with two great horns) and the rise of the kingdom of Alexander (the powerful he-goat).

As was mentioned earlier, these dreams, which 'foretell' future events as prophecy, were in fact written after the events that they describe took place. The common practice of dismissing such *vaticinia ex eventu* as merely establishing the seer's credentials for the actual prophecies that follow simply does not do justice to this material. When we consider history, as Daniel does, as the sum of not only human actions but also of divine agency, we can discern in these prophetic dreams an emphasis on the divine cause behind events similar to that which we find in Herodotus.

19.　Although Daniel encourages the king to atone for his sins by good deeds so that he may prosper (4.24), he does not state that by this course of action the king might avoid the seven-year punishment that had been decreed in the dream.

The foretelling of the event by God, whether through a dream, oracle, or portent, says something about the cause of the event itself. While human agents are inevitably involved in the unfolding of historical events, these various manifestations of the divine will point to a parallel or overarching causation which works to bring about 'what must be'.[20] While the kings in the book of Daniel are free agents acting 'as they will' (11.36), the emphatic point made throughout the book is that they are ultimately not in control of history. Just as no amount of planning or precaution by kings such as Croesus or Astyages can prevent the downfall of their kingdoms foretold through oracles and dreams, so too the various machinations of Antiochus IV will prove ineffectual in preventing his downfall revealed by God through visions.

In addition to the two dream visions of Daniel in chs. 7 and 8, there is also the extended waking vision in chs. 10 through 12. These visions, together with the prayer of Daniel and the encounter with Gabriel in ch. 9, present a unified picture of Daniel's theology of history in the second half of the book. As mentioned earlier, the question of who is in control of the course of history is central to the book of Daniel. This general concern is heightened by the historical crisis brought on by Antiochus IV which chs. 7–12 address. The theology of rule in Daniel 7–12 was insightfully addressed by Daniel Harrington in a paper delivered at the Society of Biblical Literature's annual meeting in 1999.[21] He pointed out that the theology of rule in Daniel 7–12 is in fact a theodicy of rule, answering the key questions: Who is in charge? Why is there evil now? And when is the end? The answer to the first question is unequivocal: God is in charge of the course of events. It is the heavenly court that pronounces sentence upon the earthly kingdoms. The second question is addressed in two different ways. In chs. 7, 8, and 10–12, the existence of kings and kingdoms that bring about evil is seen as a part of God's preordained plan. We are told in effect that this had to be, but we are not given any deeper explanation. Chapter 9, on the other hand, clearly links the reign of evil to Israel's sins, viewing the present moment as a continuation of the period of exile by which Israel was punished. Both ch. 9 and the remaining chapters of the second part of Daniel assure us that the end of this period of evil is near. God's plan is coming to fulfillment, and the prophesied period of exile is reaching the end of its predetermined span.

The affirmation of God's rule over the course of historical events is made through the divinely sent dreams that foretell the very events which constitute the historical crisis. The fact that the dreams are pronouncements of divine judgment

20. In Herodotus, the inability of humans to alter the course foretold in a dream or an oracle even when its meaning is clear to them clearly demonstrates that history is not merely the end result of human actions. Croesus cannot prevent the foretold end of the dynasty of Gyges in the fifth generation. Astyages cannot prevent his grandson Cyrus from usurping his throne. Xerxes cannot avoid war with the Greeks. Although Herodotus does stress the role of the individual and individual choices in his *Histories*, ultimately fate cannot be overturned. This is most clearly stated in the passage concerning Croesus where we are told that the gods may gain him a respite, but even they must bow before the power of fate.

21. Daniel J. Harrington, 'The Ideology of Rule in Daniel 7–12', *Society of Biblical Literature 1999 Seminar Papers* (Atlanta: SBL, 1999), pp. 540-51. Harrington's analysis also appears in his book: *Why Do We Suffer?: A Scriptural Approach to the Human Condition* (Franklin, WI: Sheed & Ward, 2000).

sent by God is made clear both from the imagery contained within the visions themselves and from the interpretation provided by Daniel. In Nebuchadnezzar's dream in ch. 2, the image of the stone, which was not cut by human hands, that destroys the four-metal statue points to a divine rather than a human agency that will bring about the end of the four kingdoms. The dream in ch. 4 is even more explicit when it has a 'holy watcher' (4.10) descend from heaven to pronounce judgment against the tree which represents Nebuchadnezzar. Daniel's interpretation of the first dream explicitly states that it is God who has established the kingdom of Nebuchadnezzar (2.37) and God who will put an end to the four kingdoms (2.44). Likewise, the interpretation in ch. 4 clearly identifies the dream as a judgment that God has pronounced on Nebuchadnezzar (4.21). The dreams do not neutrally recount events; rather, they judge them. They address the question of God's role in history for a nation that still finds itself in a state of 'exile' under foreign domination. The way in which the difficult question of theodicy is resolved in these passages is by asserting that judgment has been pronounced against the wicked who now enjoy dominion over the righteous. Now it is simply a matter of waiting until the sentence is carried out. The dreams thus appear as the first step of God—that of pronouncing judgment—in resolving the historical crisis. The present historical moment is then seen as existing between the promulgation of the decree of judgment and its implementation.

Even the form in which the divine message of judgment is revealed tells us something about the divine role in history. The veiled messages, which require interpretation, are emblematic of the mysterious and hidden action of God in history. It is not immediately clear from the dream visions how the enduring reign of foreign kings over the Jewish people is the result of divine action. Nevertheless, we are reminded that God has given dominion to Nebuchadnezzar (and presumably to the kings and kingdoms succeeding him as well). We are assured that God's activity does not end with the establishment of these kingdoms, but includes their destruction as well. The visions themselves do not tell us why these kingdoms must be in the first place. They simply report their rise and foretell their fall as the working of God. The only answer given to the riddle of the Jews' present suffering under the fourth kingdom is the affirmation that God has not lost control of history. Nothing has happened that God has not mandated. Hope then comes through the proclamation of the final decree foretelling the end of these nefarious kingdoms.

For a more complete answer, one must turn to ch. 9 of Daniel. There we see that the reign of these kingdoms is itself a judgment on the Jewish people. It is the period of exile decreed by God through the prophet Jeremiah (25.11; 29.10) as interpreted by Daniel to consist of seventy weeks of years (9.24). Here too we see the hidden nature of the divine in history. The apparently straightforward prophecy of Jeremiah is symbolically re-interpreted to provide a hidden meaning of God's true design. Chapter 9 of Daniel gives us one of the earliest examples of the *pesher* type of commentary that would become widely used in the community at Qumran.[22]

---

22.   There are some fifteen texts from among the Dead Sea Scrolls that have been clearly identified as *pesharim*. See M.P. Horgan, *Pesharim: Qumran Interpretations of Biblical Books*

In effect, the prophetic text (here Jeremiah) functions in a similar way to the dreams and visions. It is seen to relate symbolically the unfolding of historical events. The veiled manner of the revelation requires some special form of divinely inspired interpretation to uncover its true meaning. While it is ultimately God who reveals the meaning of such dreams and signs, the role of the human through whom the interpretation comes is also significant. To come to the 'correct' understanding of Jeremiah's prophecy, or to receive the correct interpretation of a dream, requires both prayer and study from the human side. Daniel asks his companions to pray on his behalf in ch. 2 (vv. 17-18), and he himself is diligently reflecting on Jeremiah and praying in ch. 9 (vv. 2-3) when Gabriel is sent to him with enlightenment.

In addition to the dreams of Nebuchadnezzar and Daniel and the visitation by Gabriel in response to Daniel's prayer in ch. 9, there is also the episode of the writing on the wall in ch. 5 that communicates a divine message. Although the manner of this revelation is more public than the dreams and visions, which come to individuals elsewhere in the book of Daniel, it follows the same pattern. The message is addressed to an individual, King Belshazzar, even though it is publicly manifested. Furthermore, the message is conveyed in cryptic language and its meaning is not immediately clear. It requires an interpreter just as the dreams of Nebuchadnezzar and Daniel did. Finally, the message also pertains to the dynastic succession, foretelling the end of Belshazzar's kingdom and its division among the Medes and Persians. The public and miraculous nature of this revelation has affinities with the many portents in the *Histories* of Herodotus. There, strange and miraculous phenomena are taken to be divine messages. The occurrence of naturally impossible events, such as the moving of weapons by themselves (8.37) or a mare giving birth to a hare (7.57), point to a communication from the divine. Mysterious sounds and visions, such as the voices heard coming from a cloud by Dicaeus and Demaratus (8.65) and the appearance of superhuman figures on the battlefield (6.117; 8.38), also signal the divine presence and intervention.[23] The message these phenomena convey is often one of impending destruction, much in the same way as was the message to Belshazzar. The mysterious writing on the wall presages the death of Belshazzar that very night (5.30).

b. *Heavenly Combatants*
Dreams and visions constitute the method of revealing the divine plan in history to humans in the book of Daniel. These revelations not only tell *what* God is doing or

---

(CBQMS, 8; Washington: Catholic Biblical Association of America, 1979), p. 1. These commentaries are noted for their symbolic interpretations of various prophetic texts, identifying names and words from the prophets with contemporary historical persons and events. This symbolic reinterpretation of a prophetic text (e.g. 'year' = 'week') in order to apply it to current situation is basically what ch. 9 of Daniel does. In addition to the similarities between Dan. 9 and the *pesharim* from Qumran, Dan. 11 shows many affinities to these texts as well. Its use of descriptive symbolic names for well-known persons (e.g. 'king of the north' and 'king of the south') is reminiscent of the usage at Qumran (e.g. 'teacher of righteousness' and 'wicked priest'). Both Dan. 11 and the *pesharim* also use the same symbolic name—'Kittim'—to refer to Rome.

    23. These superhuman phantoms in Herodotus will be discussed at greater length below.

about to do, they also indicate *how* God is acting in history. Divine activity in history manifests itself indirectly through the mediation of lesser heavenly beings. There appears to be a certain concern for divine transcendence, a desire to keep God above the historical fray, evidenced by the appearance of angelic beings in many of the visions. In ch. 4, it is a 'holy watcher' (עיר וקדיש), a type of heavenly being also attested in 1 En. 12.2,[24] who comes to pronounce the divine judgment upon Nebuchadnezzar. Chapter 7 has God's judgment arrive in the mysterious personage of 'One like a Son of Man' (כבר אנש) who comes upon the clouds of heaven from the 'Ancient of Days'. Perhaps most intriguing of all are chs. 10–12. There we are introduced to the 'princes' (שרים) of Persia, Greece, and Daniel's people—heavenly beings whose conflicts appear to parallel on a divine plane the struggles of the nations they represent on earth.

The term שר is found frequently in the Bible, especially in the historical books. It has a fairly broad range of meaning, denoting any of a variety of political, tribal, military, or even religious leaders. We even find the term referring to Pharaoh's chief baker and chief cupbearer in Genesis 40–41. It also occurs five times in Daniel 1, referring to Ashpenaz, Nebuchadnezzar's chief eunuch (שר הסריסים) who is responsible for the training and instruction of Daniel and his companions. The idea of leadership over or responsibility for a particular group is common to all of these uses of the term. When we come to Daniel 10, however, a new application of this word appears. For the first and only time in the Hebrew Scriptures, שר refers not to a human leader, but to a heavenly one. The 'princes' of Persia, Greece, and Daniel's people are the heavenly representatives responsible for each of these nations. The use of the term שר is significant in that while referring to a leader or commander, it is a title which of its nature is also subordinate to a higher authority: the king (מלך). This can be seen clearly in the examples above from Genesis and Daniel, as well as in virtually every passage where שר appears. It would be a mistake then to understand these divine representatives as the gods of each nation. In fact, we are told that the name of the prince of Daniel's people is Michael in 10.21 and 12.1. He is also mentioned in 10.13 as one of the chief princes. So, there is not only a subordination of these heavenly princes to what would logically be the heavenly king,[25] but there is also apparently some kind of hierarchical ordering among the princes themselves since Michael is referred to as one of the first or chief princes (אחד השרים הראשנים).

The introduction of these heavenly princes of nations who confront and combat one another points once again to divine causation in the unfolding of history. Human history is shown to be connected to a divine struggle, even though this may

24. The hendiadys ('watchers and holy ones') by which these heavenly beings are designated in Dan. 4.10 and 1 En. 12.2, is generally replaced by the simple term 'watchers' elsewhere in 1 Enoch.

25. The relationship of these heavenly princes to God is not as clear as is their relationship to the nations they represent. While Michael and Gabriel clearly act on God's behalf in defending Israel, it is unclear whether the opposition presented by the princes of Persia and Greece is understood as a necessary part of a larger divine plan in the same way as the granting of temporary dominion to the four kingdoms in chs. 2 and 7.

only be seen through the lens of a visionary experience. In this divine struggle, it is the princes of the various nations, not God, who are the participants. God remains above the conflict of history, accomplishing the divine will through other heavenly agents who interact more directly with human history. Just as God's method of revealing the divine plan in the book of Daniel is indirect, so too is the method of accomplishing that plan—through delegated agents.

2. *The Divine in Herodotus*

As previously mentioned, gone from Herodotus are the exploits of the individual Homeric gods who cavort on Olympus and descend into battle to assist their favorite hero. Herodotus is indeed preserving the great deeds of both Greeks and barbarians—he is telling a human story. At the beginning of Book 2, he explicitly states that it is his intention not to report what the Egyptian priests told him of the gods (τὰ...θεῖα), but rather to relate human affairs (ἀνθρωπήϊα πρήγματα). He desires to tell no more than the names of the gods, displaying a somewhat skeptical attitude concerning what can humanly be known about them (2.3-4). For the most part, Herodotus follows this self-imposed limit throughout his work. The few examples of actions attributed to individually named gods in the *Histories* are very insignificant.[26] Nevertheless, references to the divine (τὸ θεῖον), the gods (θεοί), or God (θεός) are plentiful in the *Histories*. Sometimes when these more generic designations are used a specific god may be referred to indirectly (as with Apollo in events concerning the Delphic oracle), but often there is no particular god that can clearly be identified. In fact, by using the more general terms listed above, Herodotus creates the impression of a singular divine force that operates in history. To repeat the observation of Ivan Linforth previously noted in Chapter 1, 'though the multiplicity of gods is never called in question, there is a disposition to speak of the divine element in the world as if it were characterized by the indivisibility of the god of the pure monotheist'.[27] While there may be implicit and explicit acknowledgment of a multiplicity of gods in Herodotus, they act as if there were but a singular divinity. Heaven no longer wars with itself as it did in the great Homeric epics.

In a fashion similar to that in the book of Daniel, this divine agency in Herodotus operates somewhat indirectly. In the first place, it reveals the course of future events through dreams and oracles, which are always somewhat cryptic, being open to (and even requiring) interpretation. Secondly, there are also lesser divinities who come into closer contact with humans through dreams and apparitions, much like the angelic mediation found in Daniel. I will now examine each of these aspects of the divine role in Herodotus.

---

26. I. Linforth lists but eleven instances in which a named god is reported to have had direct interaction with humans. These are all minor incidents (some merely genealogical claims) reported as stories of this or that ethnic group by Herodotus. Herodotus himself often denies the credibility of these accounts. See Linforth, 'Named and Unamed Gods', pp. 87-89.

27. Linforth, 'Named and Unamed Gods', p. 94.

a. *Oracles*

Oracles were an important means of ascertaining the divine will for the ancient Greeks.[28] Among the various oracles to be found throughout the Hellenic world, there was none so famous or important as the one at the temple of Apollo in Delphi. In Herodotus's narrative, the Delphic Oracle also holds a very significant position. Its pre-eminence is established in the Croesus *logos* (1.46-48) when the King of Lydia tested the various oracles at Delphi, Abae, Dodona, Amphiaraus, Trophonius, Branchidae, and Ammon. Only the Delphic Oracle succeeds in reporting what Croesus was doing on a set day, thus eliciting the worship of Croesus who acknowledges Delphi as the only oracle (μοῦνον…μαντήιον). The reputation established for Delphi in this episode early on in the *Histories* is reinforced throughout the work. Without exception the Delphic Oracle proves true in Herodotus. This consistency—the inerrancy of the Delphic Oracle—marks it as a true manifestation of the divine within the narrative of Herodotus.

While the oracle at Delphi does consistently communicate certain and accurate prophecies, these are often couched in mysterious and symbolic language. It is not enough, therefore, to receive an accurate prophecy; one must also be able to interpret it accurately. The tragic consequences of failing to do so are witnessed throughout the *Histories*. Croesus fails to interpret accurately which great kingdom he will destroy by attacking Persia and so brings himself to ruin. The Athenians, likewise, almost make a terrible mistake by misinterpreting the oracle's words as referring to an Athenian defeat at Salamis when in fact they promised victory. It is Themistocles who is able to interpret correctly the oracle, following its advice in order to achieve the favorable outcome that was prophesied.

The enigmatic revelations conveyed through oracles point to something of a gulf between the human and divine realms. This same gulf is witnessed in the mysterious dreams found in both Herodotus and Daniel. In Herodotus, the correct interpretation of an oracle or a dream is something of a hit-or-miss affair. It depends on the cunning or insight of the interpreter of the moment. In Daniel, the gulf between the mysterious divine revelation and its human recipients is always successfully transcended through either a divinely inspired human interpreter (Daniel) or a divinely sent angelic interpreter. The riddling oracles in Herodotus leave their human recipients on much more uncertain ground. While the oracles infallibly report what must happen, revealing something of the supernatural forces shaping the course of history, they offer no guarantees of a correct interpretation, thus leaving humans to their own wits in uncovering the oracles' true meaning.

It is significant that Herodotus quotes directly from the Delphic Oracle on several occasions. The preserved oracular pronouncements from Delphi were obviously an important source for Herodotus. While some scholars have downplayed the role that Herodotus ascribes to oracles and other manifestations of the divine in

---

28.   For a treatment of the role of oracles in the life of Greek states, see R. Parker, 'Greek States and Greek Oracles', in P.A. Cartledge and F.D. Harvey (eds.), *Crux: Essays Presented to G.E M. de Ste. Croix on his 75th Birthday* (History of Political Thought, VI, Issue 1/2; Exeter: Imprint Academic, 1985), pp. 298-326.

history,[29] the preservation of these oracles goes beyond Herodotus's method of simply recording what people say, without being bound to believe it (7.152). If Herodotus sometimes adds his own editorial comments, doubting the veracity of the sources he reports (e.g. 4.42) or questioning the attribution of some event to a supernatural cause (e.g. 7.189, 191), he never shows any sign of hesitancy in accepting the Delphic Oracle as a reliable divine communication. It reports what must come to pass.

While there are no oracles per se in the book of Daniel by which God might be consulted regarding future events, there is a counterpart to the oracular pronouncements of Delphi and the other shrines found in Herodotus. This counterpart is the manner in which the Scriptures are consulted in ch. 9 of Daniel. Daniel is seeking divine insight into a specific question, just as did the inquirers to Delphi. He wants to know how long the exile will be, or, more precisely, what the seventy years spoken of by Jeremiah mean. The scripture is studied, a prayer is said, and through the angel Gabriel a new and symbolic interpretation to the passage is given. As I have already noted, this interpretation is closely related to the *pesher* type of interpretation found at Qumran. By taking key words to stand for something else, the scripture is reinterpreted to bear on contemporary events. The Scriptures are reread as oracles that foretell future (now become present) events. For the Jewish author of Daniel, the Scriptures represented the authentic voice of God, much as the Delphic Oracle did for Herodotus and the Greeks. To discern or uncover the divine will and agency in history, it was necessary to consult the Scriptures and to interpret them properly. While the 'correct' interpretation appears in the text as a certainty, revealed as it is by God's angel, no doubt the author of Daniel (like the authors of the *pesharim* from Qumran) believed that many of his Jewish contemporaries failed to understand the text according to this 'correct' interpretation.

b. *Dreams*

The many dreams in Herodotus, like those in Daniel, have to do almost exclusively with dynastic succession.[30] There is the dream of Cyrus, which envisions the usurpation of the Persian throne by Darius, establishing a new branch of the Achaemenid dynasty (1.209). There are also the two dreams of Astyages, which foretell the end of his rule at the hands of his grandson and thus the passing of rule from the Medes to the Persians (1.107-108). The dream of Cambyses foresees the end of his rule at the hands of one named Smerdis, signaling the end of his line (3.30). The

---

29. One may note the minimalist treatment of divine phenomena by D. Lateiner (*The Historical Method of Herodotus* [Toronto: University of Toronto Press, 1989], pp. 197-205) who emphasizes Herodotus's 'disbelief' in what he reports concerning divine intervention in history. Lateiner appears concerned to defend Herodotus's reputation as a serious historian. He is right in asserting that Herodotus's main concern is 'the phenomenon of terrestrial experience' (p. 204), but he undervalues the role assigned by Herodotus to divine agency, which does not override but accompanies human causation. Herodotus himself explicitly states his belief in divine revelation through oracles and dreams and in divine activity in human affairs (see, e.g., 1.210; 9.100).

30. R. Bichler ('Die "Reichsträume" bei Herodot', pp. 125-47) gives a brief analysis of each of the major dynastic dreams in Herodotus.

dream of Xerxes at the beginning of Book 7 does not directly deal with dynastic succession, but it does serve to bring about the definitive decline and failure of Persian aspirations against Greece (7.12). His later dream in 7.19 speaks more directly to the end of his dynasty.

When we examine each of these dreams individually, we notice that they share in common with the dream visions of Daniel not only the theme of dynastic succession, but also several formal elements. In the dream of Cyrus, he sees Darius with a pair of wings on his shoulders, one casting a shadow on Asia and the other on Europe. In the vision in Daniel 7, the imagery of wings is also brought into relief in describing the first (Babylonian) and third (Persian) kingdoms. The meaning of this symbolism in the book of Daniel is not made as explicit as it is in Herodotus. It is often suggested that the imagery of wings connotes speed (especially in conjunction with the description of the third beast—the swift leopard),[31] but it should be noted that the plucking of the wings of the first beast most likely indicates a loss of power, not a loss of speed.[32] Furthermore, the detail we are told concerning the third beast (i.e. that it was given dominion) would appear to correspond to the imagery of its four wings as extending to the four corners of the earth.[33] In the vision of Cyrus, then, as well as in the vision in Daniel 7, we find the imagery of wings as marking out an extensive dominion for the dynasty in question.

Of the two dreams of Astyages, it is the imagery of the second that finds an echo in a dream vision in Daniel.[34] Astyages dreamed that a vine grew from his daughter's genitals and covered all of Asia. This is substantially the same imagery that we also find in the dream of Xerxes in 7.19. There he sees himself crowned with an olive bough whose branches spread out over all the earth. Then the crown suddenly

31. Montgomery, *Critical and Exegetical Commentary*, p. 289; Collins, *Daniel*, p. 298.

32. It is also helpful to interpret the imagery of the visions within the context of the entire book of Daniel. The first beast in ch. 7—the winged lion—corresponds to the head of gold in the vision in ch. 2 which is explicitly identified with Nebuchadnezzar. This identification, along with the meaning behind the imagery of the wings that are removed, is solidified when we also consider the allusions to ch. 4 in the description of the first beast. We are told in 7.4 that the beast was given a human heart (לבב אנש), the heart representing the mind or reason in the Hebrew idiom. This recalls the decree of the holy watcher in 4.13 that Nebuchadnezzar's heart be changed from that of a human to a beast's heart (לבב חיוה). Then, after seven years of this punishment, during which time Nebuchadnezzar's dominion is removed (4.28), Nebuchadnezzar once again receives his human reason. The account in the vision of ch. 7 parallels that of ch. 4. In both instances the removal of dominion (symbolized in ch. 7 by the removal of the wings) precedes the granting of a human heart to the king of Babylon. Like Croesus, Nebuchadnezzar must lose his kingdom before he can become wise. But, unlike the Lydian king, Nebuchadnezzar (at least in ch. 2) has his kingdom later restored to him.

33. This interpretation of the four wings (in conjunction with the four heads of the third beast) as referring to Persia's universal rule is argued persuasively by Montgomery (*Critical and Exegetical Commentary*, p. 290) who compares it to both the fourfold imagery in Ezek. 1, which points to God's universal rule or activity, and to the Cylinder Inscription of Cyrus in which he refers to himself as monarch of the four quarters.

34. The peculiar imagery of the first, in which Astyages dreamed that his daughter urinated to such an extent that the whole of Asia was inundated, has no counterpart in Daniel.

vanishes from upon his head. In each of these cases, the spreading plant symbolizes the spreading dominion of the ruler in question, Cyrus and Xerxes respectively. The vine in the dream of Astyages covers all of Asia (τὴν ᾿Ασίην πᾶσαν) while the shoots of the olive crown in the dream of Xerxes cover the entire earth (πᾶσαν γῆν). In the latter vision, the disappearance of the olive crown also indicates the failure to realize or maintain that dominion.

This botanical imagery for dominion that is both won and lost has a counterpart in the dream vision of Nebuchadnezzar in Daniel 4. There Nebuchadnezzar dreams of a great tree at the center of the world that could be seen to the end of the entire earth (לסוף כל־ארעא, Dan. 4.8). The great size and extent of the plant once again point to a vast empire. Yet this tree, like the olive crown of Xerxes, does not last. A holy watcher descends from heaven and orders that the tree be stripped of its branches and cut down. Only its stump is left in the ground, bound with iron and bronze fetters. The description of the great tree as dominating the 'entire earth' along with its sudden removal combine to create a particularly close affinity between the dream of Nebuchadnezzar and the dream of Xerxes. In both cases the expansionist kings are warned that their aspirations for world dominion will not ultimately be realized.

The dream of Cambyses similarly relates to the dream of Nebuchadnezzar in Daniel 4. The common element this time is the mention of the uppermost part of the person or object dreamed touching the heavens. Cambyses dreams that a messenger brings him news of Smerdis sitting on the royal throne and that his head 'reached the heavens' (τοῦ οὐρανοῦ ψαύσειε). Likewise, as we have seen in Nebuchadnezzar's dream, the great tree, which represents the king, is described as having its top (literally 'its height') touching the heavens (ורומה ימטא לשמיא). In each of these cases, the detail of reaching the heavens symbolizes supreme rule. This is clear in the dream of Nebuchadnezzar from the fact that the removal of his exercise of kingship is symbolized by the tree's being cut down. The aspect of supreme rule is also evident in the dream of Cambyses since the detail of Smerdis's head touching the heavens occurs in conjunction with his sitting on the royal Persian throne. There may likewise be an indication of *hubris* by this detail in both dreams. It is due to Nebuchadnezzar's arrogant presumption that he is castigated by God. Though not as clear in Herodotus, *hubris* may also be implied there on the part of the magus who impersonates Smerdis and usurps the throne.

As mentioned above, the lying dream at the beginning of Book 7, which urges Xerxes on to his defeat, is not strictly speaking a dynastic dream. Nevertheless, it is extremely important in bringing about a shift in power that will see the decline of Persia and the rise of Greece. There is no real imagery in the dream to be interpreted, just the imposing apparition who delivers the message. The phantom is described as a tall and well-formed man (ἄνδρα...μέγαν τε καὶ εὐειδέα).[35] He addresses Xerxes impersonally as 'Persian' and warns him against changing his

---

35. The same description is given to the figure that appears to Hipparchus in his dream (5.56). There the phantom is also described as ἄνδρα...μέγαν καὶ εὐειδέα. It may also be noted that in both instances the apparition is described as standing over (ἐπιστάντα) the dreamer.

plans to invade Greece. When the phantom appears to Xerxes a second night, he addresses him as 'son of Darius' and warns him even more sternly of the consequences should he fail to attack Greece. This imposing figure in Xerxes' dream is similar to the equally striking Gabriel who appears in Daniel's dreams. Gabriel also is described as a man (איש, 10.5) or like the appearance of a man (כמראה גבר, 8.15),[36] and his unique and impressive form is also accentuated (10.5-6). To these observations we might add that Gabriel likewise addresses Daniel impersonally as 'son of man' (8.17).[37]

The introduction of these human-like figures in the dreams of Xerxes and Daniel leads us to another sphere in which the divine will is manifested and exerts itself in history. If the course of history, particularly the fate of dynasties, is revealed through divinely sent dreams, the execution of the divine will in history is often accomplished with the assistance of heavenly figures. In Herodotus, it is not, generally speaking, the well-known gods of the Greek pantheon who directly interact in human history. Rather, a more generic divine force works its way in the *Histories* through the more indirect means of natural forces, or, as is sometimes the case, through the appearance of heavenly beings of a lesser rank. It is to these that we now turn.

3. *Heavenly Figures and Local Gods*

Although we do not encounter Athena, Apollo, or Ares on the battlefield or otherwise mingling with humans in Herodotus, there do occasionally appear manifestations of heavenly agents.[38] Often the divine agent is surmised to have acted through the occurrence of some unusual event of nature or through an unlikely accumulation of coincidental events. Such is the case with the deliverance of Croesus from the pyre. He prayed to Apollo to save him, and, although it was a clear and windless day, clouds suddenly gathered and a heavy rain fell to extinguish the flames (1.87). This is proof enough for Cyrus that the gods loved Croesus, but Herodotus is silent as to the divine agency behind this event, leaving the reader to make the inference. At other times, Herodotus clearly states his belief that a divine agency is behind some phenomenon of nature. Such is the case with the shipwreck of the Persian fleet due to a storm (8.13). Herodotus comments that all this was done by

---

36. While the apparition in ch. 10 is not explicitly named, it seems to be the same figure as in 8.17 and 9.21 where the name Gabriel does appear.

37. The form of address 'son of man' is akin to the generic address 'Persian' in that it basically means 'human'. It is also related to the patronymic address 'son of Darius' in that it can be rendered 'son of Adam'. Nevertheless, in spite of these similarities we must keep in mind that the true precedent for the single use of this form of address in Daniel is to be found in the generous use of this address in Ezekiel, where the prophet is so called by God.

38. Even one of the clearest instances of divine intervention in human affairs, the deliverance of Croesus from his funeral pyre by Apollo, is accomplished by no direct manifestation of the god, but by a sudden cloudburst to extinguish the flames following upon Croesus's supplication (1.87). It should be pointed out that Herodotus ascribes this story to what the Lydians say concerning Croesus.

God (ὑπὸ τοῦ θεοῦ) in order to reduce the superior size of the Persian fleet. Elsewhere, Herodotus sees unusual coincidences of events as evidence of divine activity. A good example of this may be found in the account of the battle of Mycale (9.100-101). Herodotus notes that this battle took place on the same day as that at Plataea. This coincidence is amplified by the fact that a rumor circulated in the Greek camp just prior to the battle of Mycale that the Greeks had won a victory over the Persians at Plataea. This rumor, which no one at Mycale could have known with certainty at the time, proved true. The mystical link that Herodotus sees between these two battles is further accentuated by the fact that both took place near a temple of Demeter. This unlikely parallelism between distant events cannot for Herodotus be due to mere chance. Rather, he sees the accumulation of coincidences as evidence of a divine ordering of events.

In addition to these indirect inferences of divine influence in history, there also appear in the *Histories* accounts of more direct and unambiguous divine interventions. Among these incidents are the portents and apparitions at Delphi when the Persians threatened to take the sanctuary (8.37-39) and the mysterious figure (noted above) that appears to Xerxes (and Artabanus) in his dream (7.12, 14, 17-18). The manifestation of divine intervention at Delphi is instructive for the many ways in which this intervention is displayed. It begins with the miraculous movement of the sacred weapons from inside the temple of Apollo to the ground in front of the shrine. This is followed by a shower of thunderbolts and the breaking off of two peaks from Mt Parnassus which come crashing down on the Persians. In conjunction with these events, a battle cry is heard coming from within the temple of Athena Pronaea.

Perhaps it is too much to suggest that the account of the separation of two large chunks of rock from the top of Parnassus bears any relationship to the imagery in the dream in Daniel 2. There too we heard of a large rock being taken from a mountain by no human hand.[39] This rock shattered the four-metal statue representing the foreign empires. Still, the imagery of a boulder (or two) being divinely separated from a mountain to crush one's enemies is not a common motif in Israel, Greece, or anyplace else in the ancient Near East. While Daniel may have conceived of this imagery on his own (a possibility that cannot be dismissed), if he did not invent the image, we have no better place to look for a source than in Herodotus. The insistence in Dan. 2.34 and 45 that this stone was cut from the mountain 'not with

---

39. When discussing the vision in ch. 2, it is important to keep in mind that we are dealing with a literary unit that almost certainly predates the visions of chs. 7–12. Even so, the element of the stone cut from the mountain appears to belong to the final composition of the book as realized by the author during the persecution of Antiochus IV. Verse 34 in MT does not mention the stone being cut 'from a mountain'. This detail does appear in LXX and Theodotion. The fact that the interpretation in v. 45 does mention that the stone was cut 'from the mountain' while the vision itself does not supply this detail suggests the possibility of a later addition. This innovation may have been prompted by v. 35 which describes the stone itself as becoming a great mountain (Hartman and Di Lella, *Book of Daniel*, p. 141). Whether this is so or not, there remains the possibility that the form of this image in Dan. 2.45 may owe something to an association with the account in Herodotus 8.37.

hands' (לֹא בִידִין) points to the divine agency in a manner similar to the account in Herodotus 8.37-39. There, just before the account of the thunderbolts and falling mountain tops, we were told that the weapons from the sanctuary were moved, but not by any human, for it was not lawful that anyone should touch them. In both instances the divine agency behind the events narrated is inferred obliquely by the insistence on the fact that what occurred did so with no human agent.

Herodotus goes on to tell of another divine manifestation at Delphi reported by the Persians themselves who survived the thunderbolts, boulders, and pursuing Delphians. They said that they had seen two hoplites of a greater-than-human stature who pursued and slew them (8.38). The people of Delphi, in turn, claimed that these two were the local heroes, Phylacus and Autonous (8.39). Thus we see yet another way in which the action of the high divinity is mediated, not only through natural phenomena (rain, thunder, etc.), but also through the appearance of semi-divine beings, or heroes. James Romm refers to the role of these heroes in Herodotus as occupying 'a kind of middle zone between heaven and earth'.[40] They can be seen as the divine agents that are active in human history in much the same way as the One like a Son of Man, or Gabriel, or Michael is in the book of Daniel. Other examples of these more-than-human or semi-divine apparitions include the figures that appear to Hipparchus (5.56), Xerxes (7.12-14) and Artabanus (7.17-18) in their dreams, and the phantom that confronts Epizelus at the battle of Marathon (6.117). Once again in this latter example, as in each of the others we have examined, the apparition is no named god, but an unnamed human figure of extraordinary size.

There is one more episode in the *Histories*, which, although relatively minor, makes a significant statement about the role played by the multiplicity of divine beings in relation to groups of humans. The passage I am referring to is the address of Xerxes to the most notable Persians before crossing the Hellespont (7.53). Xerxes concludes his speech by calling upon the Persians to pray to 'the gods who have the land of Persia as their lot' (θεοῖσι οἳ Περσίδα γῆν λελόγχασι).[41] The use of the verb λαγχάνω in the perfect points to the role of these gods as the 'tutelary deities'[42] of Persia, whose charge it is to protect it. Their function appears to be quite similar to that of the 'princes' of Greece and Persia from the book of Daniel.[43]

---

40. J. Romm, *Herodotus* (New Haven: Yale University Press, 1998), p. 143.

41. This reference to 'national gods' is somewhat unique in the *Histories*. For the most part, Herodotus identifies the Greek gods with their foreign counterparts. In 2.156 he equates Apollo and Horus, Demeter and Isis, Artemis and Bubastis, while in 3.27 Apis is equated with the Greek Epaphus. Likewise, in 1.131, he gives the various names for Aphrodite among the Assyrians (Mylitta), Arabians (Alilat), and Persians (Mitra). The last of these identifications is obviously a gross error on Herodotus's part. In spite of the general identifications made between the major gods, there is room for regional distinctiveness (see 1.131 where the original Persian deities are distinguished from those they learned from other peoples). The Persian gods to whom Xerxes refers may be akin to local heroes such as Phylacus and Autonous at Delphi (8.39) who show particular concern for the territory held sacred to them.

42. LSJ, p. 1022.

43. In Daniel there are two levels to the divine realm: that of the 'princes', or subordinate supernatural figures, and that of God. In Herodotus there is yet another level. There are the local

Each nation is seen to have a divine patron or group of divine patrons responsible for that nation's wellbeing. The protection which these beings offer their client states is expressed through battle on their behalf. Thus it is that Gabriel in Daniel 10 speaks of confrontations with the princes of Persia and Greece. Likewise, the prayer that Xerxes asks his men to make to the gods who have charge of Persia takes place after he has exhorted them to fight bravely, just before crossing the Hellespont to do battle with the Greeks. The clear assumption is that this is a prayer for assistance in the impending war with the Greeks.

Apparitions and manifestations of divine forces acting in history are thus common to both the book of Daniel and the *Histories* of Herodotus. In neither case, however, do these forces negate the very real human agency which each of these works acknowledges. Rather, there can be seen two parallel planes of activity that somehow work in tandem, although the way in which they interact is not always clear. In Daniel it would appear that the course of human history is viewed as a mirror of heavenly events. Scholars often speak of the apocalyptic world view in Daniel as one of awaiting a direct intervention from God and thus dismissing human (military) resistance such as the Maccabees as 'but a little help'.[44] In light of the dual planes of activity witnessed in Daniel (especially in the 'princes' of Persia, Greece, and Israel mirroring earthly events), it is better not to diametrically oppose human and divine activity as if one excludes the other. The divine does have precedence, but this is not to say that the book of Daniel endorses an entirely passive or quietistic position. The images of the rock torn from the mountain without a hand being put to it, or that of the One like a Son of Man coming on the clouds to pronounce judgment on the four beasts both point to a divine response. Yet it would be just as wrong to say that this divine intervention excludes human activity or is 'outside of history' as it would be to say that the activity of the 'princes' of Persia and Greece precludes any human action by Cyrus, Xerxes, or Alexander.

The same perspective can be seen in Herodotus. While there are several statements that emphasize the immutability of fate or what must be (e.g. 1.91; 7.17; 8.53, 65) and the impossibility for humans to counter the gods or destiny (e.g. 1.87; 3.43; 9.16), there are also passages that indicate that such divinely decreed events only take place through the cooperation of human agents. Such is the case with the revised advice that Artabanus gives to Xerxes after he too has experienced the king's

---

heroes or regional gods; there are also the major gods who are considered to be the same for all peoples (though called by different names); and there is fate or one's destined lot (μοῖρα) to which even the gods are subject (see 1.91, where the Pythia responds to the messengers of Croesus that none can escape their destiny, not even a god).

44. The interpretation of 'little help' in Dan. 11.34 as referring to the Maccabees goes back to Porphyry who considered them but little help because of the fact that both Mattathias and Judas were killed. The modern adaptation of this interpretation posits greater antipathy between Daniel's *maskilim* and the Maccabees (see, e.g., Collins, *Daniel*, pp. 66, 386). This has also led to something of a false dichotomy by which Daniel's less-than-enthusiastic presentation of the Maccabees is seen necessarily to imply an apocalyptic pacifism. See N. Gottwald (*The Hebrew Bible: A Social-Literary Introduction* [Philadelphia: Fortress Press, 1985], p. 594) who notes this common perception and adds that it may be a 'misimpression'. He cites Dan. 11.32 against a pacifistic interpretation, with its affirmation that 'the people who know their God shall stand firm and take action'.

dream (7.18). The dream has made him realize that God is at work in the matter of the campaign against Greece, although he mistakenly believes that the gods will bring defeat upon the Greeks. Even though he sees the coming war and its outcome as ordained by God, he urges Xerxes to do his part in bringing it about. The fact that an event is foretold as something that must happen does not negate the necessity of human activity in bringing it about. Nor does the divinely ordained nature of events exculpate human agents from their role in accomplishing these events. So it is that Croesus, although doomed to a bad end foretold by the Delphic Oracle (1.13), is equally to blame for his downfall on account of his own acts of *hubris* (1.34) and due to the superior military genius of Cyrus (1.70-71). As John Gould writes in his chapter on why things happen in Herodotus:

> parallel sets of causation, one human, the other supernatural, neither of which renders the other inoperative, are as much a feature of Greek thinking about accountability as they are of their storytelling from Homer onwards, and would not in themselves have proved in any way surprising to Herodotus' original audience... The function of supernatural causation is not, as we might think, to replace or override empirical cause and effect: ...Nor is it the function of a theory of supernatural causation to remove moral responsibility, to make men and women no longer accountable for their actions.[45]

In spite of the efforts of some scholars to defend Herodotus from his own fantastic accounts of supernatural phenomena and thus make a 'serious' historian out of him, the father of history firmly accepts the existence of gods and their active role in human history. He approaches accounts of the supernatural with the same critical appraisal with which he deals with other events that are reported to him. He does not necessarily believe every account of divine intervention, but neither does he discount them *a priori*. Indeed, sometimes the turn of historical events is so remarkable that Herodotus cannot but affirm that divine forces must be at work in it (8.13; 9.100). While certain manifestations of the divine in history may be clear to him, the realm of the divine in itself is beyond the scope of his work. As previously mentioned, he avoids repeating what the Egyptian priests told him about the gods because, as he claims, no one knows more about them than any other (2.3).[46]

If Herodotus is content to affirm the impossibility of knowing with certainty the ways in which the divine works in history, for Daniel the question appears somewhat more urgent. Both authors recognize a law of divine retribution—a nemesis that brings down the arrogant and punishes transgressors. But while Herodotus is writing of the divine envy that leads to the destruction of the enemies of Greece, Daniel must deal with an apparent suspension or delay in the law of divine retribution. The arrogant and impious King Antiochus IV is still in power and the temple

---

45. Gould, *Herodotus*, pp. 70-71.

46. As How and Wells (*Commentary on Herodotus*, I, p. 157) have noted, the meaning of ἴσον περὶ αὐτῶν ἐπίστασθαι has been much disputed. It is generally taken in a pessimistic sense concerning what can be known of divine things (see p. 84 n. 6 above). This corresponds to the qualifying statement that Herodotus adds when expressing his own opinion concerning divine affairs (9.65): εἴ τι περὶ τῶν θείων πρηγμάτων δοκέειν δεῖ. For Herodotus the divine activity in history is certain, but it is also mysterious and not wholly accessible to human knowledge.

remains desecrated at the time of Daniel's dream visions. Thus, for Daniel, the mysterious ways of God in history are communicated through puzzling dreams, cryptic writing, and symbolic scripture, but in each case a sure interpretation is provided which reaffirms the sovereignty of God over human history. So to the question 'why?' on the level of particular historical events a certain amount of uncertainty remains. The ways of God are as mysterious as the enigmatic visions that communicate them. But to the question 'why?' on a more fundamental level, the book of Daniel affirms a belief in a universal plan of God in history. God who alone is wise, God who is all-powerful, will bring about the punishment of the wicked and the glorification of the righteous to which Daniel looks forward (12.1-3). This final action of God in history that the book of Daniel reports is to be accompanied by the appearance of 'One like a Son of Man' (7.13) or the prince of Daniel's people, Michael (12.1). As we have already seen, this divine agent does not negate the very real role of human agents in the accomplishing of the divine plan in history. Rather, what is affirmed is that there are more forces at work in history than meet the human eye.

The same can be said regarding the *Histories* of Herodotus. We saw that at the beginning of his work, Herodotus points to the human agent—Croesus—who began the conflict between east and west. This marks a break from the precedent of Homer who had pointed to the god Apollo as the instigator of the Trojan War. But while Herodotus tells us of human affairs, the divine is ever lurking just below the surface. One cannot always distinguish clearly whether an event has a human or divine cause. It is rather more correct to say that events in Herodotus have both human and divine causes. As we have seen, the one does not negate the other. Perhaps the most telling statement in this regard is made at 7.139. There Herodotus informs us who was responsible for saving Greece from the Persian force led by Xerxes. It was the Athenians, but only 'after the gods' (μετά γε θεούς) who drove back the aggressor king. Thus we are given a human and a divine agency responsible for the Greek victory at the climax of Herodotus's work. While human and divine causation are both affirmed, it is the human we more often see. Still, for Herodotus no less than for Daniel, it is the divine that holds the primary position. For although this divine agency works in tandem with human agents, allowing humans to cooperate with the divine plan, there is ultimately nothing that humans can do to counter the will of heaven or what must be. This is tragically born out in the Croesus *logos*. It is also seen quite dramatically in the deceptive dream of Xerxes that urges him on to his fate.

Both Herodotus and Daniel present us with the mysterious hand of God in history. It falls to humans to try to perceive the divine will as it is manifested through various phenomena of nature, uncanny coincidences, dreams, oracles, Scriptures, and portents. By correctly interpreting these divine messages, individuals can endeavor to act in harmony with the divine force in history and so do their part to realize the divine plan. Failure to understand these enigmatic divine manifestations leads to tragic defeat, for no one can counter the will of God (Herodotus 9.16) or avert that which must be (Herodotus 7.17). The revelations given by God of future events are for their part certain and true (Dan. 2.45; 10.1).

Chapter 5

DANIEL'S THEOLOGY OF HISTORY

1. *Daniel as Greek* Historia

It has been my contention throughout the preceding chapters that the book of Daniel expresses a very real and concrete concern for history. By history I do not mean merely the end of history or eschatology, but a broad sweep of contemporary and relatively recent events connected across space and time by causal relationships. The widely disseminated views of scholars such as Martin Noth and Gerhard von Rad, who would deny the existence of any true historical interest in apocalyptic literature in general (and in Daniel in particular) simply do not hold up under scrutiny.[1] The book of Daniel covers a historical period of approximately 420 years, from the destruction of the temple by Nebuchadnezzar to its profanation by Antiochus IV. Daniel's own calculations for the duration of this period arrive at a figure of 490 years or 'seventy weeks [of years]' (Dan. 9.24). This number comes from a new, symbolic interpretation of the prophecies in Jer. 25.11 and 29.10, taking the seventy years of exile prophesied by Jeremiah to refer to weeks (of years). Thus, according to Daniel's understanding, the 490-year period with which he is concerned is the 'exile'. This clearly defined period of history is of paramount importance for Daniel who sees the unfolding events around him as having been foretold through prophecy and revealed through visions. Far from emptying history of any meaning, Daniel sees revealed in history the unfolding of the plan of God. If, by this emphasis on the divine role in history, one perceives a devaluation of history understood as human actions, then one should acknowledge the same devaluation throughout the Hebrew Scriptures and in Herodotus as well. As should be clear by now, however, neither the earlier Hebrew Scriptures, nor Herodotus, nor Daniel diminishes the significance of human actions, despite their emphasis on a divine plan or a divine will operating within history.

While the book of Daniel is not a work of history in the modern sense of the word, it nevertheless could come under the ancient category of history.[2] In the

---

1.　See Noth, 'The Understanding of History', p. 214; and von Rad, *Old Testament Theology*, II, p. 304.

2.　Echoing this judgment, P. Grelot pointed to the way Josephus made use of Daniel as a source for his own historical writing: '[Le livre de Daniel] ait pu relever de l'*historia* conçue à la manière des Grecs. Nous en avons la preuve dans les *Antiquités juives* de Flavius Josèphe, qui en fait un usage abondant (X,x, 1-7)' (P. Grelot, 'Histoire et Eschatologie dans le Livre de Daniel', in Association Catholique Française pour l'Étude de la Bible, *Apocalypses et Théologie de l'Espérance: Congrès de Toulouse [1975]* [Paris: Les Éditions du Cerf, 1977], pp. 63-109 [75]).

preceding chapters I have argued that the book of Daniel does contain accurate, although allusive, historical narratives. This historical material in Daniel was influenced by the Greek historiographical tradition, which was flourishing at the time the book of Daniel was written and which was well-known throughout the Hellenized world, including Palestine. Within the Greek historiographical tradition, it is the *Histories* of Herodotus in particular that hold a central position as the foundational work. This centrality of Herodotus's work manifests itself in two respects. In the first place, we may note how this highly original work spawned a host of other histories. Imitation and admiration of Herodotus can clearly be seen in the works of Theopompus and Ephorus in the fourth century. Even amid the implicit and explicit criticisms of a Thucydides or a Ctesias there is an undeniable debt to the father of history. Herodotus provided the blueprint for writing history with his emphasis on relating political history and on explaining the causes behind the events he relates. Secondly, we should highlight the staying power of Herodotus's *Histories*. His work continued to be widely read throughout the centuries following its publication as one of the two main exemplars of the historical genre (the other being that of Thucydides), which anyone receiving a Greek education would almost certainly know.[3] The *Histories* quickly became a classic and remained popular throughout the Hellenistic period and beyond.

The indications that the author of Daniel did indeed know this work have been abundantly cited in previous chapters. As an educated Palestinian Jew of the second century BCE, Daniel certainly had the opportunity for exposure to Herodotus's work. It should come as no surprise that this Jewish author of a work composed in Hebrew and Aramaic was also familiar with the Greek language and its literature. James Barr has carefully noted the rapid advance of the Greek language in Palestine during the Hellenistic period. The Greek correspondence of the Jew Tobias, which we find in the Zenon Papyri (c. 259–57 BCE), provides an early indication of this advance.[4] Even more telling is the fact that 'From the third century BCE on apart from the inscriptions on tombs and ossuaries and in synagogues, inscriptions in Palestine are almost entirely in Greek'.[5] The translation of the Hebrew Scriptures into Greek, begun in the third century, likewise bears witness to the diffusion of the Greek language among Jews. And although the LXX is closely associated with the Jewish community in Alexandria, the very tradition concerning this translation identifies the translators as Palestinian Jews.[6] Whether or not this was in fact the case, the account presupposes the plausibility of educated Palestinian Jews capable of translating Hebrew and Aramaic into Greek.

Greek was of course the official language of the Seleucid dynasty and the *lingua franca* of the world that had once been Alexander's empire. But even more than being simply the language of administration and international commerce, Greek

---

3. Quintilian, in his discussion of important authors to be read, gives Herodotus and Thucydides the place of honor far above all other historians (*Institutio Oratoria* 10.1.73).

4. J. Barr, 'Hebrew, Aramaic and Greek in the Hellenistic Age', in Davies and Finkelstein (eds.), *The Cambridge History of Judaism*, II, pp. 79-114 (101).

5. Barr, 'Hebrew, Aramaic and Greek', p. 102.

6. *Letter of Aristeas* 32. The account is repeated by Josephus (*Ant.* 12.2.5).

was also the language of education and culture. Although, as Barr points out, the importance of Hebrew and Aramaic as literary languages did not diminish among the Jews due to the close relation of these languages with Jewish religion, Greek became a desirable acquisition for the elite.[7] It is reasonable to suggest that a cultured Jew such as the author of Daniel, who was versant in both Hebrew and Aramaic, would also have studied the Greek language through its major literary works. To be a prominent individual in Seleucid Palestine, Greek was a *sine qua non*. And to learn Greek, one read the standard texts of poetry, philosophy, rhetoric, and history, among which Herodotus figured prominently.

The hypothesis, then, that Daniel knew the *Histories* of Herodotus is firmly grounded in the cultural climate of Seleucid Palestine. To be a pious Jew at this time (which Daniel certainly was) was by no means equivalent to being uneducated (which Daniel certainly was not). This hypothesis is born out by consideration of the many parallels between the *Histories* and the book of Daniel. The use of a scheme of successive empires, the similar accounts of the deaths of the impious kings Cambyses and Antiochus, the many dreams which foretell the rise and fall of kings and kingdoms, the intertwining of divine and human causation behind the events of history—all these elements point to Daniel's knowledge and use of Herodotus.

2. *Daniel as Apocalypse*

In arguing that the historical material in Daniel is reflective of an active interest in history, I am countering the widespread view that finds in Daniel a passive apocalyptic quietism that merely awaits God's definitive action.[8] This view often portrays apocalyptic writers and communities as despairing of any possibility of change within the present, evil world structure.[9] The only solution is presented as an end of

---

7. Barr, 'Hebrew, Aramaic and Greek', p. 101.

8. This widely held opinion of apocalyptic quietism in Daniel is succinctly expressed by J.J. Collins who states: 'Other apocalypses are quietistic. Daniel shows little enthusiasm for the Maccabees' (J.J. Collins, 'From Prophecy to Apocalypticism: The Expectation of the End', in *idem* [ed.], *The Encyclopedia of Apocalypticism*. I. *The Origins of Apocalypticism in Judaism and Christianity* [New York: Continuum, 2000], pp. 129-61 [159]). As greatly as I am indebted to the work of Collins, I cannot agree with him here. The argument is largely from silence or else from an interpretation of Dan. 11.34 which understands the 'little help' as a disparaging reference to the Maccabees. It is unclear whether this passage does in fact refer to the Maccabean resistance (which would have been in its very earliest stage of existence at the time Daniel was written) or, if it is the case that the Maccabees are here indicated, it is not certain whether the passage is even intended to be disparaging. If they are a 'little help' because of their initially small numbers and humble beginnings, they are help nonetheless. The true indictment in Dan. 11.34 is not against the little help but against those who do nothing to aid the *maskilim* or those who join them insincerely.

9. This view often finds expression in surveys of the Old Testament, contrasting the apocalyptic writers to the prophets. See, for example, the presentation of L. Boadt, *Reading the Old Testament* (New York: Paulist Press, 1984), pp. 512-13. I must emphasize once more that by questioning this widespread view on apocalyptic literature it is not my intention to deny any eschatological, quietistic, or deterministic tendencies in this literature in general. What I am saying is that

history and a salvation beyond history. I believe that this stereotypical view does not correspond to the data of the book of Daniel. It is perpetuated by a selective reading and a kind of circular reasoning that extracts an 'apocalyptic' worldview from a part of the text and then uses what was thus pulled out of the text as a key by which the rest of the text is then interpreted. A good example of this procedure can be seen in the treatment that is often given to the prayer of Daniel in ch. 9. Because the Deuteronomic theology expressed in this prayer is considered *a priori* to be contrary to the apocalyptic worldview gleaned from the rest of Daniel, it is often discounted as secondary.[10] But this does not have to be the case. It may appear to us that a Deuteronomic theology in which suffering is caused by human sinfulness is mutually exclusive of an apocalyptic theology in which suffering is either not explained or appears to result from a preordained divine plan. Yet the same interplay of human and divine causation that we saw in Herodotus is at work in the book of Daniel as well. I have demonstrated that while there is a contrast and dynamic tension between human action in history and the definitive action of God in the book of Daniel, the latter does not take place outside of history, nor is it necessarily independent of human agency. Daniel, like Herodotus, sees all historical events as an interplay between human and divine causation. The fortunes of the various human kingdoms, which undeniably involve free human actions (a fact more evident in chs. 8 and 11 than in ch. 7), have a divine level of causation no less than the final establishment of the fifth kingdom at the end of days. And this fifth and final kingdom established by God, while brought about through divine agents such as Michael or One like a Son of Man, in no way precludes the cooperative action of God's people on earth. As Bernhard Anderson has stated:

> This extreme emphasis on God's absolute sway in human affairs was not intended to encourage complacency... On the contrary, the confidence that history moves inevitably and by prearranged plan toward the Kingdom of God fired the zeal of a small band of Jews, and enabled them to act and hope when everything seemed against them.[11]

the book of Daniel, while having a great influence on later apocalypses, cannot properly be understood in relation to these other apocalypses only. To attempt to do so is to lose sight of the connections between Daniel and earlier biblical traditions. While much is similar between Daniel and other apocalypses, there is also much that is very different. Boccaccini rightly pointed out the very different thought between the book of Daniel and 1 Enoch ('È Daniele un Testo Apocalitico?', pp. 267-302). I believe that one also finds at times a tendency to read back into the book of Daniel later developments from apocalyptic writings such as *4 Ezra* or the book of Revelation. For example, one does find a heightened determinism in *4 Ezra* which postulates an 'evil heart' (*4 Ezra* 3.20-27) in humans which necessarily leads them to sin. One does not find this strict determinism in Daniel, but the coexistence of God's eternal plan with the free actions of human beings. Likewise the sharp dualism between the two worlds or ages which one finds in *4 Ezra* 7.50 is not present in Daniel.

    10.   Hartman and Di Lella (*Book of Daniel*, pp. 245-46) also give linguistic and stylistic arguments for the prayer's being a later insertion. A. Lacocque (*The Book of Daniel* [trans. D. Pellauer; Atlanta: John Knox Press, 1979], p. 180) responds to such arguments by suggesting the author of Daniel made use of traditional material, but that this material was not inserted at a secondary stage.

    11.   B.W. Anderson, *Understanding the Old Testament* (Englewood Cliffs, NJ: Prentice–Hall, 4th edn, 1986), p. 631.

The *maskilim* are called to take action on earth—an action which mirrors the heavenly struggle between the 'princes' of the kingdoms of earth.

A somewhat different approach to the question of the historical interest of the book of Daniel and to so-called apocalyptic views of history has been taken by Gabriele Boccaccini. Boccaccini does not follow the usual argument with its assumptions that apocalypticism has no real interest in history and that the book of Daniel is an apocalyptic work, therefore Daniel has no real interest in history.[12] Rather, he contrasts the historical perspective of the book of Daniel with the contemporary Book of Dream Visions (1 En. 83–90) in order to argue that Daniel is indeed truly concerned with history, but the theology of history in the book of Daniel is so contrary to that found in the Book of Dream Visions that it cannot in fact be considered apocalyptic![13] His approach has the advantage of critically evaluating the historical material in Daniel without the anti-historical assumptions so often found in analyses of apocalyptic texts. I have some difficulty, however, accepting his premise that the Enochic tradition should be regarded as somehow normative or as having precedence in defining what we should term 'apocalyptic'.[14] Given the history of the usage of the term, it seems more appropriate to speak of apocalyptic as a broader, generic category under which one might find a number of different movements and writings reflecting more particular circumstances and

12.   The negative appraisal of apocalyptic literature's conception of history has been succinctly expressed both by Noth: 'We must accept the judgment that "the concept of history...scarcely plays any marked role" for the apocalyptic writings' ('Understanding of History', p. 214) and by von Rad: 'If one compares this [apocalyptic] conception of history with those produced by Israel in earlier periods, then one will have to speak of a characteristic theological or, to be more precise, soteriological depletion of history' (*Wisdom in Israel* [Harrisburg, PA: Trinity Press International, 1972], p. 273).

13.   Boccaccini, 'È Daniele un Testo Apocalittico?'. He points out that Daniel does not share the view found in the Book of Dream Visions that the degeneration of history stems from an 'original' sin (p. 279). Rather, Boccaccini sees the historical thought of Daniel organized around two key concepts: (1) the sovereignty that belongs to God, which is given and taken away according to the divine will at the established times (chs. 2–7); and (2) the cause of the degeneration of history is found in the transgression of the covenant, which has brought upon the people the curses contained therein (chs. 8–12). In regard to this second point, I believe Boccaccini is correct in seeing the necessary connection between the prayer of Daniel in ch. 9 and the rest of the book (pp. 284-85). To summarize Boccaccini's argument: without the prayer in ch. 9 Daniel would lack any internal logic. The cause of the calamitous foreign rule of the four kingdoms extending from Nebuchadnezzar to Antiochus IV is not found elsewhere in the book of Daniel. Daniel in fact limits his view of history to this period of the four kingdoms; there is no earlier history by which to explain it such as one finds in the Book of Dream Visions with its comprehensive historical review. The cause of this 'period of exile' with which the book of Daniel is concerned is known from the Scriptures to be the transgression of the covenant (Lev. 26.27-39; Deut. 28.63-68). Daniel accepts this traditional perspective. The real question or concern for Daniel, then, is not why there exists this period of 'exile', but how long it will last.

14.   I would also like to reiterate my objection to the dichotomy between apocalyptic and earlier biblical traditions. Boccaccini tends to perpetuate this dichotomy by presenting Daniel's continuity with earlier traditions regarding the covenant as evidence against the work's being truly apocalyptic.

ideologies. Thus I would agree with Boccaccini that the book of Daniel and the Book of Dream Visions do in fact reflect very different ideologies, evidenced in part by their respective views of history. Nevertheless, they are not so totally different that we cannot call them both apocalyptic. They share not only a common genre of symbolic visions of celestial and earthly realities; they also share a common perspective of an oppressed group struggling to reconcile their religious tradition with the current crisis in which they find themselves. So, while their responses may differ, their method is largely the same. Thus we might speak of both Enochic and Danielic apocalypticism. The latter is more closely related to the earlier biblical traditions which recognized God's action in history primarily in terms of the covenant relationship.

One need not, indeed should not, define 'apocalyptic' as necessarily sectarian. Daniel is as foundational a work within the Judeo-Christian apocalyptic tradition as Herodotus is within the Greek historiographical tradition. The influence of Daniel upon later apocalypses such as the *Similitudes of Enoch*, *4 Ezra*, and the New Testament book of Revelation is enormous. Yet the book of Daniel found acceptance not only among sectarians at Qumran and Christians, but in what we might term 'mainstream' or 'common'[15] Judaism as well. Its canonical status was never called into question even while debate about other books such as Ezekiel, Qoheleth, Song of Songs, Ruth, and Esther continued well into the first century CE.[16] Since the book of Daniel was perfectly at home within a rather traditional Judaism, it should come as no surprise that traditional Jewish (or Israelite) theology is also at home in the book of Daniel. The reaffirmation of Deuteronomic theology in Daniel (as well as Daniel's connecting the current persecution to earlier events in his people's history) demonstrates the theological and historical continuity between the book of Daniel and earlier biblical traditions.

3. *Daniel's Theology of History*

a. *Continuity with Biblical Traditions*

What then are we to say about the theology of history that emerges from the book of Daniel? If it is not directly at odds with the already-existing histories of Israel and Judah, what is its relationship to these? The Deuteronomistic History placed a high premium on human free will. The human response to the divine covenant was seen as determining the course of the people's future:

15. This is the terminology used by E.P. Sanders ('Judaism as Religion', in his *The Historical Figure of Jesus* [London: Penguin Books, 1993], pp. 33-48). By 'common Judaism' he designates the common Jewish tradition that transcended party lines, realizing that 'most Jews were members of no party' (p. 48).

16. See R.E. Brown and R.F. Collins, 'Canonicity', in R.E. Brown, J.A. Fitzmyer, and R.E. Murphy (eds.), *The New Jerome Biblical Commentary* (Englewood Cliffs, NJ: Prentice–Hall, 1990), pp. 1034-54. See also J.A. Sanders, 'Canon: Hebrew Bible', in *ABD*, I, pp. 837-52. The Talmud (*Shabbath* 13b; *Hagigah* 13a; *Menahoth* 45a) tells of later objections to Ezekiel based on apparent contradictions to the Torah. Some time after 70 CE, the rabbinical school at Jamnia specifically discussed the acceptance of Qoheleth and Song of Songs.

> I call heaven and earth to witness against you today that I have set before you life
> and death, blessings and curses. Choose life so that you and your descendants may
> live, loving the LORD your God, obeying him, and holding fast to him; for that
> means life to you and length of days, so that you may live in the land that the
> LORD swore to give to your ancestors, to Abraham, to Isaac, and to Jacob. (Deut.
> 30.19-20)

According to the Deuteronomist, obedience and faithfulness to the covenant brought
prosperity and wellbeing in the land, while transgression brought castigation and
ultimately the exile. As previously mentioned, this perspective reappears in the
prayer of Daniel in ch. 9. Rather than viewing this prayer as an anomaly or a redactional interpolation, it makes more sense to realize that the traditional view expressed here is not diametrically opposed to the historical understanding expressed
elsewhere in Daniel.

We must break away from the prejudice that prunes the text of those parts which
we have already decided it could not possibly have. Such prudence is rewarded and
confirmed by the analysis I have set forth in this study; namely, that the so-called
'apocalyptic determinism' which sees all events as having their cause in God's
preordained plan of history is not opposed to human free will and the historical
understanding that flows from it. Rather, the book of Daniel, like the *Histories* of
Herodotus, conceives of two parallel planes of historical activity and causation.
Events on earth mirror those in heaven, and divine agents may even manifest themselves on the human plane to make clear that God is active in human history. Neither
Daniel nor Herodotus, however, sees this divine activity as negating human free
will and action.

By the same token, the overarching divine activity does not deprive human
activity of the praise or blame that is due to it. Herodotus has explicitly told us in
his opening words that he intends to preserve the glory of human deeds. And if
events such as the end of the house of Gyges in the fifth generation are preordained
(1.13 and 1.91), it is not fate alone that ruins Croesus. He too is to blame for his
aggressive military expansion. Herodotus singles him out for blame as the one who
first injured the Greeks (1.5). Croesus is also guilty of presumption and arrogance.
Herodotus points out the blameworthy presumption of Croesus in the exchange
with Solon (1.30-33). It is for Croesus's own sin, and not simply that of Gyges, that
divine retribution falls upon him (1.34). On an even more immediate level, the
undoing of Croesus is due to his poor military decisions compared to those of
Cyrus (1.76-84). In Herodotus, then, humans are responsible for their actions even
if they are aided or opposed by divine forces, and even if the ultimate outcome of
their actions is predetermined as 'what must be' (7.17).[17] Similarly, returning to the

---

17.   E.R. Dodds (*The Greeks and the Irrational* [Berkeley: University of California Press,
1951]) points out that throughout Greek literature, the concepts of fate and free will are not mutually exclusive. Commenting on a passage from the *Iliad* (19.86-89) where Agamemnon blames
Zeus, his fate (*moira*), and the Erinys for his actions, Dodds writes: 'by blaming his *moira* Agamemnon no more declares himself a systematic determinist than does the modern Greek peasant
when he uses similar language. To ask whether Homer's people are determinists or libertarians is a
fatalistic anachronism: the question has never occurred to them, and if it were put to them it would

book of Daniel, we can see that the perspective of the prayer in ch. 9, in which the persisting exile of foreign domination is seen as punishment for the people's sins, is fully in line with the rest of the book where the emphasis is laid upon the divine plan in history. The one does not negate the other. Predetermined events, whether by fate or God's plan, do not negate the freedom and responsibility inherent in human actions. This holds true both for Herodotus and for Daniel.

In response to those who regard the Deuteronomic prayer in Daniel 9 as secondary and irreconcilable with the theology of history in the rest of the chapter (and indeed the whole book), two comments are in order.[18] First of all, while it is true that 'the theology of history in Daniel 9 is very different from the Deuteronomic theology of the prayer [in the same chapter]',[19] these two theologies are not diametrically opposed, but rather two sides of the same coin. One emphasizes the human cause of events, the other focuses on the divine. Both are necessary elements of Daniel's overall theology of history. In the second place, the Deuteronomic theology, with its emphasis on reward or punishment based on whether the people remain faithful to the covenant or not, is not entirely absent from the rest of the book of Daniel. The 'holy covenant' is conspicuously mentioned twice in Daniel 11 at vv. 28 and 30. These verses also make a clear distinction between those who forsake the covenant and those who do not. We are told that the king of the south will 'pay heed' (וְיָבֵן) to the former group. Regardless of the precise meaning of the Hebrew verb בִּין in this context, the point I would like to make is that the two groups receive different treatment based upon their actions in relation to the covenant.[20] The same can be said of those who will be resurrected in Dan. 12.2; some receive the reward of life, others the punishment of disgrace. Human free will and responsibility are clearly implied by the reward accorded to some and the punishment to others. Verse 3 then explicitly connects this retribution with human action.

---

be very difficult to make them understand what it meant' (p. 7). With regard to Herodotus in particular, Dodds highlights the fact that 'history is overdetermined' (p. 30), being the outcome of both human actions and divine jealousy or *phthonos*. The same point is made regarding the Jewish apocalyptic writers by D.S. Russell (*The Method and Message of Jewish Apocalyptic* [Philadelphia: Westminster Press, 1964], p. 232): 'So it is also with the apocalyptic writers. The clash of human freedom and divine control had not as yet become a conscious problem, so that these two apparently contradictory points of view could be expressed side by side without any intellectual difficulty.'

18.   I should also mention here that the attempt itself to separate 'secondary' from 'primary' material is not without its assumptions and value judgments. While it can be a useful enterprise in understanding the history and formation of a text, it can also give an exaggerated importance to 'earlier' forms, neglecting the fact that for at least someone (and especially for the communities that accepted the 'final' form of the text as normative), the present arrangement of the text was meaningful. When considering a book with such an obvious compositional history as Daniel, the terms 'primary' and 'secondary' become almost meaningless. Though the visions were obviously written at a later date than the court tales, it makes little sense to speak of chs. 7–12 *in toto* as secondary. They are essential to the book of Daniel as we know it.

19.   Collins, *Daniel*, p. 360.

20.   The basic meaning of the root בִּין is 'to discern' or 'distinguish'. It is unclear what specific action of Antiochus is being hinted at here.

It is those who act wisely and those who lead many to righteousness who receive the reward. So, while this traditional covenant dynamic of divine retribution of free human actions is embedded within the larger framework of God's preordained plan for history, it is not annihilated by it. Within the divine plan of history found in Daniel, there is still the acknowledgment that human individuals are active and free participants in the historical drama, and that as such their actions will receive their due reward or punishment.

The false dichotomy between human and divine causation in history that has been applied to Daniel and other apocalyptic works (and which has led to the so-called 'apocalyptic' worldview of divine determinism which negates or minimizes the importance of human free will) is further aggravated by the division scholars make between the historical and the eschatological components of Daniel's visions. While we can detect a distinct break where Daniel departs from recounting history through *ex eventu* prophecies and proceeds with actual speculation about the future, it would be a mistake to identify Daniel's future prophecies exclusively with the end of time and history. It is highly doubtful that Daniel shared our abstract conception of the end of time which we have read back into his many references to 'the end'.[21] Expressions such as 'at the end of days' can simply mean 'after some days have passed' or 'after awhile'.[22] It certainly need not imply that no further days will

---

21. J.J. Collins ('The Meaning of "The End" in the Book of Daniel', in H.W. Attridge, J.J. Collins and T.H. Tobin [eds.], *Of Scribes and Scrolls: Studies on the Hebrew Bible, Intertestamental Judaism, and Christian Origins* [New York: University Press of America, 1990], pp. 91-98) finds a variety of meanings for 'the end' (קץ) in Dan. 7–12. This expression is associated with the end of the persecution, the restoration of the temple cult, and the resurrection of the dead. At least with regard to the first two of these three referents, Daniel was looking towards a historical event and not history's end. As we have seen, the book of Daniel is not concerned with the whole of history, but with a particular period of history—the period of the 'exile' of foreign domination. The end of this period is indeed envisioned, but this does not justify the claim that Daniel points to an end of history. It is more accurate to say that Daniel anticipates a new period of history marked by the kingdom of God's holy ones.

22. Similar to the expression לקץ הימין (usually translated 'at the end of days', this is the phrase with which the Hebrew portion of Daniel ends) are the Aramaic and Hebrew expressions באחרית יומיא and באחרית הימים found in Dan. 2.28 and 10.14 respectively. Both refer to visions of the future. But as these visions are *ex eventu* prophecies, they refer to historical events that have already happened—events that are part of history. There is no need, then, to suggest an end to history when speaking of the non-*ex eventu* prophecies. These prophecies (death of Antiochus, restoration of temple cult, resurrection of dead) refer to a new historical period after that of the 'exile'. And while the resurrection of the dead certainly implies for the modern reader a metahistorical category, it is not necessarily such for Daniel. It is certainly closely connected to the vision in Ezek. 37 as an image of restoration. If Daniel moves beyond this in proposing an actual resurrection as integral to that restoration, it still does not necessitate an end to history. Rather, history's continuation is implied in resurrected life, which is not the same concept as that which we commonly refer to as afterlife. One may compare the account in the book of Revelation where history is envisioned as continuing for a thousand years after the first resurrection (Rev. 20.4). One may also compare the use of the similar expression מקץ ימים found elsewhere throughout the Bible (Gen. 4.3; 2 Sam. 14.26; 1 Kgs 17.7; Jer. 13.6). Once again, what is referred to is the passing of an indeterminate amount of time, not an 'end of days' in the sense of history coming to an end with no more days following.

follow those being described. The visions in Daniel are undoubtedly speaking about a significant moment in history when they describe God's establishment of a definitive kingdom 'at the end of days'. But this need not imply an event at the end or outside of history. The temptation for us is to read the symbolic imagery of Daniel literally when we pass beyond those images that we can identify historically. But the coming of 'One like a Son of Man' or the victorious battle of Michael is still the heavenly counterpart of what Daniel sees as a very real and anticipated historical event on earth—the ending of the exile through the re-establishment of an autonomous Jewish kingdom. Although in the future and not yet realized, the cosmic imagery of these final visions reflects a historical reality no less than the fantastic imagery of the beasts (chs. 7 and 8) or the patron spirits (ch. 10), which we readily identify with earthly kingdoms and historical events.

We have to ask ourselves whether the cataclysmic upheaval depicted in chs. 7 and 12 refers necessarily or exclusively to the end of the world or the end of time. Does it not more immediately refer to the end of foreign domination and the end of exile which are the immediate concerns of the book of Daniel? I do not wish to deny that there are eschatological implications in these passages. Rather, I wish simply to affirm that just as significant moments in Israel's past (such as the Exodus or the return from Babylon[23]) were recounted as definitive works of God by using cosmic imagery, so too this latest act of God which Daniel sees unfolding is so presented. In none of these cases is the role of human agents working to bring about God's will denied. Moses and Cyrus are chosen by God to bring about the great events of the Exodus and liberation from exile; their human actions are necessary causes of the events. Yet we are consistently told in the biblical accounts that it was God who did these things. In the same way in Daniel, it is God who establishes and brings down kings and kingdoms. It is God who will establish the everlasting kingdom of Daniel's people. Yet we must not imagine this as taking place in some far-off world of apocalyptic eschatology devoid of any human activity. As we have seen, the wise, the *maskilim*, are called to take decisive action.

b. *The Influence of Greek Historiography*

The question must now be asked: If the historical vision of the book of Daniel can be explained by the pre-existing Jewish tradition, why bring in Greek historiography at all? My response is that although in continuity with the Jewish tradition that came before it, the book of Daniel also presents us with a distinctive development that cannot be explained by that tradition. An ancient, whether Jewish or Greek, would have no trouble describing historical events as the result of both human actions and a preordained divine will. We may notice a certain shift in emphasis in the book of Daniel, which gives more weight to the factor of divine predestination as opposed to the earlier Jewish tradition that emphasized human free will and divine reward or punishment for these freely chosen actions. The truly significant development, however, is the broadened historical focus, which takes in not only Israel or Judah (along with those nations that immediately interact with them), but

23. See, e.g., Exod. 15; Ps. 114; Isa. 43.

embraces a truly universal perspective. Commenting on this development, Robert H. Charles said: 'The O.T. prophet dealt with the destinies of this nation or that, but took no comprehensive view of the history of the world as a whole... Hence Daniel was the first to teach the unity of all human history, and that every phase of this history was a further stage in the development of God's purposes.'[24]

This universal history is markedly different from earlier historical writings in the Bible that followed the story of Israel's election by God, the Exodus from Egypt, settlement in the promised land, and the rise and fall of the kingdoms of Israel and Judah. The history we find in the book of Daniel is the story of the world's great empires. This is a story to which Israel had previously not belonged. Rather than following the thread of Israel's story, with reference to foreign powers only when they interact with the chosen people, Daniel follows the succession of world empires, with reference to the Jewish people only when the fourth kingdom comes to bear oppressively upon them. Then do we hear of 'the holy ones of the Most High' taking their place in this imperial series as a fifth and final kingdom.

A comparison of the historical surveys found in the book of Daniel and in the contemporary book of Dream Visions (1 En. 83–90) helps illuminate how unique Daniel's historical focus is within Judaism. While both apocalyptic works recount history as prophecy *ex eventu* through symbolic visions and animal imagery, the history they tell is quite different. The Book of Dream Visions repeats the history we are used to hearing in Israel, with references to Adam and Eve (85.3), Cain and Abel (85.4), Noah and the flood (89.1-9), the Exodus (89.16-27), the united and divided kingdoms (89.41-67), the exile and return (89.68-72). It situates the persecution of Antiochus IV and the activity of Judas Maccabeus in relation to this biblical history (90.1-12). The visions in Daniel take an entirely different approach. They focus on the successive kingdoms of Babylon, Media, Persia, and Greece (chs. 2 and 7), the ascendancy of Greece over the kingdom of the Medes and Persians (ch. 8), and the rivalry between the Ptolemaic and Seleucid kingdoms (ch. 11). No Israelite history is mentioned leading up to the conflict between the Jewish people and Antiochus IV with which each of these visions culminates. The book of Daniel radically reorients the history of the Jewish people. It does not look back to a restoration or return to ancient glories, but looks forward to a new place among the powers of this world. Daniel does not speak of the restoration of the past Davidic dynasty, but of the establishment of a new and definitive kingdom of God's holy people. Anticipating the end of the powers of this world, which have heretofore oppressed his people, Daniel looks to a new kingdom, established by God, that will succeed these oppressors and take its place as the definitive world empire.

The historical perspective that appears in the book of Daniel is pre-eminently Greek. As we have seen, it was the Greeks who first came up with the idea of a succession of world empires, among which they situated themselves after the conquest of Alexander.[25] This interest in the rise and fall of great powers began with

---

24. Charles, *Critical and Exegetical Commentary*, pp. cxiv-cxv.

25. See Chapter 2 for a complete discussion of this point. To reiterate the main points, the theory of imperial succession is not to be confused with the theory of the declining ages or races of

Herodotus himself. In his own lifetime he witnessed the rise of imperial Athens and the beginnings of the Peloponnesian War. To what extent the experience of these events influenced the composition of his *Histories* must be left open for debate.[26] For whatever reason, Herodotus took as the subject for his *Histories* the rise of Persia to a position of predominance over Asia, and ultimately the conflict between the Persians and the Greeks. Before coming to speak of the war between Persia and Greece that dominates Books 6-9, Herodotus describes at length the Persian rise to dominance over Asia, a position in which it was successor to the previous rule of the Assyrians and Medes (1.95). Thus we have the first three of the four kingdoms, with the fourth already hinted at by the Greek victory over the Persians. Herodotus relates the failure of the Persians and the success of the Greeks to the differing forms of government of the two peoples. The Greeks prove superior to the Persians by virtue of their superior νόμος. They are able to halt the imperialistic expansion of the Persians, borrowing the words of Demaratus, because they fight as free men under their master, the law, and not as slaves to a human despot (7.104).

This pattern of history that Herodotus laid down proved to be extremely influential. After Alexander, the Greeks firmly claimed their place in this imperial succession. The Greek interest in political and military history then came to have a deep impact on the peoples with whom they came in contact and over whom their rule and cultural hegemony extended, including the Jews. In the west, the Romans quickly regarded themselves as the fifth kingdom.[27] And in a remote corner of the Seleucid kingdom, a Jewish author suggested a surprising candidate for the fifth kingdom in the series. Although the Greek kingdom was by now fragmented and in decline itself, it is easy to imagine a self-satisfied Antiochus IV laughing at the suggestion of the book of Daniel (were he to hear of it) that this puny people could overcome his kingdom. Xerxes laughed at the similarly preposterous notion of Demaratus that a small band of Spartans could resist his mighty army. Yet Daniel, like Demaratus, focuses not on sheer numbers, but on a quality that cannot be

---

the world (golden, silver, bronze, and iron) which is found in Hesiod and combined with the four-kingdom schema in Dan. 2. The four-metal theory of world ages is much older than the four-kingdom schema and appears to have been more widely known across ancient cultures. By way of contrast, the theory of four kingdoms appears only in Greek authors and in later writers dependent upon the Greek tradition. This latter group is essentially made up of Roman historians and the author of Daniel. I should also reiterate that while Daniel integrates the imagery of the four-metal scheme into the vision in ch. 2, the underlying historical perspective does not become part of Daniel's theology of history. One might argue that in Daniel the final 'iron' kingdom is indeed the worst, but on the other end of the metallic spectrum it is untenable to regard Nebuchadnezzar's Babylonian kingdom as a golden age. For Daniel, the kingdoms represented by gold, silver, bronze, and iron are all bad.

26. J.A.S. Evans (*Herodotus, Explorer of the Past* [Princeton, NJ: Princeton University Press, 1991], pp. 38-40) discusses the link between Herodotus's focus on the imperialist impulse and the current events during the period in which he researched and wrote his *Histories*. With Athens dominating the Aegean world and with Persia in a state of decline, 'It was time to ask what had been the nature of the impulse behind [Persian expansionism]' (p. 38)

27. If Swain is correct in his dating of Aemilius Sura, the Romans may have appropriated this schema as early as c. 180 BCE (Swain, 'Theory of the Four Monarchies', pp. 2-3).

quantified. As the Greeks overcame the Persians because of their νόμος which they obey, the holy ones of the Most High will possess the kingdom (7.18, 22, 27) because of their God whom they serve.

We can see that not only does the schema of successive world empires come from Herodotus and the Greek historiographical tradition that followed him, but the detailed account of the Seleucid and Ptolemaic dynasties in Daniel 11 also must have its origins in the Greek tradition. Nowhere else does the Bible give such a detailed and accurate account of what is by and large non-Israelite or non-Jewish history. Its examination of international political-military history comes straight out of Greek historiography. In fact, because of the allusive nature of the history re-counted in this chapter, we would have no way of identifying the persons and events described in it if we did not have Greek historians (most notably Polybius) who describe the same people and events in unveiled language. It is clear, then, that ch. 11 borrows from non-Jewish sources, a point further accentuated by the difficult Hebrew in this chapter which may indicate the incorporation of material from some other language.[28] I believe the foreign sources behind this chapter must have been Greek, since it is only in Greek historiography that we find the type of material recounted in Daniel 11.

The close link between Daniel 11 and Greek historiography is supported by the fact that where the 'history' leaves off and gives way to 'prophecy' about future events (this transition can clearly be seen in the description of the events surround-ing the death of the impious 'king of the north'[29]) the 'fictional' account that follows appears to be based upon the narrative in Herodotus which describes the death of Cambyses. To finish the as-yet-unfinished history of Antiochus IV, Daniel finds a counterpart to Antiochus IV in the *Histories* of Herodotus on which he can pattern the conclusion of his vision (11.40-45). The impious King Cambyses, who was noted for his transgression of laws both Egyptian and Persian, provides a suitable model on which to base Daniel's prophecies concerning the end of Antiochus, who likewise disregarded the laws and customs not only of Jews but also of his own people (11.37). The striking parallels that I have noted between Daniel's portrayal of Antiochus and Herodotus's portrait of Cambyses point to a connection between the two works that goes beyond the appropriation of structuring elements. It appears that Daniel also uses Herodotus to help fill out details within his prophetic narrative and to help characterize his arch-fiend, Antiochus IV.

---

28. Charles, *Critical and Exegetical Commentary*, pp. 268-70; Barton, 'Composition of the Book of Daniel', pp. 62-66; Lebram, 'König Antiochus', pp. 760-61; Hartman and Di Lella, *Book of Daniel*, pp. 266-74; Collins, *Daniel*, pp. 377-90. Lebram suggests an Egyptian propaganda docu-ment, but he does so largely upon a reconstruction of Egyptian traditions concerning King Cam-byses gleaned from Herodotus! I suggest eliminating the middle man and recognizing that the traditions about Cambyses that appear in Dan. 11 come directly from Herodotus.

29. The break occurs at v. 40. Although Porphyry considered the entire chapter as historical, there is no evidence for a third campaign against Egypt as recounted in vv. 40-45. Rather, Anti-ochus IV spent the last year and a half of his life on campaign in the east where he died (see Otto Mørkholm, *Antiochus IV of Syria* [Copenhagen: Glydendalske Boghandel, 1966], pp. 20, 166-80).

c. *The Scope of History in Daniel*

As we have seen, the parameters of history in the book of Daniel are markedly different from earlier biblical histories. There is no mention of Israel's pre-exilic history such as one finds in the Enochic Book of Dream Visions.[30] The limits of history under consideration in the book of Daniel are very clearly defined. They extend from the reign of Nebuchadnezzar and the initial 'profanation' of the temple in his time[31] to the current reign of Antiochus IV and the profanation of the temple during his persecution of the Jewish religion. The nature of the history recounted is also quite different from earlier biblical accounts. As we have seen, it is decidedly international in focus. It is not simply the history of Israel and the account of God's saving actions on behalf of this chosen people. Rather, it is largely a secular history—the accounts of world empires and foreign kings to whom the Jews were subject. Yet this too, like Israel's earlier history, is seen as the unfolding of a divine plan. God not only is at work in Israel or among the Jews, but directs and governs even the seemingly profane world which has come to dominate the Jewish people. The hope and promise expressed is that Daniel's people themselves—the Jewish people—will eventually take their rightful place among these worldly kingdoms as the final and definitive kingdom established by God.

It is clear from the abundant historical allusions that the book of Daniel was written in response to the crisis at the time of Antiochus IV. The cult of YHWH in the temple had been interrupted and replaced by the 'abomination that makes desolate' (11.31). Daniel, however, does not view the prohibition of the Jewish religion at the time of Antiochus IV in isolation. It is related to the historical events that preceded it. This we can see clearly from the synopsis of history from Persia to Antiochus IV in ch. 11. The visions in chs. 2 and 7 also relate the immediate moment for Daniel (the fourth kingdom which is Greece) to its three predecessors. Finally we may note once more that the book of Daniel is structured around the successive reigns of Nebuchadnezzar, Belshazzar, Darius, and Cyrus, with visions of the 'future' Greek kings Alexander and Antiochus IV who remain nameless under various images. In all of these instances (whether we look at the tales, the visions, or the overall structure of the book), Daniel begins his 'history' with the person of Nebuchadnezzar.[32] Nebuchadnezzar and Antiochus IV are the bookends

---

30. Under the imagery of various animals, 1 En. 85–90 recounts the entire biblical history from Adam (the snow-white bovid of 85.3) to Judas Maccabeus (the horned ram of 90.9).

31. Dan. 1.2 does not in fact mention the destruction of the Jerusalem temple by Nebuchadnezzar, but only the deportation of some of the temple vessels to Babylon. This datum sets up the anticipated restoration or rededication of the temple in the time of Antiochus IV (Dan. 12.11) as the close of the historical period in question. It is as if Antiochus picks up where Nebuchadnezzar left off, and the rebuilding of the temple centuries earlier is entirely overlooked. It is rather the restoration of the daily sacrifice to YHWH which is seen (in conjunction with the demise of the great persecutor Antiochus IV) as the end of the period of exile.

32. With regard to the visions, it is true that the visions of ch. 8 and chs. 10–12 begin with Persia, or more precisely with the defeat of Persia at the hands of the Greeks. This focuses one's attention on the reigning fourth kingdom as embodying the period of most intense persecution. Nevertheless, these chapters continue and build upon the visions of chs. 2 and 7 that situate this

within which the book of Daniel subsists. They represent the limits of the period of history with which Daniel is concerned.

Although the situation in Herodotus is a bit more complex, given his many digressions in the narrative, there is nevertheless something quite similar going on. The figures of Croesus and Xerxes form a similar framework within which the story of the *Histories* takes place. Xerxes represents for Herodotus the apex of Persian expansion and aggression against the Greeks much in the same way that Antiochus is the culmination of the foreign powers that oppress Daniel's people. And just as Herodotus began his *Histories* with the account of the man whom he knows to have been the first to injure the Greeks, Daniel also began his book with tales of the man whom he knows to have first injured the Jews.[33] The oppression and humiliation of Daniel's people began with Nebuchadnezzar who captured Jerusalem and removed some of the vessels from the temple (Dan. 1.1-2). The exile, which began in his time, reached its culmination in the further initiatives against the Jews and defilement of the temple under Antiochus IV.

Since the book of Daniel has so carefully and so clearly defined the limits of the period of history under its consideration, one should not hastily situate Daniel's understanding of a definitive divine intervention outside of that history. This was the position taken up by Gerhard von Rad and insightfully critiqued by Antonio Bonora.[34] Bonora's conclusion, put quite simply, is that the hope held out by the book of Daniel to the Jewish people in their moment of crisis pertains to the present world and its history. Just as Daniel's history does not start 'in the beginning' with the very beginning of history as it were, so too there is no sufficient reason to suppose that it concludes with the end of history. Rather, Daniel is anticipating the end of a very specific and carefully delineated period of history. The hope held out by Daniel for an end to the wicked oppressor (7.26; 11.45; 12.7) and the restoration of the true cult (8.14; 12.11) pertains to terrestrial, historical realities. As such it not only implies but would seem to demand a historical continuation when Daniel's people are free from foreign oppression and the temple sacrifice is restored. As Bonora points out, even when the element of resurrection from the dead is brought in (12.2), it still has the character of an earthly hope.[35] Pierre Grelot has also argued that the perspective in the book of Daniel does not at all resemble an escape from

---

final kingdom within a fourfold structure. When we consider the visions as a whole, they begin (like the connected series of tales in chs. 1–6) with Nebuchadnezzar of Babylon.

33.   Once again, I must emphasize that this is so for the historical period of the 'exile' with which Daniel concerns himself. There is no mention of earlier oppressors from the Pharaoh of the Exodus to the Assyrians. For Daniel the injury *par excellence* is the exile marked by foreign domination and the suppression of the authentic temple cult.

34.   Von Rad, *Wisdom in Israel*, p. 273. Von Rad spoke of a 'soteriological, depletion of history', claiming that in Daniel salvation is moved to the margins of history. Bonora claims that for Daniel the divine intervention is not beyond history; even the 'end' and the divine judgment are not thought of as metahistorical events, but as happening within the horizon of history (Antonio Bonora, 'La Storiografia nel Libro di Daniele', in *La Storiografia nella Bibbia: Atti della XXVIII Settimana Biblica* [Bologna: Edizioni Dehonaine, 1986], pp. 77-91 [78]).

35.   Bonora, 'Storiografia', p. 78.

the present world into the beyond. A new age is indeed anticipated in which the plan of God for Daniel's people will be realized, but while this perspective is eschatological in the sense that the decreed end of the desolator (9.27b) is envisioned, the opening onto an absolute future does not imply the end of the present world.[36]

If the book of Daniel were truly dualistic and presented the present age as being hopelessly within the power of malignant forces, then the anticipated divine intervention might be seen as an event beyond the horizons of this world and its history. Then might this present world necessarily come to an end in order for God's plan to be accomplished. But it is precisely because Daniel presents the whole of the 'exilic' period of history—bad though it may be—under the ultimate control of God's plan that the awaited moment of divine deliverance cannot be understood as being distinct from the rest of history or outside of it. The awaited deliverance is the fulfillment of God's plan in history. It completes the divine scheme for this period of history; it does not negate that history.

d. *The Typological Use of History*

When Porphyry pointed out to his Christian adversaries that the book of Daniel was not in fact written by a Jewish exile in Babylon during the reigns of Nebuchadnezzar, Belshazzar, Darius, and Cyrus, but by a Palestinian Jew at the time of Antiochus IV, his arguments were dismissed as pagan malice and unbelief. Believers, both Jewish and Christian, continued to adhere to the judgment of Josephus that Daniel was among the greatest of the prophets because he not only accurately foretold what would happen, he even told when it would happen.[37] The point of bringing this up is that for believers and non-believers—for pagans, Jews, and Christians—the historical allusions in Daniel were clear enough that none could deny that the major focus of the book centered around the persecution of Antiochus IV. They only differed as to whether these events were being foretold or recounted after the fact. However, in spite of the many clear allusions to Antiochus IV in the book of Daniel, he is never mentioned by name. This anonymity, which envelops Antiochus and the other main characters of this period, gives to the history recounted in the book of Daniel a typical quality. As a type of impious opposition to God, it does not make much difference whether the king being spoken of or alluded to is Antiochus, Nebuchadnezzar, or Belshazzar. What is important is that the divine plan in history always ultimately prevails over the machinations of impious human powers.

Behind the figures of Nebuchadnezzar and Belshazzar (and perhaps even Darius) in the court tales, there stands the ever-looming presence of Antiochus IV. One can see this, for example, in the reference to Nebuchadnezzar's plundering of the temple in ch. 1, in his setting up an idol in ch. 3, and in his arrogant boasting in ch. 4. These are all actions attributed to Antiochus IV in the visions of the latter part of the book of Daniel (11.31, 36). Belshazzar in ch. 5 is also noted for his defiling of the temple vessels, paralleling the desecration of the temple by Antiochus. Even the well-meaning but foolish Darius in ch. 6 agrees to the decree that no prayers may

---

36. Grelot, 'Histoire et Eschatologie', p. 103.
37. Josephus, *Ant.* 10.11.7.

be offered to any god or human except himself for thirty days. This action attributed to Darius may very well be used as a mirror for the disregard Antiochus showed towards the gods and for his self-exaltation above all gods (11.37). Such presumption would constantly be before the Jewish people subject to him in the inscription found on his coinage beginning around 173 BCE: ΒΑΣΙΛΕΩΣ ΑΝΤΙΟΧΟΥ ΘΕΟΥ ΕΠΙΦΑΝΟΥΣ.[38]

The various crimes of Antiochus IV, then, are recounted through the stories of the kings who preceded him. They are typical actions of any foreign king to which Daniel's people is subject in the period of their exile. Antiochus IV is not a unique individual for Daniel, nor is his persecution of the Jews seen as a solitary event. Rather, Antiochus and his measures against the Jews are seen as the culmination of a pattern begun with Nebuchadnezzar. Within the fourth kingdom, Antiochus appears as the full maturation of the evil begun by Alexander. Such is the perspective of the visions in chs. 8 and 11, which begin with a description of Alexander's victory over Persia and culminate with the outrages of Antiochus. But this fourth kingdom itself is the evil heir to the three that preceded it. This even broader perspective can be seen in the visions of chs. 2 and 7, as well as in the structure of the entire book.

Antiochus IV is not only prefigured in the kings and kingdoms that come before him (inasmuch as the sins of Nebuchadnezzar, Belshazzar, and Darius are foreshadowings and allusions to what Antiochus was doing in Daniel's time), but where he himself is referred to in the visions of the latter half of Daniel his portrait takes on a cosmic dimension as the incarnation or epitome of all evil. It is no wonder that Jerome could understand the historical descriptions of Antiochus in Dan. 11.21-39, as well as the non-historical vv. 40-45, as referring to the Antichrist. His furious assault against the holy covenant (11.30-35) and his blasphemous self-deification (11.36-37), while having concrete historical referents, are presented in terms that are allusive and vague enough so as to invite a larger interpretation. Antiochus, as the culmination of all the evil kings and kingdoms that preceded him, becomes the symbol and standard bearer for evil. Like the four-metal statue in ch. 2, which in one image represented four kingdoms, Antiochus represents the sum of all his predecessors. When he finally comes to his deserved end (11.45), the whole complex of kings and kingdoms—the whole period of the exile—will come crashing down with him.

What, then, is the effect of this typical presentation of Antiochus IV? As grave a threat as he posed to the Jews at this critical juncture of their history, his menace is no different in kind from those who came before him. His is a difference only in degree, being the culminating moment of the prolonged period of exile. This difference is brought out most explicitly in Dan. 7.23-24. First, in v. 23, the fourth beast is interpreted as a fourth kingdom 'different from all the other kingdoms'. Then in

---

38.   Otto Mørkholm, *Antiochus IV of Syria* (Copenhagen: Gyldendal, 1966), p. 113. Beginning in 169 until the end of his reign, the inscription ΝΙΚΗΦΟΡΟΥ was added as well. These dates apply to the great mint at Antioch. The mint at Acco, which would have been the closest royal mint to Judea, began using the longer legend in 168.

v. 24, where the ten horns of this fourth beast are interpreted as ten kings, we hear of a final horn coming after them that is 'different from the former ones'. Thus, of all the kingdoms, the fourth and final one is the most powerful and oppressive. And of all the kings of this fourth kingdom, it is the final one who is the most arrogant, blasphemous, and nefarious towards the holy ones of the Most High (7.25). But even if he achieves such power as to prevail over these holy ones for a time, the fate of him and the whole complex of kings and kingdoms he represents is already sealed. Though different in degree, Antiochus and the fourth kingdom are yet closely related to the other three beasts. Together they represent this singular period of dark history for Daniel and his people. In the vision in ch. 7, they are all seen losing their dominion together (7.11-12). This unity of the four kingdoms as a single entity from the perspective of the book of Daniel appears even more clearly in ch. 2 where, under the image of a single statue, they are all crushed simultaneously by the stone from the mountain (2.34-35).

We can say, then, that the book of Daniel does regard the 'Greek' kingdom and Antiochus in particular as different from their predecessors. Yet they are not unique or distinct from them. For Daniel, Antiochus cannot be understood apart from Nebuchadnezzar and the whole history of the 'exile'. The hoped-for 'end' to which the book of Daniel looks forward, is not simply the end of this impious king, but an end to the entire structure of foreign oppression. So it is in ch. 2 that when the feet of the statue (the fourth kingdom) are struck, the entire statue (all four kingdoms) crumbles. Likewise in ch. 7, when the fourth beast is slain, the other three beasts lose their dominion with it. The individual kings, and even the individual kingdoms, are part of a larger complex of forces in opposition to God. This entire complex will be destroyed all together and at once according to the prophetic vision of Daniel.

In the parallel realms of historical causation—the human level and the divine—the scales are weighted in favor of the latter. It may be for this reason that the individual players on the human level remain anonymous, identifiable only through allusion. Their individual actions are all part of a greater whole that God will overthrow. This is in keeping with the central theme of the book of Daniel that dominion and kingship belong to God alone, who has authority over all earthly and heavenly powers (4.31-32). That is not to say that human actions and individuals do not matter. The author of Daniel realized the uniqueness of the fourth kingdom and its blasphemous little horn, while at the same time acknowledging that this new and unique crisis would be overcome in typical divine fashion.

e. *The Human and the Divine*
As we have seen, Daniel does not negate or deny the influence of human actions and human causation in history. The book of Daniel does not represent a quietistic or pacifistic response to the historical crisis at the time of Antiochus IV. It does not despair of history, yearning only for the consummation and end of history to be brought about by the definitive action of God alone, independent of any human initiative. While the book of Daniel does present us with a new vision of the divine sovereignty in and over history which encompasses not only Israel but follows the

story of the world's empires, this universal divine dominion does not eliminate the human factors in history which may either cooperate with God or oppose the divine will.

In Daniel, the divine plan for history is worked out both through and in spite of human agents. The historical struggle depicted is real enough; it should not be interpreted as God's simply pulling the puppet strings of otherwise powerless humans. We are told in ch. 7 that the impious little horn of the fourth beast will even prevail over the holy ones of the Most High for a time. The power of human agents to affect history has been duly felt by Daniel and his people in the persecution of Antiochus IV. The reality of human ability to oppose the divine will and influence history is a terrible experience that is too immediate possibly to deny. Yet, while affirming the alarming ability of evil human forces to shape the course of events, the book of Daniel affirms a larger divine plan against which no human power can prevail. Impious human agents may hold sway for a time, two times, and a half time, just as Croesus may gain from the gods a brief postponement from his inevitable doom. But the final triumph of the divine plan in history, the accomplishment of that which must be, is assured.

More difficult to ascertain is the position of Daniel regarding human action or initiative not in opposition to God but on God's behalf. Does Daniel regard the Maccabean movement as 'but a little help'? Does Daniel advocate a sectarian separation from the political and religious center of Judaism? Are his 'holy ones' a pacifistic, elitist group that relies on God to combat the evil human agents in history, a group that quietly watches and waits? The classical representation of apocalyptic dualism would have us answer yes to each of these questions. An unbiased look at the theology of history in Daniel, however, presents us with a different answer. In the first place it would appear only natural and logical that if Daniel presents us with evil human agents who are able to affect history, then good human agents should be able to do so as well. To this one might object that God needs no help in overcoming evil human forces—that the conflict expressed is between the human and divine spheres. The power of God prevails over the human powers of this world. This objection does not hold, however, because as we have seen, the conflict is expressed equally on the divine and human levels. The evil forces do not just consist of human agents, but include the 'princes' or angelic protectors of the various nations. As the princes of Persia and Greece have their human counterparts in the various kings referred to in the narrative, so too Michael and the One like a Son of Man represent the Jewish people. Their activity in the divine realm is not a matter of acting solely on behalf of or in place of the Jewish people. Rather, it is the revelation of a deeper dimension to the unfolding historical drama. This revealed dimension entails a cosmic battle between heavenly forces, but rather than denying the human counterparts to these heavenly agents, it necessitates them. There must be an earthly reality corresponding to the heavenly one.[39]

---

39.   The same close relationship between what is attributed to a divine representative and what takes place in human history can be seen in earlier biblical texts. Jeremiah speaks of Milcom dispossessing Gad (49.1) and of Milcom's subsequent punishment of going into exile (49.3). This is

Part of the difficulty in unraveling the roles of human and divine agents in Daniel's theological history is the very ambiguity of the term 'holy ones' (Hebrew: קדשׁים, Aramaic: קדּישׁין). Usually referring to heavenly beings, 'holy ones' can also refer to human beings in the Hebrew Bible (e.g. Ps. 34.10) as well as in the Dead Sea Scrolls, the Deuterocanonical Books (Wis. 18.9), and the Pseudepigrapha.[40] Its usage in Daniel, where there is a close connection between humans and their heavenly representatives, appears to benefit from the very ambiguity inherent in the term. It is capable of referring to both the holy people (see Dan. 7.27 where the additional noun 'people', עם, is explicitly supplied) and their heavenly advocates. The literal phrasing of Dan. 7.27—'people of the holy ones of the Most High'—is paralleled in the *War Scroll* from Qumran: 'people of the holy ones of the covenant' (1QM 10.10). In both cases a human referent is clearly implied, but these humans are described in relation to heavenly beings. A similar connection between the holy ones in the heavenly sphere and the holy ones on earth can be seen in the Similitudes of Enoch (1 En. 37–71). This work, which probably dates to the first century BCE and is itself dependent upon Daniel, contains numerous references to 'holy ones' as humans, while also referring to 'the holy ones who dwell in the heavens' (47.2).[41]

The holy ones on earth in the book of Daniel, that is to say Daniel's people or the Jewish people, are not without their role to play in history. If Michael, the prince of Daniel's people, is fighting against the princes of Persia and Greece (10.20-21), this means that Daniel's people as well are engaged in combat with the peoples represented by those guardian spirits. The heavenly vision is revelatory of what is taking place on earth. And although the conflict in the book of Daniel is not necessarily military in nature, it would be a mistake to see Daniel as simply dismissing the Maccabean resistance. The action Daniel advocates, however, is primarily a religious one of non-compromise, rejecting the religious initiatives of Antiochus that amount to idolatry (7.25; 8.13; 9.27; 11.31-32). He urges fidelity to Jewish laws at a time when many were abandoning these same laws in favor of greater assimilation with the Greeks. Daniel's primary weapons are wisdom and instruction. The people must know the law and remain faithful to it. This is hardly some elitist or

a rather poetic way of referring to the Ammonites, the people being represented by their god, Milcom, who dispossessed Gad and were sent into exile. No one would claim that because Jeremiah uses this type of representative language that he is denying any historical role to the Ammonites themselves. The situation is similar in Daniel. When speaking of the figures of Michael or the One like a Son of Man, Daniel does not make a clear distinction between the heavenly representative and the Jewish people. This is clear especially in ch. 7 where we first hear that dominion and kingship are given to the One like a Son of Man (v. 14), while later in the interpretation, the same dominion and kingship are bestowed upon the holy people of the Most High (7.27).

40. For a thorough listing of the evidence and the history of the interpretation of this term, see Collins's Excursus in his commentary on Daniel (*Daniel*, pp. 313-17). As he points out, the human interpretation of this term in the book of Daniel was favored until Noth's significant study: 'The Holy Ones of the Most High'. Since then, the angelic interpretation has gained in popularity, although there is still significant debate over the issue.

41. See Collins, *Daniel*, pp. 316-17, and C.H.W. Brekelmans, 'The Saints of the Most High and their Kingdom', *OTS* 14 (1965), pp. 305-29.

separatist call. It is simply an exhortation to remain faithful to the covenant so as to receive the blessings of the covenant—the restoration of national autonomy in the land.

It makes little difference whether we ascribe to Daniel pacifist or revolutionary tendencies. In either case his view of the proper human response to the historical crisis in which he lived is primarily one of cooperating with God's plan of establishing a definitive kingdom. Daniel's perception of the role of the human in history can apply equally to the Maccabees who besieged the defiled temple in order to purify and restore it, and to those Jews who fled to the desert and refused to fight on the Sabbath.[42] Each in their own way sought to cooperate with the plan of God in history as they perceived it. Since God is the primary agent in history, the success of this venture lies ultimately in the realm of the divine and not with humans. What Daniel and his people for their part must do is remain faithful to the covenant and laws of God. Like Themistocles, they must have the wisdom and knowledge to interpret correctly the divine word that has come to them. They must consult their oracle—the Scriptures—to discern God's plan being worked out on their behalf. Thus they will be able to cooperate fully with God, and they will not despair of the seemingly hopeless situation in which they find themselves. They will not lose heart and compromise their identity and convictions by abandoning their ancestral traditions and law. Like the Spartans at Thermopylae, they will fight bravely for their law which they serve. They will not cowardly embrace servitude to an arrogant despot who menaces them.

Unlike the first book of Maccabees, which judges the correct course of action to be armed resistance even on the Sabbath (1 Macc. 2.41), the book of Daniel leaves the question open as to the proper way for humans to actualize the divine plan. Whereas 1 Maccabees judged the course of the pacifists to be a failure (2.40), Daniel envisions a larger perspective which includes the hope of a resurrection for those fallen in faithfulness to God's laws (12.2). Writing while the outcome of the Antiochian persecution still hangs in the balance, Daniel is not in a position to say who has correctly discerned the divine plan so as to act in accord with it. On the level of specific actions, there is no Themistocles who chooses the right course by building ships, just as there is no Croesus who chooses the wrong course by marching against Persia. For Daniel, any Jew who rejects the syncretistic cult and adheres to the Jewish law is cooperating with the divine plan. There is a divine guarantee of ultimate success regardless of what the immediate historical result might indicate.

This brings us to the question of whether there is a more individualistic perspective on salvation in the book of Daniel than in the previous Hebrew Scriptures. On the one hand, it is very clear that for Daniel what is at stake is the fate of his people—the nation—in opposition to the foreign oppressor kingdoms. As stated earlier, the primary conflict is not found within Judaism (a perspective that can be seen in the opening chapters of 2 Maccabees) but between the Jewish people as a whole and the foreign nations. On the other hand, we can catch a glimpse of the internal

---

42.   The story of this ill-fated group is told in 1 Macc. 2.31-38. They are not to be confused with the Hasideans (Hasidim) who are described as fighting with the Maccabees (2.42-44).

Jewish struggle between those who collaborate with the evil kingdoms (Dan. 11.30, 32) and those who resist. We have seen that only some will rise again 'to ever-lasting life', while others will rise 'to shame and everlasting contempt' (Dan. 12.2). This individualistic emphasis should not be overstated. Just as in Herodotus there were individual Greeks who collaborated with the Persians, failing to unite with the Greek resistance and betraying their own people, so too we find such traitors in Daniel. But the overall picture that Herodotus presents to us is one of the triumph of Greece as a whole over Persia. So too Daniel envisions the ultimate triumph of his people as a whole, as a nation or kingdom, replacing the kingdoms that have come before it.

Daniel, like Herodotus, is concerned with his nation's history and its place among the kingdoms of this world. Like Herodotus, he is able to see the finger of God in human affairs, guiding history forward to bring about what must be, without taking away from human freedom and responsibility. Contemplating his people's exile from the time of Nebuchadnezzar to the persecution of Antiochus IV, he looks forward to its prophesied end. As Solon calculated the days of a man's life, Daniel calculates the days until this end. But while the point of Solon's exercise was to show to Croesus the fickleness of fortune, Daniel's aim is to affirm the faithfulness of God. Daniel's message is not so much a warning against arrogant complacency, but a declaration of hope in a time of crisis that urges us to 'look to the end'.

APPENDIX

THE TEXT OF DANIEL 11.2B

The difficulty in the text of Dan. 11.2b manifests itself in the various ways translators have rendered this passage. Three representative examples will serve my
purpose:

> Behold, three more kings will arise for Persia, and the fourth will amass greater
> wealth than all. When he is strong in his wealth he will stir up everything, even the
> kingdom of Greece. (Collins)

> Three kings of Persia are still to arise, and the fourth will acquire the greatest riches
> of them all. When he feels strong enough because of his riches, he will incite the
> whole kingdom of Greece. (Hartman)

> Three more kings shall arise in Persia. The fourth shall be far richer than all of them,
> and when he has become strong through his riches, he shall stir up all against the
> kingdom of Greece. (NRSV)

Where these translations significantly differ is in the relationship between the word
כל ('everything', 'whole', or 'all') and מלכות יון ('the kingdom of Greece'). Is
the author referring to 'everything, including the kingdom of Greece' (Collins),
'everything within the kingdom of Greece' (Hartman), or 'everything outside the
kingdom of Greece' (NRSV)?

The diversity of translations results both from a difficult Hebrew text and from
a significantly different rendering in the LXX. To return to the Hebrew text of Dan.
11.2b, we read: הנה־עוד שלשה מלכים עמדים לפרס והרביעי יעשיר עשר־גדול
מכל וכחזקתו בעשרו יעיר הכל את מלכות יון. The difficulty is in the final
clause. First of all, in regard to the verb used, the MT has יעיר, a hiphil imperfect
meaning 'to rouse' or 'stir up'. The LXX, however, translates the verb as ἐπανασ-
τήσεται, a future middle meaning 'to rise up against'. The loss of transitivity in the
Greek text probably reflects a reading of the Hebrew verb as a niphal, יעור, but this
understanding is difficult to reconcile with the final words of the verse. It requires
both the addition of a preposition not found in the Hebrew text,[1] and the difficult
adjectival use of הכל as modifying מלכות יון. However, were הכל modifying
מלכות יון it would not have the article attached to it, nor would there be the
particle את between it and what follows. That the Greek translators were perhaps
struggling with a difficult Hebrew text which they freely adapted is also suggested
by the additional change from 'kingdom of Greece' in the MT to '[every] king of

---

1. With the exception of but two medieval manuscripts containing the preposition אל.

the Greeks' (βασιλεῖ Ἑλλήνων) in the LXX. The reading in MT is supported by the oldest extant manuscript of the book of Daniel, 4QDanᶜ which dates to the end of the second century BCE, only about 50 years after the composition of the text.[2]

Accepting the reading in the MT, which is attested also at Qumran, one is still confronted with making sense of the peculiar text. Literally, it appears to read: 'he will stir up everything, the kingdom of Greece'. The verb עור in the hiphil means 'to rouse' or 'incite to action', as when the Lord incites Cyrus to act on behalf the exiled Jews: 'I have *aroused* Cyrus in righteousness, and I will make all his paths straight' (Isa. 45.13). This verb also frequently has implicit or explicit military overtones as when Jeremiah speaks of God rousing the nations to move against Babylon: 'For I am going to *stir up* and bring against Babylon a company of great nations from the land of the north' (Jer. 50.9). Ezekiel speaks of a similar military mustering against Judah in allegorical terms: 'Therefore, O Oholibah, thus says the Lord GOD: I will *rouse* against you your lovers from whom you turned in disgust, and I will bring them against you from every side' (Ezek. 23.22). These last two examples in particular provide a key for interpreting the passage in Daniel as a military mustering. The fourth Persian king is stirring up, rousing, calling to action everything and everybody (הכל). What is being roused is the entire world or universe. Given that the object of this 'stirring up' is the world itself, 'the kingdom of Greece' cannot be a second object in apposition to or amplifying the first. Rather, it is the motive, the target, the direction towards which this great stirring up is moving. The use of את rather than the expected על (Jer. 50.9; Ezek. 23.22) for distinguishing the objective of this military force is really the source of most of the confusion surrounding this passage. Still, one does not need to posit some sort of scribal error for this change since the preposition את (meaning 'with', as opposed to the direct object marker) sometimes carries a directional sense of 'towards' (cf. Isa. 66.14; Ps. 67.2) and is also frequently used with verbs of fighting or contending (cf. Gen. 14.2, 8, 9; Num. 20.13; Isa. 45.9; 50.8; Ps. 35.1),[3] which, as we have seen above, is often implied or made explicit where the verb עור is used. Thus, one might even literally render this passage in English as 'he will rouse up everyone [to make war] with the kingdom of Greece'. This is a fairly accurate summary of Herodotus's account of the campaign of Xerxes against Greece. Herodotus himself sums up the universal mustering of forces against Greece by posing the question: τί γὰρ οὐκ ἤγαγε ἐκ τῆς Ἀσίης ἔθνος ἐπὶ τὴν Ἑλλάδα Ξέρξης; ('For what nation did Xerxes not lead out of Asia against Greece?', 7.21).[4]

2.   Assuming the reliability of paleographic dating (F.M. Cross, *The Ancient Library of Qumran* [Garden City, NY: Doubleday, 1961], p. 43) and the widely accepted scholarly consensus that chs. 7–12 were composed during the actual persecution of Antiochus IV, before the rededication of the Temple (167–164 BCE). This consensus rests largely on the 'incorrect' prophecies in Daniel concerning the time of the restoration of the Temple (8.14; 12.11-12) and the circumstances of Antiochus IV's death (11.45).

3.   BDB, p. 86.

4.   My translation.

BIBLIOGRAPHY

Albrektson, B., *History and the Gods: An Essay on the Idea of Historical Events as Divine Manifestations in the Ancient Near East and in Israel* (Lund: C.W.K. Gleerup, 1967).

Anderson, B.W., *Understanding the Old Testament* (Englewood Cliffs, NJ: Prentice–Hall, 4th edn, 1986).

Asheri, D., *Erodoto: Libro I: La Lidia e la Persia* (Milan: Fondazione Lorenzo Valla, 1988).

—*Erodoto: Libro III: La Persia* (Milan: Fondazione Lorenzo Valla, 1990).

Astin, A.E., *Scipio Aemilianus* (Oxford: Clarendon Press, 1967).

Astour, M.C., *Hellenosemitica: An Ethnic and Cultural Study in West Semitic Impact on Mycenaean Greece* (Leiden: E.J. Brill, 1965).

Attridge, H., 'Philo the Epic Poet', in *OTP*, II, pp. 781-84.

Barber, G.L., *The Historian Ephorus* (Chicago: Ares Publishers, 2nd edn, 1993).

Barr, J., *Biblical Words for Time* (London: SCM Press, 1962).

—'Hebrew, Aramaic and Greek in the Hellenistic Age', in Davies and Finkelstein (eds.), *The Cambridge History of Judaism*, II, pp. 79-114.

Barton, G.A., 'The Composition of the Book of Daniel', *JBL* 17 (1898), pp. 62-86.

Bauer, J., *Die Benutzung Herodots durch Ephoros bei Diodor* (Leipzig: Teubner, 1879).

Baumgartner, W., 'Zu den vier Reichen von Daniel 2', *Theologische Zeitschrift* 1 (1945), pp. 17-22.

Berti, S. (ed.), *Essays on Ancient and Modern Judaism* (trans. M. Masella-Gayley; Chicago: University of Chicago Press, 1994).

Bichler, R., 'Die "Reichsträume" bei Herodot: Eine Studie zu Herodots schöpferischer Leistung und ihre quellenkritische Konsequenz', *Chiron* 15 (1985), pp. 125-47.

Bickerman, E., *Der Gott der Makkabäer* (Berlin: Schocken Verlag, 1937).

— *Four Strange Books of the Bible* (New York: Schocken Books, 1967).

—'The Historical Foundations of Postbiblical Judaism', in L. Finkelstein (ed.), *The Jews: Their History* (New York: Schocken Books, 4th edn, 1974), pp. 72-118.

—*The Jews in the Greek Age* (Cambridge, MA: Harvard University Press, 1988).

Blenkinsopp, J., *Ezra–Nehemiah: A Commentary* (OTL; Philadelphia: Westminster Press, 1988).

Boadt, L., *Reading the Old Testament* (New York: Paulist Press, 1984).

Boccaccini, G., 'Daniel and the Dream Visions', in *idem*, *Middle Judaism: Jewish Thought, 300 BCE to 200 CE* (Minneapolis: Fortress Press, 1991), pp. 126-60.

—'È Daniele un testo apocalittico? Una (ri)definizione del pensiero del Libro di Daniele in rapporto al Libro dei Sogni e all'Apocalittica', *Henoch* 9 (1987), pp. 267-302.

Boman, T., *Hebrew Thought Compared with Greek* (trans. J.L. Moreau; London: SCM Press, 1960).

Bonora, A., 'La Storiografia nel Libro di Daniele', in *La Storiografia nella Bibbia: Atti della XXVIII Settimana Biblica* (Bologna: Edizioni Dehonaine, 1986), pp. 77-91.

Brekelmans, C.H.W., 'The Saints of the Most High and their Kingdom', *OTS* 14 (1965), pp. 305-29.

Brown, R.E., and R.F. Collins, 'Canonicity', in R.E. Brown, J.A. Fitzmyer and R.E. Murphy
    (eds.), *The New Jerome Biblical Commentary* (Englewood Cliffs, NJ: Prentice–Hall,
    1990), pp. 1034-54.
Buchanan, G.W., *The Book of Daniel: Intertextual Commentary on the Book of Daniel*
    (Lewiston, NY: Edwin Mellen Press, 1999).
Bultmann, R., 'γιγνώσκω', in *TDNT*, I, pp. 689-719.
—'History and Eschatology in the New Testament', *NTS* 1 (1954–55), pp. 5-16.
Caponigro, M.S., 'Judith, Holding the Tale of Herodotus', in J.C. VanderKam (ed.), *'No One
    Spoke Ill of Her': Essays on Judith* (SBL: Early Judaism and Its Literature, 2; Atlanta:
    Scholars Press, 1992), pp. 47-59.
Cereti, C.G., *The Zand i Wahman Yasn: A Zoroastrian Apocalypse* (Rome: Istituto Italiano per
    il Medio ed Estremo Oriente, 1995).
Chariton, *Chariton's Chaereas and Callirhoe* (trans. W.E. Blake; Ann Arbor: University of
    Michigan Press, 1939).
Charles, R.H., *A Critical and Exegetical Commentary on the Book of Daniel* (Oxford:
    Clarendon Press, 1929).
Colless, B., 'Cyrus the Persian as Darius the Mede in the Book of Daniel', *JSOT* 56 (1992),
    pp. 113-26.
Collins, J.J., 'Artapanus: A New Translation and Introduction', in *OTP*, II, pp. 889-903.
—'The Court-Tales in Daniel and the Development of Apocalyptic', *JBL* 94 (1975), pp. 218-34.
—*Daniel: A Commentary on the Book of Daniel; with an essay 'The Influence of Daniel on the
    New Testament', by Adela Yarbro Collins* (ed. F.M. Cross; Hermeneia; Minneapolis:
    Fortress Press, 1993).
—*Daniel with an Introduction to Apocalyptic Literature* (ed. R. Knierim and G.M. Tucker;
    FOTL, 20; Grand Rapids: Eerdmans, 1984).
—'From Prophecy to Apocalypticism: The Expectation of the End', in J.J. Collins (ed.), *The
    Encyclopedia of Apocalypticism. I. The Origins of Apocalypticism in Judaism and
    Christianity* (New York: Continuum, 2000), pp. 129-61.
—'The Meaning of "The End" in the Book of Daniel', in H.W. Attridge, J.J. Collins and T.H.
    Tobin (eds.), *Of Scribes and Scrolls: Studies on the Hebrew Bible, Intertestamental
    Judaism, and Christian Origins* (New York: University Press of America, 1990),
    pp. 91-98.
—'New Light on the Book of Daniel from the Dead Sea Scrolls', in F. García Martínez and
    E. Noort (eds.), *Perspectives in the Study of the Old Testament and Early Judaism: A
    Symposium in Honour of Adam S. Van der Woude on the Occasion of his 70th Birthday*
    (Leiden: E.J. Brill, 1998), pp. 180-96.
Coxon, P.W., 'Greek Loan-Words and Alleged Greek Loan Translations in the Book of Dan-
    iel', *Transactions of the Glasgow University Oriental Society* 25 (1973–74), pp. 24-40.
Craven, T., 'Artistry and Faith in the Book of Judith', *Semeia* 8 (1977), pp. 75-95.
—*Artistry and Faith in the Book of Judith* (SBLDS, 70; Chico: Scholars Press, 1983).
Cross, F.M., *The Ancient Library of Qumran* (Garden City, NY: Doubleday, 1961).
Davies, G.I., 'Apocalyptic and Historiography', *JSOT* 5 (1978), pp. 15-28.
Davies, P.R., 'Daniel Chapter Two', *JTS* 27 (1976), pp. 392-401.
—*In Search of 'Ancient Israel'* (JSOTSup, 148; Sheffield: JSOT Press, 1992).
Davies, W.D., and L. Finkelstein (eds.), *The Cambridge History of Judaism*, II (Cambridge:
    Cambridge University Press, 1989).
Delcor, M., 'L'Histoire selon le Livre de Daniel', in Van der Woude (ed.), *The Book of Daniel*,
    pp. 365-86.

Diodorus of Sicily, I (trans. C.H. Oldfather; 12 vols.; LCL; Cambridge, MA: Harvard University Press, 1933).

Dionysius of Halicarnassus, *The Roman Antiquities of Dionysius of Halicarnasus*, I (trans. Earnest Cary; 7 vols.; LCL; Cambridge, MA: Harvard University Press, 1937).

Dodds, E.R., *The Greeks and the Irrational* (Berkeley: University of California Press, 1951).

Doran, R., 'Pseudo-Eupolemus: A New Translation and Introduction', in *OTP*, II, pp. 873-82.

Easterling, P.E., and B.M.W. Knox (eds.), *Greek Literature* (Cambridge History of Classical Literature, 1; Cambridge: Cambridge University Press, 1985).

Eddy, S.K., *The King is Dead: Studies in the Near Eastern Resistance to Hellenism 334–31 BC* (Lincoln: University of Nebraska Press, 1961).

Egger, B., 'Looking at Chariton's Callirhoe', in Morgan and Stoneman (eds.), *Greek Fiction*, pp. 31-48.

Enslin, M.S., and S. Zeitlin, *The Book of Judith* (JAL; Leiden: E.J. Brill, 1972).

Evans, J.A.S., *Herodotus, Explorer of the Past* (Princeton, NJ: Princeton University Press, 1991).

Fallon, F., 'Eupolemus: A New Translation and Introduction', in *OTP*, II, pp. 861-72.

Feldman, L.H., 'How Much Hellenism in Jewish Palestine?', *Hebrew Union College Annual* 57 (1986), pp. 83-111.

Fitzmyer, J.A., *The Acts of the Apostles: A New Translation with Introduction and Commentary* (AB, 31; New York: Doubleday, 1998).

Flusser, D., 'The Four Empires in the Fourth Sybil and in the Book of Daniel', *Israel Oriental Studies* 2 (1972), pp. 148-75.

Fohl, H., *Tragische Kunst bei Herodot: Inaugural-Dissertation zur Erlangung der Doktorwürde der hohen philosophischen Fakultät der Universität Rostock* (Borna-Leipzig: Buchdruckerei Robert Noske, 1913).

Fornara, C., *The Nature of History in Ancient Greece and Rome* (Berkeley: University of California Press, 1983).

Fröhlich, I., *Time and Times and Half a Time* (JSOTSup, 19; Sheffield: Academic Press, 1996), pp. 73-76.

Frost, S.B., 'Apocalyptic and History', in J.P. Hyatt (ed.), *The Bible in Modern Scholarship: Papers Read at the 100th Meeting of the Society of Biblical Literature, December 28-30, 1964* (Nashville: Abingdon Press, 1965), pp. 98-113.

Garbini, G., *History and Ideology in Ancient Israel* (New York: Crossroad, 1988).

Glasson, T.F., *Greek Influence in Jewish Eschatology* (London: SPCK, 1961).

Gottwald, N., *The Hebrew Bible: A Social-Literary Introduction* (Philadelphia: Fortress Press, 1985).

Gould, J., *Herodotus* (New York: St Martin's Press, 1989).

Grabbe, L., 'Reconstructing History from the Book of Ezra', in P.R. Davies (ed.), *Second Temple Studies*. I. *Persian Period* (JSOTSup, 117; Sheffield: JSOT Press, 1991), pp. 98-106.

Grayson, A.K., *Babylonian Historical-Literary Texts* (Toronto Semitic Texts and Studies, 3; Toronto: University of Toronto Press, 1975).

Grelot, P., 'Histoire et Eschatologie dans le Livre de Daniel', in Association Catholique Française pour l'Étude de la Bible, *Apocalypses et Théologie de l'Espérance: Congrès de Toulouse [1975]* (Paris: Les Éditions du Cerf, 1977), pp. 63-109.

—'L'Orchestre de Daniel III, 5, 7, 10, 15', *VT* 29 (1979), pp. 23-38.

Gruen, E.S., *Heritage and Hellenism: The Reinvention of Jewish Tradition* (Berkeley: University of California Press, 1998).

Hadas, M., *Hellenistic Culture* (Morningside Heights, NY: Columbia University Press, 1959).

Hanhart, K., 'The Four Beasts of Daniel's Vision in the Light of Rev. 13.2', *NTS* 27 (1981), pp. 576-83.

Hanson, P., *The Dawn of Apocalyptic* (Philadelphia: Fortress Press, 1975).

Harrington, D.J., 'The Ideology of Rule in Daniel 7–12', in *Society of Biblical Literature 1999 Seminar Papers* (Atlanta: SBL, 1999), pp. 540-51.

—*Why Do We Suffer?: A Scriptural Approach to the Human Condition* (Franklin, WI: Sheed & Ward, 2000).

Hartman, L.F., and A.A. Di Lella, *The Book of Daniel* (AB, 23; New York: Doubleday, 1964).

Hartog, F., *The Mirror of Herodotus: The Representation of the Other in the Writing of History* (trans. J. Lloyd; The New Historicism: Studies in Cultural Poetics, 5; Berkeley: University of California Press, 1988).

Hengel, M., 'The Interpenetration of Judaism and Hellenism in the Pre-Maccabean Period', in Davies and Finkelstein (eds.), *The Cambridge History of Judaism*, II, pp. 167-228.

—*Judaism and Hellenism: Studies in their Encounter in Palestine during the Early Hellenistic Period* (2 vols.; Philadelphia: Fortress Press, 1974).

Herodotus, *Herodoti Historiae* (ed. K. Hude; Oxford: Clarendon Press, 3rd edn, 1927).

—*The Histories* (trans. A. de Sélincourt; revised with introductory matter and notes by J. Marincola; New York: Penguin Books, 1996).

Hesiod, *Works and Days* (ed. with prolegomena and commentary by M.L. West; Oxford: Clarendon Press, 1978).

Hofmann, I., and A. Vorbichler, 'Herodot und der Schreiber des Esther-Buches', *Zeitschrift für Missionswissenschaft und Religionswissenschaft* 66 (1982), pp. 294-302.

Horgan, M.P., *Pesharim: Qumran Interpretations of Biblical Books* (CBQMS, 8; Washington: Catholic Biblical Association of America, 1979).

How, W.W., and J. Wells, *A Commentary on Herodotus* (2 vols.; Oxford: Clarendon Press, 1928).

Huber, L., 'Herodots Homerverständnis', in H. Flashar and K. Gaiser (eds.), *Synusia: Festgabe für Wolfgang Schadewalt zum 15 März 1965* (Pfullingen: Neske, 1965), pp. 29-52.

Immerwahr, H.R., *Form and Thought in Herodotus* (ed. W. Morris; Philological Monographs, 23; Cleveland: Press of Western Reserve University, 1966).

Jacobson, H., *The Exagoge of Ezekiel* (Cambridge: Cambridge University Press, 1983).

Jacoby, F., *Die Fragmente der griechischen Historiker* (Leiden: E.J. Brill, 1954–64).

—'Herodotos', in W. Kroll (ed.), *Paulys Real-Encyclopädie der classischen Altertumswissenschaft: Supplement* (15 vols. [to the Supplement]; Stuttgart: J. B. Metzler, 1894–1963), pp. 205-520.

Jerome, *S. Hieronymi Presbyteri Opera*. I,5 (Corpus Christianorum; Series Latina, 75A; Turnholt: Brepols, 1964).

Jones, B.W., 'Ideas of History in the Book of Daniel' (unpublished doctoral dissertation, Graduate Theological Union, 1972).

Krischer, T., 'Herodots Prooimion', *Hermes* 93 (1965), pp. 159-67.

Labonté, G.G., 'Genèse 41 et Daniel 2: Question d'Origine', in A.S. Van der Woude (ed.), *The Book of Daniel*, pp. 271-84.

Lacocque, A., *The Book of Daniel* (trans. D. Pellauer; Atlanta: John Knox Press, 1979).

Lambert, W.G., *The Background of Jewish Apocalyptic* (London: Athlone, 1978).

Laqueur, R., *Hellenismus* (Giessen: Alfred Töpelmann, 1925).

Lateiner, D., *The Historical Method of Herodotus* (Toronto: University of Toronto Press, 1989).

Lattimore, R., 'The Wise Adviser in Herodotus', *CP* 34 (1939), pp. 24-35.

Lebram, J.C.H., 'König Antiochus im Buch Daniel', *VT* 25 (1975), pp. 737-72.

Lemche, N.P., 'The Old Testament—A Hellenistic Book', *JSOT* 7 (1993), pp. 163-93.

Lesky, A., *A History of Greek Literature* (trans. J. Willis and C. de Heer; New York: Thomas Y. Crowell, 1966).

Linforth, I., 'Named and Unnamed Gods in Herodotus', in L. Tarán (ed.), *Studies in Herodotus and Plato* (New York: Garland Publishing, 1987), pp. 75-119.

Lucian (trans. A.M. Harmon and K. Kilburn; 8 vols.; LCL; New York: Putnam's, 1921–67).

MacKenzie, D.N., 'Notes on the Transcription of Pahlavi', *BSO(A)S* 30 (1967), pp. 17-29.

Mandell, S., and D.N. Freedman, *The Relationship between Herodotus' History and Primary History* (Atlanta: Scholars Press, 1993).

Marincola, J., *Herodotus: The Histories* (trans. A. de Sélincourt; revised with introductory matter and notes by J. Marincola; New York: Penguin Books, 1996)

Mendels, D., 'The Five Empires: A Note on a Propagandistic Topos', *AJP* 102 (1981), pp. 330-37.

Meyer, E., *Ursprung und Anfänge des Christentums* (Berlin: Cotta, 1921).

Milik, J.T., '"Prière de Nabonide" et autres écrits d'un cycle de Daniel', *Revue Biblique* 63 (1956), pp. 407-15.

Miller, M.C., *Athens and Persia in the Fifth Century BC: A Study in Cultural Receptivity* (Cambridge: Cambridge University Press, 1997).

Momigliano, A., 'Biblical Studies and Classical Studies', in Berti (ed.), *Essays on Ancient and Modern Judaism*, pp. 3-9.

—'Daniel and the Greek Theory of Imperial Succession', in Berti (ed.), *Essays on Ancient and Modern Judaism*, pp. 29-35.

—'Eastern Elements in Post-Exilic Jewish, and Greek, Historiography', in *idem*, *Essays in Ancient and Modern Historiography*, pp. 25-35.

—*Essays in Ancient and Modern Historiography* (Oxford: Basil Blackwell, 1977).

—'Jews and Greeks', in S. Berti (ed.), *Essays on Ancient and Modern Judaism*, pp. 10-28.

—'J.G. Droysen between Greeks and Jews', in *idem*, *Essays in Ancient and Modern Historiography*, pp. 307-23.

—'The Origins of Universal History', in R. Friedman (ed.), *The Poet and the Historian: Essays in Literary and Historical Biblical Criticism* (HSS, 26; Chico: Scholars Press, 1983), pp. 133-55.

—'The Place of Herodotus in the History of Historiography', in *idem*, *Studies in Historiography* (London: Weidenfeld & Nicolson, 1966), pp. 127-42.

—*Storiografia Greca* (Turin: Einaudi, 1982).

—'Time in Ancient Historiography', in *idem*, *Essays in Ancient and Modern Historiography*, pp. 179-204.

Montgomery, J.A., *A Critical and Exegetical Commentary on the Book of Daniel* (ICC; Edinburgh: T. & T. Clark, 1927).

Moore, C.A., *Judith* (AB, 40; Garden City, NY: Doubleday, 1985).

Morgan, J.R., and R. Stoneman (eds.), *Greek Fiction: The Greek Novel in Context* (New York: Routledge, 1994).

Mørkholm, O., *Antiochus IV of Syria* (Copenhagen: Gyldendal, 1966).

Morris, S.P., *Daidalos and the Origins of Greek Art* (Princeton, NJ: Princeton University Press, 1992).

Murphy, R.E., *The Tree of Life: An Exploration of Biblical Wisdom Literature* (Grand Rapids: Eerdmans, 2nd edn, 1996).

Murray, O., 'Herodotus and Hellenistic Culture', *CQ* 22 (1972), pp. 200-13.

Myres, J.L., *Herodotus: Father of History* (Oxford: Clarendon Press, 1953).

Nagy, G., 'Herodotus the Logios', *Arethusa* 20 (1987), pp. 175-84.

Nicklesburg, G.W.E., *Jewish Literature between the Bible and the Mishnah* (Philadelphia: Fortress Press, 1981).

Nielsen, F.A.J., *The Tragedy in History: Herodotus and the Deuteronomistic History* (JSOTSup, 251; Sheffield: Sheffield Academic Press, 1997).

Noth, M., 'Das deuteronomistische Werk [Dtr]', in *idem, Überlieferungsgeschichtliche Studien: Die sammelnden und bearbeitenden Geschichtswerk im Alten Testament* (Schriften der Königsberger gelehrten Gesellschaft; Geisteswissenschaftliche Klasse 18; Halle: Max Niemeyer, 1943), pp. 45-152.

—'The Holy Ones of the Most High', in *idem, The Laws in the Pentateuch*, pp. 215-28 (first published in *Norsk Teologisk Tidsskrift* 56 [1955] [= Festschrift Sigmund Mowinckel], pp. 146-57).

—*The Laws in the Pentateuch and Other Studies* (trans. D.R. Ap-Thomas; Edinburgh: Oliver & Boyd, 1966).

—'The Understanding of History in Old Testament Apocalyptic', in *idem, The Laws in the Pentateuch*, pp. 194-214.

Parker, R., 'Greek States and Greek Oracles', in P.A. Cartledge and F.D. Harvey (eds.), *Crux: Essays Presented to G.E.M. de Ste. Croix on his 75th Birthday* (History of Political Thought, VI, Issue 1/2; Exeter: Imprint Academic, 1985), pp. 298-326.

Pfeiffer, E., 'Herodots Geschichten und das Buch Esther', *Deutsches Pfarrerblatt* 62 (1958), pp. 544-45.

Pfeiffer, R.H., *History of New Testament Times with an Introduction to the Apocrypha* (New York: Harper & Brothers, 1949).

Pietersma, A., 'Holophernes', in *ABD*, III, p. 257.

Polybius, *The Histories* (trans. W.R. Paton; 6 vols.; LCL; New York: Putnam's, 1922–27).

Quintilian, Marcus Fabius, *Institutio Oratoria* (trans. H.E. Butler; 4 vols.; LCL; Cambridge, MA: Harvard University Press, 1922).

Rad, Gerhard von, *Old Testament Theology.* II. *The Theology of Israel's Prophetic Traditions* (trans. D.M.G. Stalker; New York: Harper & Row, 1965).

—*Wisdom in Israel* (Harrisburg, PA: Trinity Press International, 1972).

Rajak, T., 'The Sense of History in Jewish Intertestamental Writing', in *Crises and Perspectives: Studies in Ancient Near Eastern Polytheism, Biblical Theology, Palestinian Archaeology and Intertestamental Literature: Papers Read at the Joint British–Dutch Old Testament Conference held at Cambridge, UK 1985* (OTS, 24; Leiden: E.J. Brill, 1986), pp. 124-45.

Reardon, B.P., *Collected Ancient Greek Novels* (Berkeley: University of California Press, 1989).

Romm, J., *Herodotus* (New Haven: Yale University Press, 1998).

Rowley, H.H., *Darius the Mede and the Four World Empires in the Book of Daniel: A Historical Study of Contemporary Theories* (Cardiff: University of Wales Press Board, 1935).

Russell, D.S., *The Method and Message of Jewish Apocalyptic* (Philadelphia: Westminster Press, 1964).

Sanders, E.P., 'Judaism as Religion', in *idem, The Historical Figure of Jesus* (London: Penguin Books, 1993), pp. 33-48.

Sanders, J.A., 'Canon: Hebrew Bible', in *ABD*, I, pp. 837-52.

Schmid, W., *Geschichte der griechischen Literatur: Die griechische Literatur in der Zeit der attischen Hegemonie vor dem Eingreifen der Sophistik* (Munich: Beck, 1934).

Smith, M., *Palestinian Parties and Politics that Shaped the Old Testament* (London: SCM Press Ltd., 2nd corrected edn, 1987).

Stoneman, R., 'The *Alexander Romance*: From History to Fiction', in Morgan and Stoneman (eds.), *Greek Fiction*, pp. 117-29.

Stoneman, R. (trans., with an introduction and notes), *The Greek Alexander Romance* (New York: Penguin Books, 1991).

Swain, J.W., 'The Theory of the Four Monarchies: Opposition History Under the Roman Empire', *CP* 35 (1940), pp. 1-21.

Tarn, W.W., *Alexander the Great*, I (2 vols.; Cambridge: Cambridge University Press, 1948).

—*Hellenistic Civilisation* (London: Edward Arnold & Co., 3rd edn, 1952).

Thompson, T.L., *Early History of the Israelite People: From the Written and Archaeological Sources* (SHANE, 4; Leiden: E.J. Brill, 1992).

Thucydides, *History of the Peloponnesian War* (trans. R. Warner with an introduction and notes by M.I. Finley; Baltimore: Penguin Books, 1972).

Torrey, C.C., *The Apocryphal Literature* (New Haven: Yale University Press, 1945).

Turro, J.C., and R.E. Brown. 'Canonicity', in R.E. Brown, J.A. Fitzmyer and R.E. Murphy (eds.), *The Jerome Biblical Commentary* (Englewood Cliffs, NJ: Prentice–Hall, 1968), pp. 515-34.

Van der Woude, A.S. (ed.), *The Book of Daniel in the Light of New Findings* (Leuven: Leuven University Press, 1993),

Van Seters, J., *In Search of History: Historiography in the Ancient World and in the Origins of Biblical History* (New Haven: Yale University Press, 1983).

Wacholder, B.Z., *Eupolemus: A Study of Judaeo-Greek Literature* (Cincinnati: Hebrew Union College, 1974).

Walbank, F.W., *A Historical Commentary on Polybius*, III (Oxford: Clarendon Press, 1979).

Waters, K.H., *Herodotus on Tyrants and Despots* (Historia, 15; Wiesbaden: Franz Steiner Verlag, 1971).

West, E.W. (trans.), *Pahlavi Texts, Part I* (ed. F.M. Müller; The Sacred Books of the East, 5; Oxford: Clarendon Press, 1880).

—*Pahlavi Texts, Part IV* (ed. F.M. Müller; The Sacred Books of the East, 37; Oxford: Clarendon Press, 1892).

West, S., 'Herodotus' Epigraphical Interests', *CQ* 35 (1985), pp. 278-305.

Westermann, C., *Die Geschichtsbücher des Alten Testaments: Gab es ein deuteronomistisches Geschichtswerk?* (TB, 87; Gütersloh: Chr. Kaiser/Gütersloher Verlagshaus, 1994).

Wills, L.M., *The Jew in the Court of the Foreign King: Ancient Jewish Court Legends* (Harvard Dissertations in Religion, 26; Minneapolis: Fortress Press, 1990).

—*The Jewish Novel in the Ancient World* (Ithaca, NY: Cornell University Press, 1955).

INDEXES

INDEX OF REFERENCES

DANIEL

1–6	2, 53, 85, 87, 118	2.17-18	91		76-78, 84, 86, 88, 92, 96, 97, 119
1–4	55	2.20	76		
1	53, 75, 92, 119	2.21	76		
		2.23	76		
1.1–2.4a	53	2.25	53, 86	4.4	81
1.1-2	118	2.27-30	86	4.5	77
1.1	32, 37	2.27	76	4.6	77
1.4	87	2.28	76, 112	4.8	97
1.5	32	2.30	76, 80	4.10	90, 92
1.13	88	2.32	32	4.13	87, 96
1.19-21	53	2.33	32	4.17	58
1.20	54	2.34-35	121	4.21	90
1.29	79	2.34	99	4.22	88
1.32	46	2.37-38	65	4.24	88
2–7	108	2.37	43, 65, 85, 90	4.25	58
2	2, 7, 8, 27, 30, 31, 33-36, 40, 43, 53, 56-58, 60, 66, 76-78, 84, 86-88, 90-92, 96, 99, 114, 115, 117, 120, 121	2.38	36	4.27	66
		2.39	30, 32	4.28	88, 96
		2.40	30	4.30	66
		2.41	32	4.31-32	121
		2.44	57	4.31	76
		2.45	86, 99, 103	4.34	58
		2.46	87	5	53, 60, 62, 76, 77, 86, 91, 119
		2.47	56	5.7	81
		2.48	87	5.11	77, 87
		3	1, 53, 57, 58, 75, 119	5.12	62
2.1	86, 87			5.18-23	59
2.2-4	75			5.18	85
2.4b–7.28	53	3.13	57	5.20-23	85
2.10-11	86	3.16	70	5.20	77, 85
2.10	81	3.19	57	6	59, 75, 84, 119
2.12	57	4	43, 53, 57, 58, 60,		
2.14	62, 76			6.13	59

Daniel (cont.)

6.16	59	8.8	41, 63	11.4	44
6.17	59	8.9-12	69	11.5	63
7–12	44, 53, 89, 99, 111, 126	8.13	123	11.6	63, 64
		8.14	8, 118, 126	11.11-12	64
		8.16	78	11.11	64
7	2, 3, 7, 27, 31, 35, 40, 41, 43, 55, 60, 61, 63, 64, 66, 84, 86, 88, 89, 92, 96, 107, 113, 114, 117, 120-23	8.17	78	11.12	64
		8.20-21	61	11.13	44
		8.23-25	62	11.14	64
		8.24	62	11.15	64
		8.25	62	11.16	43, 44
		8.27	78	11.17	64
		9	46, 54, 63, 78, 84-86, 89-91, 95, 108, 110, 111	11.18	64
				11.19	64
				11.20	43, 44, 64
				11.21-39	120
				11.21	64
7.1	78			11.23	64
7.2	41	9.2-3	91	11.24-25	44
7.4	43, 96	9.21	44, 78	11.24	64
7.6	41	9.24	90, 104	11.25	44
7.7	3	9.27	123	11.27	64
7.11-12	121	9.27b	119	11.28	44, 64, 111
7.14	123	10–12	78, 84, 86, 88, 89, 92, 117		
7.15	78			11.29	44
7.16	78			11.30-35	120
7.17	60	10	61, 63, 89, 92, 101, 113	11.30	44, 64, 70, 111, 125
7.18	116				
7.19	3, 96			11.31-32	123
7.21	126	10.1	88, 103	11.31	70, 117, 119
7.22	116	10.5-6	98		
7.23-24	120	10.5	98	11.32	101, 125
7.23	60, 120	10.8	78	11.33	54
7.24	60, 121	10.13	92	11.34	106
7.25-26	60	10.14	45, 112	11.35	54
7.25	61, 70, 121, 123	10.20-21	123	11.36-37	120
7.26-27	45	10.21	92	11.36	70, 119, 89
7.26	61, 118	11	7, 43-47, 55, 60, 63, 69, 71, 91, 107, 111, 114, 116, 117, 120	11.37-38	70
7.27	116, 123			11.37	116, 120
7.28	78			11.40-45	45, 116, 120
8–12	108				
8	7, 35, 55, 61-64, 67, 84, 86, 89, 107, 113, 114, 117, 120	11.1	41	11.40	70, 116
		11.2-39	46	11.44-45	71
		11.2	43-45	11.44	70
		11.2b	42, 126	11.45	118, 120, 126
		11.3	43, 44	12	89, 113
8.1–12.13	53	11.4-30	44	12.1-3	46, 103

12.1	92, 103	12.3	54	12.11-12	8, 126
12.2	111, 118,	12.7	118	12.11	117, 118
	124, 125	12.10	54		

HERODOTUS

1.1	4	2.106	15	6.117	91, 100
1.3-4	83	2.113-20	83	6.119	72
1.5-6	65	2.125	16	6.137	20
1.5	110	2.143	20	7	23, 83, 96,
1.6-92	65	2.156	100		97
1.8	21	3-4	72	7.3	62
1.13	102, 110	3.14	68	7.6-9	49
1.26	65	3.16	68	7.6-7	73
1.29-33	66	3.25	69	7.6	80
1.30-33	110	3.27	69	7.10c	79, 80
1.30	79	3.29	69	7.10e	74, 77, 80
1.32	79	3.30	69, 95	7.11	73
1.34	66, 102,	3.31-32	69	7.12-14	100
	110	3.33-37	69	7.12	96, 99
1.46-48	94	3.36	62	7.13	103
1.70-71	102	3.43	101	7.14-15	73
1.76-84	110	3.61-79	22	7.14	99
1.80	67	3.64	69	7.15-17	21
1.87	98, 101	3.65	69	7.16b	80
1.89	62	3.68-69	21	7.17-18	99, 100
1.91	101, 110	3.79	21	7.17	101, 103,
1.95	7, 28, 115	3.86	72		110
1.104	15	3.89-97	21	7.18	102
1.105	15	3.89	67, 72	7.19-21	43
1.107-108	66, 95	3.91	15	7.19	96
1.108	21, 67	3.102	50	7.24	74
1.119	21	3.132	73	7.29	73
1.130	7, 28	3.133-37	73	7.35	74, 100
1.131	100	3.153	40	7.39	73, 74
1.178	37	3.155	37	7.45-46	74
1.184	37	3.160	40	7.46	79
1.185	37	4.3-4	67	7.48-49	74
1.206	61	4.27	100	7.54	74
1.207	62, 64	4.39	15	7.57	91
1.209	66, 72, 95	4.42	95	7.101-105	74
1.210	95	4.134	73	7.104	115
1.212	68	4.191	50	7.139	103
1.214	68	5.30	91	7.143	81
2	29, 83, 93	5.56	97, 100	7.152	95
2.3-4	93	5.106-107	73	7.189	95
2.3	102	6-9	115	7.191	95
2.24	84	6.57	47	7.235	62

138   *The Human and the Divine in History*

Herodotus (cont.)		8.38	91, 100	9.21	98
8.13	15, 19, 49, 98, 102	8.39	100	9.53	47
8.15	98	8.53	101	9.65	84, 102
8.17	98	8.65	15, 91, 101	9.79	21
8.27-29	43	8.238	21	9.100-101	99
8.37-39	99, 100	9	29	9.100	95, 102
8.37	15, 91, 99	9.16	101, 103	9.109	21
				9.110-13	21

OTHER BIBLICAL REFERENCES

Genesis		*Deuteronomy*		24.2	55
4.3	112	10.17	57	24.13-15	55
5.24	53	28.63-68	108		
14.2	126	29.25-27	18	*2 Chronicles*	
14.8	126	30.19-20	110	36	56
14.9	126			36.6-7	55
39.6	87	*Joshua*		36.22-23	56
40–41	92	10.13	20		
41	86			*Ezra*	
41.1	86, 87	*Judges*		1.1-4	56
41.8	86	3.8	56	4.5-7	42
41.9-13	86	3.12	56	4.5	42
41.16	86	4.2	56	7.12	65
41.25	86	7	19		
41.28	86	7.2	19	*Nehemiah*	
41.30	87	7.12	19	12.22	42
41.38	87				
41.39-40	87	*2 Samuel*		*Esther*	
		1.18	20	1	22
Exodus		14.26	112	1.1	21
14	51			1.11	21
14.21	51	*1 Kings*		3.1	21
15	113	14.19	55	4.13-14	21
		14.29	55	5.3	21
Leviticus		17.7	112	6.2	21
26.27-39	108			6.7-11	21
		2 Kings		7.6-10	21
Numbers		1.2	55	8.9	21
12	16	2.8	51	9.12-15	21
12.8	62	2.14	51	9.14	21
13.25-33	16	17.6-7	56	9.18-19	21
14.1-10	16	17.7-8	18	9.30	21
16.1-11	16	17.19-20	18		
16.12-24	16	22.16-17	18	*Psalms*	
20.13	126	24–25	56	34.10	123
		24.1-4	55	35.1	126

37	63	27–28	56	**New Testament**	
67.2	126	29.10	90, 104	*Matthew*	
114	113	49.1	122	24.14	1
136.2-3	57	49.3	122	24.15-16	1
		50.9	126		
Proverbs		51.11	41	*Acts*	
11.18	63	51.28	41	6.1	10
26.16	76				
		Ezekiel		*Revelation*	
Isaiah		1	96	13.1-3	41
7.17-20	56	14.14	53	20.4	112
13.17	40	14.20	53		
43	113	23.22	126		
45.1	44	28.3	53		
45.9	126	37	112		
45.13	126	40	85		
50.8	126	40.45-46	85		
66.14	126	41.22	85		
		42.13-14	85		
Jeremiah		43.6-7	85		
1.11-14	84				
13.6	112	*Zechariah*			
25.11	90, 104	10.11	51		

OTHER ANCIENT REFERENCES

Deuterocanonical Books/		12.15	23	4.9	10
Apocrypha		15.13	23	4.10-15	8
Tobit				4.11	8
14	35, 41	*1 Maccabees*		4.12	10
		2.31-38	124	4.13	9, 10
Judith		2.40	124	4.14	10
1.1	37	2.41	124	5.11	69
2.1-3	24	2.42-44	124	5.21	69
2.7	23, 24	3.30	64	9	70
2.28	25	6.1-17	71	9.1-29	71
3.7	23	6.1-16	71	9.1-28	71
3.8	23, 25, 38	6.12	70		
3.9-10	24	7	70	*Wisdom of Solomon*	
4.4	25	8.17	8	18.9	123
4.6	25	9.4-7	70		
4.7	24	9.11-17	70	**Pseudepigrapha**	
5	23	9.19-27	70	*1 Enoch*	
6.2	38			12.2	92
7.8-11	24	*2 Maccabees*		37–71	123
7.30	38	4.9-15	10	47.2	123

1 Enoch (cont.)
83–90   108, 114
85–90   117
85.3   114, 117
85.4   114
89.1-9   114
89.16-27   114
89.41-67   114
89.68-72   114
90.1-2   114
90.9   117

4 Ezra
3.20-27   107
7.50   107
12.22-23   41
14.37-48   14

Letter of Aristeas
32   105

Qumran
1QM
10.10   123

Talmuds
Hag.
13a   109

Men.
45a   109

Shab.
13b   109

Josephus
Ant.
10.11.7   1
12.2.5   105
12.7.2   64
12.9.1   71

Patristic Literature
Jerome
Commentariorum in
Danielem
3.11.2b   43

Eusebius
Praeparatio Evangelica
9.39.4   8

Tertullian
De Praescriptione
Haereticorum
7   9

Greek and Roman
Literature
Appian
Libyca
132   28

Appian
Syrian Wars
47   39

Ctesias
Persika
10–14   22

FGrH
588   28

Diodorus Siculus
1.46.8   49
1.69.7   49
2.15.1   29
2.32.2   29
2.32.3   29
2.32.5–34.6 8
11.13.1   49
11.14.2-4   49
16.47.4   38
17.5.3   38
31.19.2-3   38
31.19.7   39
32.24   28

Dionysius of
Halicarnassus
1.1.2   29
1.1.3   29
1.3.4   29

Eupolemus
39.4   39

Ezekiel
Exagoge
3.30   50
7.19   50
7.35   51
7.41   51
198   51
224-28   51
229   51

Hesiod
Works and Days
109-201   30

Homer
Iliad
2   80, 83
6.289-92   83
19.86-89   110

Homer
Odyssey
4.227-30   83
4.351-52   83

Lucian
Herodotus or Aëtion
1   48

True History
1.16   50

Pliny
Natural History
5.75   71
13.41   38

Plutarch
De fortuna aut virtute
Alexandri Magni
4.328b   11

Polybius
1.2   28
1.1.5   45
3.1.4-5   45
3.5.2   38
14.12.3-4   64
26.10   64

28.18-23	44	Vellius Paterculus		Ancient Near Eastern	
29.12.11	45	1.6.6	29	Texts	
29.12.6	45			*Babylonian Dynastic*	
29.21	28	Xenephon		*Prophecy*	
29.21.4	8	*The Education of Cyrus*		i 10	35
29.26-27	44	8.7	68	i 13	35
31.9	69, 71			i 20	35
32.10	38	Persian Literature		i 23	35
33.6	38	*Bahman Yasht (Zand i*		i 24	35
33.9	71	*Wahman Yasn)*		ii 11	35
38.21	28	1.6-11	31	ii 17	35
		2.19	34	iii 9	35
Quintilian		2.24	33		
Institutio Oratorio		2.50	33	Ugaritic Texts	
10.1.73	50, 105	3.8	33	*2 Aqhat*	
		3.34	34	V.7-8	53
Thucydides					
History of the		*Denkard*			
Peloponnesian War		9.8.2-5	33		
1.1	47				
1.20	47				

INDEX OF AUTHORS

Anderson, B.W. 107
Asheri, D. 16, 40, 71
Astin, A.E. 28
Astour, M.C. 13, 30
Attridge, H. 10

Barber, G.L. 28
Barr, J. 6, 105, 106
Barton, G.A. 43, 63, 116
Bauer, J. 49
Baumgartner, W. 29
Bichler, R. 66, 95
Bickerman, E. 2, 5, 12, 13, 30, 43, 46, 57
Blenkinsopp, J. 65
Boadt, L. 106
Boccaccini, G. 26, 107, 108
Boman, T. 5
Bonora, A. 118
Brekelmans, C.H.W. 61, 123
Brown, R.E. 109
Buchanan, G.W. 26
Bultmann, R. 6

Caponigro, M.S. 24, 25
Cereti, C.G. 31, 33
Charles, R.H. 62, 114, 116
Colless, B. 72
Collins, J.J. 1, 2, 36, 39, 41, 43, 52, 54,
    63, 87, 96, 101, 106, 111, 112, 116,
    123
Collins, R.F. 109
Coxon, P.W. 2
Craven, T. 25, 37
Cross, F.M. 127

Davies, G.I. 7
Davies, P.R. 17, 86

Delcor, M. 69
Di Lella, A.A. 42, 53, 61, 99, 107, 116
Dodds, E.R. 110, 111
Doran, R. 39

Eddy, S.K. 2, 32, 33
Egger, B. 40
Enslin, M.S. 38
Evans, J.A.S. 115

Fallon, F. 8
Feldman, L.H. 9, 12
Fitzmyer, J.A. 10
Flusser, D. 2, 32, 34
Fohl, H. 15
Fornara, C. 4
Freedman, D.N. 6, 13-16
Fröhlich, I. 60
Frost, S.B. 7

Garbini, G. 14
Glasson, T.F. 2
Gottwald, N. 101
Gould, J. 45, 102
Grabbe, L. 14
Grayson, A.K. 2, 34-36
Grelot, P. 3, 104, 119
Gruen, E.S. 9, 10

Hadas, M. 23
Hanhart, K. 60
Hanson, P. 6, 7
Harrington, D.J. 89
Hartman, L.F. 42, 53, 61, 99, 107, 116
Hartog, F. 80
Hengel, M. 11, 12
Hofmann, I. 21

Horgan, M.P. 90
How, W.W. 84, 102
Huber, L. 20

Immerwahr, H.R. 68, 72

Jacobson, H. 50, 51
Jacoby, F. 49
Jones, B.W. 7

Krischer, T. 83

Labonté, G.G. 87
Lacocque, A. 107
Lambert, W.G. 2
Laqueur, R. 11
Lateiner, D. 95
Lattimore, R. 78, 79
Lebram, J.C.H. 43, 69, 116
Lemche, N.P. 17
Lesky, A. 47
Linforth, I. 15, 93

MacKenzie, D.N. 31
Mandell, S. 6, 13-16
Marincola, J. 4, 37, 83, 84
Mendels, D. 28, 29, 35
Meyer, E. 2
Milik, J.T. 58
Momigliano, A. 1, 3, 5, 6, 8, 11, 13, 17,
    23, 27-30, 48
Montgomery, J.A. 42, 43, 63, 96
Moore, C.A. 25
Morgan, J.R. 38, 39
Mørkholm, O. 70, 116, 120
Morris, S.P. 13
Murphy, R.E. 75
Murray, O. 49, 51
Myres, J.L. 15

Nagy, G. 83
Nickelsburg, G.W.E. 38
Nielsen, F.A.J. 6, 14, 15, 18, 19
Noth, M. 2, 20, 29, 31, 61, 104, 108

Parker, R. 94
Pfeiffer, E. 21
Pfeiffer, R.H. 37-39
Pietersma, A. 39

Rad, G. von 2, 6, 75, 104, 108, 118
Rajak, T. 10
Reardon, B.P. 40
Romm, J. 100
Rowley, H.H. 40
Russell, D.S. 111

Sanders, E.P. 109
Sanders, J.A. 109
Schmid, W. 16, 48
Smith, M. 12
Stoneman, R. 38, 39
Swain, J.W. 28, 29, 115

Tarn, W.W. 11
Thompson, T.L. 17
Torrey, C.C. 37

Van Seters, J. 5
Vorbichler, A. 21

Wacholder, B.Z. 8, 39
Walbank, F.W. 28
Waters, K.H. 63, 65
Wells, J. 84, 102
Westermann, C. 18
Wills, L.M. 22, 39, 86, 87

Zeitlin, S. 38